What people are saying about

Compassion Based Living Course

It is with great pleasure that I recommend this introduction to compassion written by Heather & Choden. The world is being swamped by books and articles on this topic so readers may wonder why yet another? The reason is simple — this is a practical D.I.Y. for those who might be interested in the Compassion Based Living Course which is offered by the Mindfulness Association. I know that hundreds of people have done and benefitted from this course so feel confident in suggesting that many more people, including you, will benefit from it.

Rob Nairn, author of *A Diamond Mind*

T0244681

Compassion Based Living Course

Compassion Based Living Course

Choden and Heather Regan-Addis

MANTRA
BOOKS

London, UK
Washington, DC, USA

CollectiveInk

First published by Mantra Books, 2024
Mantra Books is an imprint of Collective Ink Ltd.,
Unit 11, Shepperton House, 89 Shepperton Road, London, N1 3DF
office@collectiveinkbooks.com
www.collectiveinkbooks.com
www.mantra-books.net

For distributor details and how to order please visit the 'Ordering' section on our website.

Text copyright: Choden and Heather Regan-Addis 2023

ISBN: 978 1 80341 676 2
978 1 80341 709 7 (ebook)
Library of Congress Control Number: 2023949059

A CIP catalogue record for this book is available from the British Library.

Design: Lapiz Digital Services

UK: Printed and bound by CPI Group (UK) Ltd, Croydon, CR0 4YY
Printed in North America by CPI GPS partners

We operate a distinctive and ethical publishing philosophy in all areas of our business, from our global network of authors to production and worldwide distribution.

Contents

Previous Titles

Mindfulness Based Living Course. Choden and Heather Regan-Addis. O-Books (2018). ISBN 978-1785358326

Mindfulness to Insight. Rob Nairn, Choden and Heather Regan-Addis. Shambala Publications Inc. (2019). ISBN 978-1611806793

Dedicated to our dear friend Prof. Graeme Nixon, whose kindness, patience and intelligence will be missed by all who knew him.

***

Developed by Mindfulness Association CIC.

Acknowledgements

We have many people to thank for their advice, support and encouragement. We are truly fortunate and grateful to our teachers, family, friends and colleagues. We would like to thank our friend, teacher and co-founder of the Mindfulness Association, Rob Nairn, for his teaching, support and friendship and for his genius formulation of the compassionate mess. We would also like to thank special colleagues we have worked with over the years and who have informed and influenced our approach to teaching compassion, especially Prof. Paul Gilbert, Dr Chris Germer and Dr Kristin Neff. We would also like to thank teachers who we have not worked with and who have nevertheless informed and influenced our approach to teaching compassion, especially Pema Chodron and Aura Glaser. We have dedicated this book, with gratitude, to our dear friend Prof. Graeme Nixon, who will be missed by all who knew him, and our Mindfulness Association team who are all extraordinary people, deeply committed to sharing compassion-based mindfulness with the world. Special thanks to Lisa Hellier and Jacky Seery for proofreading and formatting the text, to Lisa Hellier for the cover image and to Heather Grace Bond and Alex Tang who set up our Mindfulness Based Living Apps, including the guided audio practices from this book.

Finally, we would like to thank our many course participants over the years for their engagement with this Compassion curriculum as it has developed. This book would not exist without you.

We hope that this book will help to bring freedom from the conditioning that governs and limits our lives, in particular freedom from the inner self-critic, so that our human potential to bring love and kindness to the world is able to flourish and grow.

Introduction

Do You Want to Be Compassionate?

Since you have picked up this book then our presumption is that you want to become a more compassionate human being. But the question, 'Do you want to be compassionate?' is an important one for us to explore right at the outset.

If we do not think about the implications of the question then the obvious answer is *Yes*, of course, as a good human being I want to be compassionate. Thinking about this question more deeply, however, may give us cause to doubt our original certainty.

We might discover that we do not really want to be compassionate. At first glance compassion sounds like an attractive virtue, something we feel that we ought to cultivate if we are an intelligent, sensitive human being. It appeals to the image of our better self. But once we reflect on how compassion really takes birth — being willing to face ourselves, our destructive habits, and our selfishness — our initial enthusiasm might start to wane.

We will quickly realise that compassion goes against a deeply entrenched habit of doing what we want and avoiding things we do not like. Even though we might come to see that this is a prison that limits our full potential as a human being, it is still a very comfortable and familiar prison. And so, when our advocate — our own deepest wisdom — hands us the key to get out of the prison, we might just leave it lying on the floor of our cell and stay where we are!

But the key point here is that genuine compassion is about getting to know and accepting this conflict in ourselves; that one part wants to be compassionate and another part wants to stay selfish. If we can face this dilemma honestly, with a touch of humour, then the real journey of compassion can begin. This journey is being willing to embrace our messy, imperfect humanity; to begin to love and accept the parts of us that do not co-operate, that do not want to be good and virtuous, and that just want to stay in the same old familiar prison. We might come to see that these parts have a life of their own and they have been around for a long time, so we will need to approach the path of compassion in a gradual, realistic way.

Compassion, by its very nature, requires us to face the suffering of the world. We start by facing our own suffering. Once we do this, then we are in a better position to recognise and face the suffering of others. We might prefer, however, to live in so-called 'blissful ignorance', out of touch with the suffering of ourselves and those around us. Many of us live this way and gloss over the pain and difficulties in life, staying busy and finding ways to distract ourselves.

But what do we mean by suffering? It is rather a loaded word implying great pain and strife. However, suffering can be anything from a nagging sense of things not feeling right — an underlying sense of dissatisfaction — to profound anguish and grief.

More inconvenient still, compassion by its very nature requires us to do something to relieve suffering, as best we can, wherever we encounter it. Again, we start with ourselves and then once we know how to relieve our own suffering, we are in a much better position to help others. Acting to relieve suffering, however, often requires us to act against our own self-interest and to go against the grain of long-held habits of self-absorption that are painful to break.

In short, practising compassion requires us to face our selfishness and to act in the service of the greater good, rather than in the service of our own limiting desires. Practising compassion requires us to be brutally honest about our self and our activity in the world and this takes great courage.

Do you still want to be more compassionate? The important thing is for you to explore this question for yourself. You can do this by engaging with Practice One at the end of this chapter.

It can be useful to explore the different layers of response when we reflect on the question of whether we want to be compassionate. The first layer might be, 'Yes of course, I want to be a good and upstanding citizen!' The next layer might be, 'I am not sure, that is asking a lot, I am fond of doing the things I like and I am very clear about the things I do not like'. The next layer might be uncertainty and fear of changing what is comfortable and familiar. A deeper layer might be, 'No way, I want to stay just the way I am and forget all this compassion stuff, it is not for me!' But if we are patient and continue reflecting on this question, we might touch a deep, barely audible voice that says, 'YES, I really do want to be compassionate because then I will fulfil my deepest potential'. The important thing is for you to go through the process of reflection yourself and see what comes up for you.

So far we have been focusing on the difficulties surrounding compassion training. On the plus side, however, cultivating compassion generates more openness, joy and ease in how we live in the world. Our problems and challenges become more workable and this can result in a deep and abiding wellbeing. By living compassionately, we are living more in touch with ourselves, those around us and the wider world. We live from the understanding that all of life is interdependent and how we think, speak and act affects other people, insects, animals and the Earth we depend on. It results in a deep sense of love and care for the extraordinary life that we are part of. This is the fruition of the path of genuine compassion, and this book is about how to tread this path.

Recognising How Much Compassion You Already Have

A useful starting point in treading this path is recognising how much compassion we already have. Many people think that they are not compassionate at all. They think that compassion is reserved for famous saints like Mother Theresa and the Dalai

3

Lama or great statesmen like Nelson Mandela and Ghandi. But many of us are kind and compassionate in small ways every day, but we tend not to give ourselves credit for this. It can be very helpful to reflect on our small acts of compassion or on harmful acts we would never contemplate doing. This becomes a foundation for building our compassionate capacity. The second reflective practice in this chapter will explore this further.

Practicalities

This book takes you step by step through the Compassion Based Living curriculum. Although it is written in a self-help style, our intention is that this book is either an encouragement to undertake compassion training or an accompaniment to such a training. For more information about our training, to join our free online daily guided meditation sessions, or to join our membership please visit www.mindfulnessassociation.net.

Guided audio of many of the practices in this book are available in the Compassion section of the Mindfulness Association's free Mindfulness Based Living app, which is available from the Google Play Store for Android devices and from the Apple App Store for iOS devices. The guided audio can also be streamed or downloaded from this web page: www. mindfulnessassociation.net/cblc-book.

Practice Section

In this introductory chapter we offer two reflection practices. They follow the reflection instructions below.

Reflection Instructions

Have a pen and paper handy. Then place your body in a meditation posture. Choose a posture that is comfortable, with the bottom half of your body grounded and the upper half dignified and alert. Then focus on the rising and falling of your body as you breathe. To help settle your mind, try deepening your in-breath a little and lengthening your out-breath. See if you can regulate your breathing so that the in-breath and out-breath are of a similar length and rhythm. You might like to count to three or four on the in-breath and a similar count on the out-breath. Then when your mind begins to settle a little (this may take several minutes) let go of counting and allow your breathing to find its natural rhythm. Next, switch your focus to physical sensations in your body. Do you notice any prominent sensations? Feel from the inside how these sensations manifest. Feel the sensations in your hands where they rest on your lap. Feel the sensations in your sitting bones where they rest on your seat. Feel from the inside the sensations of your feet where they rest on the ground. Then scan your body from your feet upwards to become aware of the sensations throughout your body. Then, lightly focus on your breathing as a support. Whenever you notice that your mind wanders during this practice, bring your attention back to feeling your feet on the floor, aware of your body as a whole resting on your seat with a light focus on your breathing.

Now let a question drop into your mind, like dropping a pebble into a pond, and observe the ripples. You are not thinking about the question; you are simply observing the mind's response to dropping in the question. Whenever you notice that you are thinking too much about the question or you are distracted by random thoughts, bring your attention back to feeling your feet on the floor, aware of your body as a whole resting on your seat with a light focus on your breathing. Once you feel settled and grounded, pose the question again and let it drop into the mind once more. Repeat this process three times and write down anything that comes up, even if what you write does not seem to make any sense. At the end of the practice reflect on what you have written and ask yourself 'How do I feel about this?'

Practice 1: Do You Want to Be Compassionate? (15 – 20 minutes)
This reflection entails posing the following questions to yourself
(following the instructions above):

- *Do I want to be more compassionate?*
- *Do I recognise that I will have to be less self-focused and less attached to my likes and dislikes?*
- *Do I recognise that the human condition makes it difficult to be compassionate, and this is not my fault?*
- *Do I still want to become more compassionate?*

It is important to be honest with yourself. You may not like some
of the answers that emerge and you may get in touch with a self-
centred part of you that prefers the status quo. Nevertheless, try
to welcome whatever comes up. The main point of compassion
practice is to accept ourselves as we are, even the bits that we do
not like. They are part of us and they deserve our compassion
too. Our intention is to take care of the entire mixed bag of who
we are. After all, we don't have a spare self, which is hung up in
a cupboard somewhere!

**Practice 2: Recognising How Much Compassion You Already
Have** (15 – 20 minutes)
Many of us think that we are not compassionate at all and that
we are not up to the task of becoming compassionate people. To
dispel this illusion, answer the following questions (following
the reflection instructions above):

- *Do I care about others?*
- *Would I like others to be happy?*
- *Would I knowingly cause suffering to another living being?*
- *How would I feel if I discovered I had harmed a person or an animal?*
- *Would I put myself out to help someone in distress?*

- *Do I ever do small things for others, such as offering a warm smile, helping someone carry their bags, or listening attentively to someone who is in difficulty?*

If the answer to some of these questions is 'Yes' then you already have some compassion. It is useful to see where compassion shows up in our lives because often it goes unrecognised. Then we think that we are not compassionate and this becomes another reason to be hard on ourselves. The training that we are about to embark on builds on the compassion that we all already have.

A useful daily life practice that builds on this practice is the following:

At the end of each day, spend five minutes reflecting back on all the things you did that day to take care of yourself, other people and the world at large. Pay attention to small acts of kindness. Reaffirm to yourself that you already have some compassion and it is a foundation on which you can now build. You might like to keep a record of these daily reflections in a diary or journal.

As the Dalai Lama once famously remarked, 'Perform random acts of kindness, and if you cannot help living beings, at least do not harm them'.

Chapter One

The Seed of Compassion Is Already within Us

Compassion Is Innate

When some people first hear about the idea of training in compassion, they often react and say, 'Oh no that is not for me, I am not a compassionate person'. We all too easily identify with our selfish, neurotic traits and put ourselves down. Others might think, 'I am not a compassionate person, but maybe I can introduce some compassion into my life by taking a compassion pill'. The underlying belief is that we are not already compassionate people and the only way to get compassion is from the outside. But the fundamental premise of this book is that you are *already* compassionate. It is a seed that you have within you. You do not need to get it from the outside. The important first step is to recognise and own this fact. We started this process by offering the practice of 'recognising how much compassion you already have' in the Introduction. When you do this, then you empower yourself and the question then becomes, 'How do I cultivate this seed of compassion that is already within me?'

We draw on various sources in this book. One is the science of Evolutionary Psychology and another is Cultural Evolution. From an evolutionary perspective one might think that compassion goes against the evolutionary drive to survive and procreate and pass on our genes to the next generation. We see this powerful drive all around us in society today, manifesting as a competitive drive to earn more money and to get more power and resources. We do this to bolster the security of people like 'us', often without caring about the consequences of our actions for those 'others' who are from a different country, race, species or social rank.

As human beings, however, care and compassion are qualities that are endowed to us by the evolutionary process too. Our brains are hard-wired to care for others, specifically those who form part of our kith and kin. Human beings cannot survive alone and so we have evolved the capacity to take care of each other in groups. As human culture has evolved, the size of the groups within which we collaborate and prosper have grown from small hunter gatherer groups to village groups, to city states, to whole countries, until now we have global organisations, such as the United Nations. Over the evolution of human culture, it has served our survival as a species to cooperate and care for each other, first in smaller and then in larger groups.

For example, in the United Kingdom all working citizens contribute payments to support the National Health Service so that everyone in our society can receive the health care they need to survive and flourish. Furthermore, the United Nations was set up to maintain international peace and security, to protect human rights and to deliver humanitarian aid and it is now a collaboration of 195 of the 197 countries in the world. Interestingly, both these institutions were set up after the Second World War in response to a period of intense global suffering.

In a recent episode of the television program *Gogglebox*, a group of children were filmed watching a nature program in which a family of monkeys were trying to cross a crocodile-infested river. There was a father monkey who led the way by jumping between two overhanging trees so as to cross the river. It was a long jump. Then the mother monkey who was holding her baby had to make the jump. The anxiety of the watching children was palpable, and they were desperately rooting for the mother and child to be successful in making the jump. But when they did so they were unsuccessful and fell into the river, much to the distress of the watching children. Then, to their relief the mother and baby out-swam the crocodiles and escaped to safety. This was an example of children of one species watching a family from another species and caring deeply for their safety and wellbeing. It is yet another testament to the fact that compassion is an intrinsic quality within us human beings.

Another source we draw on in this book is Buddhism. The emergence of a secular training in compassion in the last 15 to 20 years has come from a lively interaction between Buddhism, Neuroscience and Psychology. This is not to say that other religious and spiritual traditions do not value and practise compassion too. Indeed, they do. One of the themes underlying so many religious traditions is the Golden Rule: 'Do unto others as you would have them do unto you'. This lies at the heart of compassion.

The fundamental view of Mahayana Buddhism is that we are all Buddhas but do not realise it. By 'Buddhas' we do not mean Eastern ascetics sitting on gilded thrones, but we are referring to our intrinsic nature of wisdom and compassion. We tend to think of ourselves as limited and flawed with a big haversack of personal issues that weigh us down. But the view of Buddhism is that our true nature is flawless, free and whole. It is replete with qualities that are waiting for the opportunity to glisten and shine if we give them the chance.

The classic image in Buddhist scriptures is that of a pauper who spends his whole life living in a dilapidated shack on top of a big pile of dung. He spends his days lamenting his poverty and feeling sorry for himself but he does not realise that beneath the pile of dung is a large piece of gold ore. Tragically, he goes to his grave thinking he was poor when in fact all along he was richer than his wildest dreams!

If we reflect on this story, how many of us are sunk in poverty mentality like the pauper on the dung heap? One of the reasons why we train in compassion is to discover the gold ore for ourselves within the dung of our everyday lives, and then to begin the slow, yet joyful process of refining the gold ore so that it can shine and enrich the lives of ourselves and others.

Compassion Requires Training

Sometimes when we talk about training in compassion, people are puzzled because they think that either you are compassionate or you are not. Often, when we talk about people we ascribe fixed qualities to them, such as 'he is kind', or 'she is very bright', or 'he is an arrogant fool'. Through the way we talk, it sounds like these qualities or faults are set in stone. In reality people are changing all the time and someone whom we might remember as being selfish when they were young and immature might turn out to be a kind and caring parent in later years.

The same applies to compassion. Although it is innate within us, it requires some application and effort for it to mature in our experience. In the example of the pauper living on top of the dung heap, if he were told that there is a big piece of gold beneath the dung, he would still need to put in the effort to dig through the dung to get to the gold.

Another analogy is that of going to a gym to build up our muscles. We would all readily agree that it takes consistent hard work over an extended period of time to tone our bodies and build up our muscles. Similarly, we can think of compassion as a heart muscle that needs its own very special kind of training. The fact that the heart muscle is there means that we can develop and train it, but we still have to put in the hard work.

Realising that we can cultivate compassion through a process of training is very empowering. It is all too easy to disempower ourselves by thinking that other people have special qualities but not me; other people can become compassionate but not me. The starting point for training in compassion, however, is owning the fact that it is already in us. All we have to do is to cultivate it. This requires that we form the intention to do so and put in the right amount of effort and apply the right kind of skills. In a nutshell, this is what this book is all about.

On the other hand, it is important to bear in mind that human beings are capable of great destructiveness and aggression. Along with compassion, these tendencies are hard-wired into us by the evolutionary process too. The prevalence of violence and war throughout human history provides ample evidence of this fact. There are many examples of long term friends and neighbours, who have lived harmoniously side by side for many years, and then turn on each other in the name of race, religion or access to resources, such as water or oil.

As we will see through this book, we can train to *refrain* from mindlessly acting out these tendencies. We can learn to overcome habits of anger, opposition and fear and replace them with kindness, collaboration and courage. In this way we can begin to free ourselves from some of the evolutionary hard-wiring in our brain.

We are also evolutionarily primed to get what we want, for ourselves, our families, our tribe or our country. Our culture in the West has become increasingly individualistic over the last 50 years and we find ourselves in a dog-eat-dog society. Each person is striving to get more of what they want, regardless of whether there is anything left for others. This has resulted in a small minority of people becoming extremely wealthy and being in a position to indulge their every whim. At the same time the rest of the world has got poorer, resulting in great deprivation and suffering. Interestingly, evidence shows that nobody gets happier, not even the wealthy ones.

It is important to recognise that our hard-wired evolutionary drives and passions are *not our fault*. We did not choose to be born a human being with a tricky brain that is beset by powerfully conflicting drives and emotions; nor did we choose to be born into a particular culture or time in history; and nor did we choose to be born into a loving or abusive family — all of which powerfully shape the kind of person we become. But once we wake up to the situation we find ourselves in, we can take responsibility for it by training in compassion.

In short, we have two opposing evolutionary tendencies:

- One towards selfishness, fighting for what we and our immediate clan wants, regardless of the cost to others;
- And another towards compassion, doing what's necessary so that everyone (including ourselves) is cared for and has what they need.

The tendency that becomes stronger is the one that we cultivate. This amounts to a choice between whether we go with our hard-wired circuitry of selfishness and tribalism, or whether we cultivate the brain circuitry that fosters compassion.

Thankfully, our brains are adaptable. They have neuroplasticity. This means that how we think, speak and behave is habitual, based on the habits we have repeated in the past. When we behave in a particular way repeatedly over time, this way of behaving becomes hard-wired in our brain and we begin to embody it.

An example of this is when we learn a new skill, such as learning to drive a car or play a musical instrument. To begin with we have to think about each action we take. But with practise, these actions become hard-wired into the brain so that we no longer have to think about them. They become habitual and automatic. We can drive a car without thinking about it and we can seamlessly translate dots on a piece of paper into music without thinking about it too.

Refraining from a habit is difficult, as anyone who has given up a bad habit knows all too well. But if we refrain from a habit repeatedly, the brain rewires itself so that the habit becomes less hard-wired. Over time we gradually become free of that habit.

For example, if we have spent a lot of our lives worrying, this habit becomes hard-wired within our brain and nervous system. It becomes a part and parcel of who we are: a worrier. Through mindfulness and compassion practice, however, we can train to refrain from the habit of worry while at the same time learning to cultivate the qualities of curiosity and courage. As we train in these new qualities, they become hard-wired into our brain and nervous system. Curiosity and courage become part and parcel of who we are: a warrior of compassion!

Therefore, thanks to the plasticity of the brain we can train our innate capacity for compassion while at the same time weakening the innate tendency of selfishness, both of which are hard-wired into us by the power of natural selection.

The Blocks and Obstacles Are the Path

Training in compassion is not theoretical. It is rooted in our everyday lives. It emerges from our struggles and from the struggles of those around us.

We often observe in our own practice and when teaching compassion-based mindfulness to others that periods of life without challenge can lead to a relatively calm meditation practice, which is pleasant to experience, but it does not lead to much personal growth. Personal growth seems to come during and after times of great challenge, in which our meditation practice is often chaotic, seemingly distracted, and full of strong emotion or numbness and zoning out. In this way, the blocks become the path of compassion.

Compassion is a natural human response to suffering and if there is no suffering then there is no possibility for cultivating compassion. That being said, we are not wishing on ourselves heaps of suffering as this can be overwhelming. We skilfully start our compassion training by engaging with challenges and difficulties that are big enough to grow our compassion, but not so big as to overwhelm us.

Each of us has our own level of capacity to tolerate difficulties and respond skilfully to them. If that capacity is breached, we can get overwhelmed. If it is not challenged we will not grow. So, we start where we are. Over time, as we practise compassion we develop the resources within us to tolerate more difficulties and larger scale issues and our compassionate capacity grows. It is often a messy process that involves a lot of emotion, and that is also part of the path.

One major yet subtle block to the practice of compassion is fear of change. If we become more compassionate, what will happen? What might we lose? How might our relationships with loved ones be affected? As human beings we tend to prefer the status quo, even if it is unpleasant. We generally fear change and yet compassion entails significant inner change. Our egocentric self-interest can put up quite a battle when we begin to practise compassion. It does not want to lose power over its familiar terrain.

We may have expectations that our practice of compassion should progress in an orderly manner, but generally that is not what happens. At times we might become overwhelmed and need to take a break. At other times we might experience numbness or agitation; we might resist our practice or feel that it is chaotic and not progressing at all. At other times we might experience volcanic surges of anger; we might descend into the depths of sadness or become ensnared in a whirlwind of anxiety. Our training is simply to allow whatever is unfolding to do so with acceptance and kindly curiosity. All of these experiences and states of mind are part of the practice; nothing falls outside the domain of our practice.

While we are training in compassion we may feel that our practice isn't improving. There doesn't seem to be any major breakthrough. However, we may notice in our daily lives that we are responding differently to the people we are with and the situations we find ourselves in. This is significant because the fruition of our compassion practice happens first and foremost in our daily lives and not necessarily on the meditation cushion.

Life generally obliges us by offering up some tasty difficulties and juicy challenges. The instruction here is to adopt these onto to the path. In this way our compassion practice becomes a practical laboratory to which we bring our life experience. To assist with this process, at the end of each chapter we will be offering informal practices for bringing compassion into our daily lives.

A Metaphor for Compassion

There is a very useful metaphor about the blocks and obstacles being the path. It is that of a lotus flower growing out of the mud at the bottom of a lake. We will return to it later in the book and explore it in more detail but it might be useful at this point to give the basic outline of this ancient Buddhist myth because it goes to the heart of what the practice of compassion is all about.

According to the myth there is a very deep lake and at its bottom there is a great heap of mud and sludge that has accumulated over a long period of time. We can think of the mud as being all the disowned, shadowy and suppressed parts of our personality that we have accumulated in this life — what people often call 'their baggage'. It is all those things we prefer other people did not know about us, and even things we ourselves prefer not to know about!

The key part of the story is that beneath the mud and sludge there is a seed that has lain dormant for a very long time. It is the seed of our wisdom and compassion. We are not aware of it because it is covered by the mud. This is similar to the story we mentioned before of the pauper sitting on a heap of dung with the piece of gold lying hidden beneath it. Nevertheless, the seed is within us — compassion is innate within us — but it only exists as a potential and has not matured in our life experience.

The moral of the story is that the mud and the sludge are not to be rejected. They are vital because they are the manure for the growth of the lotus flower of compassion. As soon as we genuinely form the intention to cultivate compassion, a process deep within us is initiated. The seed begins to germinate and all the things we normally do not like about ourselves become the manure for the gradual emergence of ourselves as a compassionate person. All our anxiety and sadness, all our fits of anger and frustration, and all our feelings of despondency and worthlessness — all of these have great value because they help the seedling of compassion to grow.

For example, if someone had a problem with addiction to alcohol or drugs, this would be part of their mud, along with the associated feelings of low self-worth, depression and anger. If this person then formed the intention to honestly work through their addiction, all of these issues and feelings would become part of their distinctive manure fertilising the seedling of compassion within them. And once this seedling matured into a fully grown lotus flower that bloomed on the surface of the lake, they would be uniquely equipped to help other people like them. They would understand what other people with addiction were going through and they would be in a position to help people in this difficult life situation because *they had been there themselves*. This is the meaning of the blocks and obstacles being the path.

Start with Self-Compassion

It is important to bear in mind that compassion is a life force that flows in different directions. This is something we will return to later in the book, but we will touch on it briefly now. When most people think of compassion, they take it to mean being compassionate to others. Of course, this is important, but it is only part of the process.

Compassion also means being willing to *receive* kindness and compassion from others. Many people struggle to be on the receiving end of compassion. They may not feel worthy of compassion, subtly undermined to be on the receiving end, or fear that they will become indebted to the person offering compassion. They are much more comfortable being the one giving compassion. Furthermore, many people find giving compassion to themselves is not easy at all. In our society this is often associated with self-indulgence and weakness.

In our approach all three types of compassion are very important: others to self, self to self and self to others. If you reflect on this for a moment it is self-evident. If we just give out and do not take in, and if we do not take care of ourselves, it follows that we will run out of steam and burn out. This happens to so many people in caring roles, whether this be in the context of the family, or professionals such as nurses, doctors, therapists and care workers. Therefore, it is so important to stimulate the flow of compassion in these different directions. And not only compassion, but also kindness, joy and gratitude too.

For the vast majority of people, the place to start is self-compassion. Many of us are so terribly hard on ourselves. One of our teachers, Rob Nairn, once commented that if someone spoke to us in the way we habitually speak to ourselves, we would not stick around with this person for longer than a day; but in our own case we just roll over and succumb to the vicious attacks and beatings of our self-critic, often for an entire lifetime!

Until we face the self-critic, understand where it is coming from and bring some compassion to this wounded part of ourselves, we will not be able to embark on a path of authentic compassion. The worst-case scenario that is all too common these days is to constantly beat ourselves up whilst also being a martyr to others, constantly looking after the needs of everyone else whilst ignoring our own. This approach is doomed to failure.

For these reasons starting with self-compassion is a sane and important step.

Clarifying Our Motivation

It is important to be very clear what our motivation is for being compassionate otherwise our efforts at being compassionate can backfire.

Some people are motivated by a wish to be liked or approved of. Their actions may be motivated by an expectation of reciprocation: 'If I do this for you, then you will do something similar for me'. There is nothing wrong with this approach, but it is useful to be clear about our underlying motivation or we might become resentful if our assumption is not met.

Furthermore, we have worked with many people over the years who have low self-esteem and have spent their lives looking after everyone around them at the expense of themselves. They feel that they are not worth the kindness and care that they give to others. This approach is unbalanced and can lead to burnout, resentment and a martyr complex. As our teacher, Rob Nairn, always used to say, 'There is no need for self-sacrifice'. Genuine compassion balances our needs with those of everyone else and it is unconditional, but this takes time and practise.

An issue related to that of our basic motivation, is whether the way that we are being kind and caring is actually helpful in getting to the root of a problem or whether it is merely prolonging the problem. This type of kindness and caring may be the path of least resistance. It is a way to stay liked and approved of by those around us, but often we don't recognise this. One example might be always doing the washing and cooking for our teenage children, but the upshot is that they do not learn to do this for themselves and so cannot look after themselves when they leave home. It might be quite tough to ask our children to do this for themselves because it is what we have always done and it keeps the peace at home, but in the long term it is not in their best interests.

Another example is commiserating with someone who is always complaining, and in the process reinforcing their habit of resentment. It might take a lot of courage to respond in a different way to this person by not just going along with their litany of complaints, but by helping them to see that their habit of complaining is the real issue. Genuine compassion requires us to do something different from following the path of least resistance, and this might mean acting in a way that might make us less popular, at least in the short term.

By seeing deeply what causes us to suffer — including our underlying expectations, assumptions and habits — we can begin to see what causes others to suffer. By understanding how to relieve our own suffering at its root, we begin to recognise how to do this for others. This equips us to help others in an authentic and meaningful way. This will not always be easy for us or pleasing for others, but it is more likely to get to the root of the problem.

Practice Section

For each of the practice sections offered at the end of each chapter in this book, we recommend that you do a formal daily sitting practice of 20 to 45 minutes per day, as well as some informal, daily life practices. You might also like to keep a journal and record any observations about your practice. Make a few notes at the end of each practice about anything you have noticed. You can also journal about daily life practice at the end of each day. Then, once week or so, read over what you have written and reflect on it. If you notice any patterns beginning to emerge, write them down. You can ask yourself, 'How do I feel about this?' and journal your response to this question.

Formal Sitting Practice

Practice 3: Reflection on Intention and Motivation (15 – 20 minutes)

Once you have prepared your mind by following the reflection instructions on pages 4-5 of the Introduction, pose the following questions to yourself in a reflective way:

- *What am I intending to do in order to become more compassionate?*
- *Why do I want to be more compassionate?*
- *What is my deepest motivation for practising compassion?*
- *Can I express this as a heartfelt personal vision?*

Make a note of your intention and motivation at the front of your journal or write it on a piece of paper that you keep in your purse or wallet so that you can refer to it regularly. Each time you do a formal compassion meditation practice start by bringing to mind your intention and motivation. This is important because your intention reminds you of _what_ you are meaning to do whilst your motivation reminds you _why_ it is important to you. Intention sets your direction of travel. Motivation provides the energy to keep you moving in that direction.

Although, some core aspects of your intention and motivation may stay the same, over time you might notice that other aspects of your intention and motivation change. Keep a note of any changes in your journal.

If you so choose, you can end your session with the wish to carry forward any benefit from your practice into your daily life, so that it may be dedicated to the welfare of both yourself and others. This helps to ensure that you don't leave all your good intentions behind when you get up off your cushion.

Chapter Two

Why Practise Compassion?

Pain and Suffering

We practise compassion because all of us suffer *needlessly* and compassion practice can relieve this needless suffering.

There is unavoidable pain in life. The Buddha pointed this out over 2600 years ago in his famous teaching on the *Four Noble Truths*. He identified sickness, old age and death as key components of unavoidable pain. But there are many other forms too, such as grief and loss, losing what we hold dear and encountering what we feel aversion towards, along with all manner of ups and downs in life. We cannot do much about these since they are part and parcel of our fragile, impermanent lives.

But suffering is optional. This is what we add to the unavoidable pain by resisting it. Our friend and teacher, Rob Nairn, once remarked that actual pain amounts to 10% of the problem while our resistance and seeking to avoid pain amounts to 90% of the problem. When we resist pain, we compound it by thinking about it over and over again. This gives rise to strong emotions that stimulate more thinking as we tell ourselves stories about the pain. We then buy into these stories, and before we know it we have woven for ourselves a painful habit of suffering.

An example of this might be noticing a pain in our knee as we are doing sitting meditation practice. A sane approach would be to move our legs and if the pain persists simply to allow it to be. We might experiment with gently breathing into the area of pain, curious about the pattern of physical sensations that our mind labels as 'pain'. We might also place a hand on our knee as a gesture of self-soothing and feel the warmth and kindness implicit in this gesture. Our attitude here is to allow the pain to be as it is without resisting it or trying to get rid of it. There is just the pain.

Another approach might be to get angry about the pain in our knee. We might start ruminating on how we were clumsy and tripped yesterday and this why we are feeling pain now. We might then become frustrated and start berating ourselves for being a clumsy idiot — and then amplify this by ruminating on how we have always been careless and foolish! The more we buy into this story, the more worthless and demoralised we feel. And then, in the midst of our ruminations, we recall that we tripped over something that our equally careless neighbour left out on the path. Now we start blaming the neighbour and get ourselves worked up about how they are so messy and are bringing the entire neighbourhood down! We then imagine ourselves giving them a real talking to the next time we see them. All of this makes the pain feel so much worse. There is no longer just the pain; there is the self-created suffering too.

Alternatively, the pain in our knee might trigger our tendency to worry. We might worry that it will get worse and we might need an operation — or worse still, a knee replacement! Then we might be out of work for months on end and might even lose our job. We might then not be able to keep up our mortgage payments and end up homeless on the streets on crutches! The more we dwell on these stories, the more we buy into them and the more we trigger our fight and flight response. We feel shaky and our heart beats a lot faster. It is no longer just a pain in our knee, it is now a full-on catastrophe!

This example of unavoidable pain is a physical one. The same applies to emotional pain, such as grief and anger. We might tell ourselves stories of how we are alone in our grief and how no-one understands what we are going through; we then buy into these stories and pile on lashings of suffering. Similarly, we might blame other people for making us angry and for losing our temper, without it ever occurring to us to look inwardly and notice how our own self-created habit of anger is piling on the 90%.

We each have different styles of resisting our pain, depending on our habitual patterns. This is not our fault; it is simply part of the human condition. It is a habit that has been hard-wired into our brain by our conditioning. But when we recognise how we turn our pain into suffering, then change can occur.

Sutra of the Two Arrows

There is an ancient story that illustrates very well the difference between pain and suffering. Originally it was an oral teaching given by the Buddha. Many years after the Buddha died these oral teachings were recorded in writing by his students, and they became known as the 'sutras'.

According to this sutra, even the good and the wise are struck by one arrow in life, and this is the unavoidable pain that is part and parcel of being alive. Each one of us experiences change; we get sick, we get old and we die. Nobody can avoid these stark realities of life, even those who are saintly and wise. Furthermore, the first arrow strikes us over and over again, often on a daily basis, in the form of minor setbacks, fatigue, heartache and loss.

But most of us are struck by a second arrow which lands very close to where the first arrow struck, in the part of the body that is inflamed by the original wound. The Buddha described the second arrow as *resistance obsession* which is a wonderfully apt term for describing the unwillingness to feel the pain of the first arrow. This avoidance can take the form of suppressing the pain of the first arrow by actively pushing it away, by fixating on something else in order to distract ourselves, or by simply tuning out and becoming numb.

Each of us can reflect on the many ways these three reactions occur in our own experience. For example, we might receive some bad news in an email — someone we relied on to do something has let us down. Instead of coolly acknowledging the reality of the situation and taking care of our hurt feelings, we might immediately launch into a tirade of anger to our partner who has the misfortune of sitting next to us. Or we might distract ourselves from the feelings of hurt by going onto Facebook to find something appealing to focus on. Or we might consciously go numb by drinking one glass of wine after another!

Each of these reactions represent the second arrow of *resistance obsession*. The good and the wise are less susceptible to the second arrow because they have learnt from experience to stay with the present situation, to calmly weigh up the facts and take care of their hurt feelings. In this way their relationship to pain and setbacks is more straightforward, simple and effective. They have learnt from experience that reacting to pain creates an extra layer of problems and makes the situation worse. Basically, they have learnt that the first arrow is 10% of the problem and *resistance obsession* is 90% of the problem. This is what makes them wise! They feel the pain but they uproot the causes of suffering.

One of our colleagues, Clive Holmes, said once in a memorable teaching that there is a third arrow for those of us living in these modern times. He went on to say that this arrow is even more devastating than the first two because it strikes at our very identity. It is the tendency to put ourselves down and feel shamed for having been struck by the first two arrows. Shame is the killer blow because it renders us immobilised and powerless — it makes us feel that we are a flawed and unworthy human being.

In the practice of compassion, the key thing is to accept the first arrow, and to learn to work with the second arrow by cultivating acceptance of our reactive tendencies. We work with the third arrow by stepping into our power as a compassionate being, and from this place we hold the feelings of shame with kindness and understanding. We will come to this later in the book when we cultivate the compassionate self.

It will be useful to hold in the mind the image of the three arrows as we continue on our compassion journey because they provide a useful indicator of where we can get stuck, as well as being rich manure for our emergence as a compassionate person. Each of you can explore how the dynamic of the three arrows is unfolding in your own life by doing the practice of *Noticing Suffering* at the end of this Chapter.

A Path of Practice

Through our practise of mindful compassion, we begin to cultivate the resources to face the inevitable pain of life. We begin to develop the skills to spot the stories we tell ourselves, to drop them and to simply be with the underlying experience of original pain. As our teacher Rob Nairn has said repeatedly: 'There is no exemption certificate!'

We have to feel the original pain. But if we can do this with acceptance and without resistance, then the suffering can be avoided, or at least reduced.

We start by recognising how we pile on the 90% for ourselves. Once we begin to see how we do this to ourselves, we also see how others do it to themselves. There is no blame here. There is simply a recognition of how the human condition sets us all up to suffer. As we stop buying into our own suffering, we naturally stop buying into the suffering of those around us. When this happens we are much less likely to become overwhelmed. This creates the space for a skilful response to emerge so as to respond empathically to the suffering of others.

The practice of compassion is not theoretical. It is about facing the challenges and messiness of our day to day lives. Our life experience is the main ingredient in the experimental laboratory of our compassion practice. Bear in mind that:

'We are all spectacularly flawed.' John Paul Sartre
'...but this is completely OK.' Rob Nairn

Working Definition of Compassion

Since compassion is a response to suffering, it is important first to clarify what we mean by 'suffering'. This is what we have done in the section above. Now we can turn our attention to what we mean by 'compassion'.

We have a simple working definition of compassion. What we mean by a 'working definition' is one that is useful to us when we put compassion into practise. Compassion is a highly complex and nuanced human faculty and this working definition does not cover all the many aspects of compassion. It is not a comprehensive definition. What it seeks to do is clarify where our focus should be when we come to practise.

The working definition of compassion that we use in this book is attributed to the Dalai Lama:

'A sensitivity to the suffering of ourselves and others, along with a deep desire to relieve that suffering and its causes.' (Tsering, 2008.)

We can see from this definition that there are two main aspects to compassion. In the book Choden co-authored with Professor Paul Gilbert, *Mindful Compassion* (2013), Paul referred to these as the *two psychologies* of compassion because each of them entails different mental competencies and they draw on different parts of our motivational and emotional makeup. Therefore, each of them entails a different psychology. However, in this book we are choosing the simpler term of the *two aspects* of compassion.

The first aspect is developing a sensitivity to the suffering of ourselves and others. In the case of our own experience, we become closely attentive to what is going on for us in the present moment. We notice our habits of thinking around a difficulty or issue. We notice the emotional feelings associated with this difficulty, such as anger, fear or denial. We notice any physical sensations that we are experiencing in relation to the difficulty.

We notice, too, how we are relating to the difficulty, and become curious about any expectations, assumptions or stories that we are buying into.

So, the first aspect entails turning towards what is difficult, and not turning away. It involves welcoming what is there, even if it is unpleasant, rather than avoiding it. We learn to allow and make space for the pain and suffering that shows up in our lives. This does not mean that we need to dwell on it and become immersed in it. We simply allow it to be there *because it is there*, and we make room for it in our hearts and minds. This is a skill that comes from practising mindfulness and acceptance.

We also become curious about the pain and explore its different shades. This is what is meant by 'sensitivity'. It means that we see it, we allow it to be present and we become curious about it — rather than lapsing into unawareness and blocking it out. There is a profound wisdom here because avoidance and denial does not remove the problem; it just complicates it and makes it worse. As we discovered above, we end up getting struck by the second and third arrows and these compound our suffering.

Once we have attuned ourselves to what is there, compassion is a call to respond to the suffering we find. This brings us to the second aspect. Before we can respond, however, we need to develop the capacity to do so. Otherwise, it is like someone who is deeply moved by the sight of a drowning person (first aspect) jumping into a fast-flowing river to save the person before first learning how to swim! In this case two people end up drowning rather than one. In Buddhism this is called 'idiot compassion'. Therefore, what is called for in the second aspect of compassion is to build our capacity to respond to suffering and to cultivate the resources that are needed to do so.

In general, we could say that the first aspect of compassion is developed by training in mindfulness and acceptance, and the second aspect of compassion is developed by training in compassion *per se*. We could go on to say that the second aspect involves learning two things: building our capacity and then learning how to skilfully respond. Both go hand in hand with compassion training.

Often people remark that mindfulness is all about being and compassion is all about doing. We have found that some mindfulness practitioners even have a resistance to compassion training for this very reason. But this is only partially true. The second aspect of compassion also concerns the quality of being we bring to a situation and does not always involve doing something. The common understanding of compassion implies doing tangible things to help people, like giving food to someone who is starving, or giving protection to someone who is in danger etc.

But we could think of a situation where someone is dying of cancer. There might be very little we can do for them in a tangible way. All forms of treatment might have run their course and the person is lying in a hospital bed waiting to die. Yet compassion still has an important role here. We might sit by their bedside and allow ourselves to be touched by their suffering. This is the first aspect and relates to empathy. Furthermore, if we had trained in loving-kindness and compassion, the way we looked at them, the way we spoke to them, and the way we held their hand — all of these gestures would be infused with the energy of loving-kindness and compassion. Our very presence and way of being would emanate an energy of safe holding and support to this person. We could just sit with them and listen to them and offer a kind receptiveness. People can feel the compassionate presence of another person and oftentimes this can be far better than saying or doing something. This is all part of the second aspect of compassion and is more a quality of being than one of doing.

In practical terms, the second aspect of compassion entails cultivating inner emotional resources so that we are able to withstand the difficulties we experience, without becoming overwhelmed, and so that we can respond skilfully to what arises. These resources develop our compassionate capacity so that over time we are able to face more challenging circumstances without becoming overwhelmed. This requires us to develop inner resources of feeling safe, cheerful, kind, curious and allowing. These in turn develop into the *Four Immeasurable Qualities,* which we will come to later in the book. These qualities include loving kindness, sympathetic joy and equanimity. They also include compassion, which has specific qualities of courage and commitment, strength and stability, kindness and warmth, wisdom and understanding.

We will begin now by cultivating one of these resources. The reason for approaching things in this way (i.e. cultivating the second aspect before the first) is that before we approach suffering we need to feel confident that we are able to contain and deal with what we encounter, otherwise we might end up feeling overwhelmed and depleted. This might make us feel demoralised and reluctant to proceed further with compassion training. To avoid this we first build up some capacity.

If we think about preparing to run a marathon we don't immediately begin by running up a very long hill. It might be too much. So we start by running on a treadmill in a gym or doing some shorter runs first. This builds our strength and confidence so that we can keep going for the long haul. Training in compassion is just the same.

Cultivating Joy

One of the main messages of our teacher, Choje Lama Yeshe Rinpoche, is quite simply, 'Joy, joy and more joy!' When Lama Rinpoche gives a public talk he always emphasises the importance of a joyful attitude to life and recruits as many people as he can to his 'Joyful Club'. Whenever Lama Rinpoche speaks, he exudes an infectious glow of kindness and joy. Over the years this has rubbed off on us and we have recognised the power of an ongoing practice of cultivating joy because this provides a counterbalance to the focus on suffering that is inherent within compassion training.

Many of us have a 'glass half empty' approach to life. This is also known as a poverty mentality. We habitually focus on what is wrong with us and all the things that we do not have. We go around moaning about our lives and we tend to see only the negative qualities in people around us. Many of us end up meeting people sunk in poverty mentality too, and we end up becoming partners in crime, continually winding each other up about all the things that are wrong with everything. Clearly, this is not the path to happiness!

It is worth pausing here and recognising that as human beings we are hard-wired to recognise and respond very quickly to threats and challenges. This is described by neuroscientists as our *negativity bias*. This default setting in our brain has enabled us to survive in harsh conditions as we evolved as a species. These days, however, the issue is less about tigers jumping out of bushes and threatening our survival, and more about the tigers that live in our own minds. We find many of our own thoughts and feelings to be threatening.

By comparison, there is no survival imperative to recall and respond to all the good things in our lives. Sadly, we are not evolved for happiness; we are evolved for survival. Therefore, most of us pay little attention to the many daily occurrences of beauty and delight that are everywhere present as we go about our lives. Therefore, it takes discipline and practise to notice and appreciate these simple good things long enough for them to be installed as joyful traits within our minds.

Research from neuroscience recommends noticing the good things in life, savouring them and allowing them to enter deeply into our mind and body, as a way of re-wiring the brain for happiness. According to Rick Hanson (2009) the brain is good at learning from bad experiences, but bad at learning from good experiences. It is Velcro for negative experiences and Teflon for positive ones. This negativity bias of the brain derives from the fact that we are threat focused and primed for survival. So we need to actively work on cultivating positive neural pathways. From his research, Hanson suggests a three-fold approach:

1. Tune in — notice positive things around you — this is like lighting a fire.
2. Enrich — spend some time appreciating these things — this is like adding wood to the fire.
3. Take in the good — actively absorb the positive experience — this is like receiving the warmth of the fire.

Therefore, to support our compassion practice we might want to re-balance this negativity bias. Fleeting attention to positive occurrences is not enough. Research tells us that we need to attend to these occurrences for at least 20 to 30 seconds, actively appreciate them, and then consciously absorb their positive energy. Therefore, throughout this book we will be focusing on the cultivation of joy and will suggest daily life practices to build this capacity within ourselves.

Sphere of Energy in Your Heart

As a way of cultivating joy, we can imagine a sphere of energy in our heart centre — in the centre of our chest (i.e. not where our physical heart is located). We can imagine it being any colour that best represents compassion for us. This sphere of energy is a symbol of our emerging wellbeing and joy. It is like a cup that we are pouring our joy into and storing within ourselves so that we can offer it to whomsoever we choose. The visual image is not the main thing. The important thing is the felt sense of joy that is communicated by the image.

We are always imagining things. For example, if we are in love then we often bring to mind our loved one, the places we go to and the things we do together. These images become charged with feeling, and whenever we then bring an image of our loved one to mind our body resonates with the feeling of love. A similar principle is at play here. We imagine that the sphere of energy in our heart holds a feeling charge of joy. If you cannot imagine clearly, or if imagining a sphere of energy does not work for you, then just focus on the feeling of joy in your heart centre growing stronger and stronger.

Some people have strong visual imaginations and generate clear images in their minds of what they are calling forth. Other people have a 'felt sense' imagination and are able to generate clear feelings of what they are imagining. Yet other people have more of a story-telling imagination, in which a story unfolds as a series of thoughts and images when they bring something to mind. Most of us have a combination of these styles. The trick is to just go with the flow of how your own imagination works.

Once we have imagined the sphere of energy in the heart, whenever we notice something good and wholesome, such as the sound of birdsong or falling autumn leaves in a wooded park, we can pause and pay attention. We can spend some time feeling gratitude for this moment and notice how this makes us feel. And then, instead of glossing over this moment and moving on with our chores, we can stay present a little longer and simply appreciate the wonder of this fleeting moment. Then we can breathe in any sense of joy that arises from our gratitude and appreciation, breathing it into the sphere of energy in our heart and imagining that our heart glows with joy. Then, as we breathe out we can imagine breathing out this energy of joy to our loved ones and to the wider world. We might do this for ten breaths or so as a way of installing this experience of joy into our heart/mind circuitry. This is a skilful way of beginning the process of re-balancing the negativity bias within our brains.

Practice Section

Formal Sitting Practice

Practice 4: Noticing Suffering (20 minutes)
Begin by sitting in a relaxed and comfortable posture. Feel the weight of your body on the ground while sitting dignified and alert. Then pay attention to the rising and falling of your body as you breathe. To help settle your mind, try deepening your in-breath a little and lengthening your out-breath. See if you can regulate your breathing so that the in-breath and out-breath are of a similar length and rhythm. You might like to count to three or four on the in-breath and a similar count on the out-breath. When your mind begins to settle a little (this may take several minutes) let go of counting and allow your breathing to find its natural rhythm. Next, switch your focus to physical sensations in your body. Do you notice any prominent sensations? Feel from the inside how these sensations manifest. Feel the sensations in your hands where they rest on your lap. Feel the sensations in your sitting bones where they rest on your seat. Feel the sensation of your feet resting on the ground. Then scan your body from your feet upwards to become aware of the sensations throughout your body. Then, lightly focus on your breathing as a support. Whenever you notice that your mind wanders during this practice, bring your attention back to feeling the contact between your feet and the floor, aware of your body as a whole resting on your seat with a light focus on your breathing.

Now, pay closer attention to how you are feeling. In particular, become aware of any areas of pain or discomfort in your body. Also notice if any difficult emotions are present, perhaps held in the body too. Notice too if any distracting or unsettling thoughts are occurring in your mind. This is the first arrow. Reflect that other people also experience the unavoidable pain of life, not just you.

Now notice if there is any resistance to the discomfort you are feeling — not wanting to feel what you are feeling, or not wanting to be present. Notice if there is a tendency to avoid: either by suppressing your feelings or getting lost in fantasy or distraction. Become aware of the sense of suffering that is tied up in the compulsion to resist. This is the second arrow. Reflect on the fact that other people are also caught up in resistance obsession, not just you.

Now notice any feelings of unworthiness or self-attacking that spring up from the first two arrows: that subtle feeling that 'something is wrong with me because I feel bad and I don't want to feel like this'. This is the third arrow. Reflect that other people experience this too.

Now rest without any specific focus.

In the second part of the practice, reflect back on last week. Notice how you were feeling in general and how much of your experience was difficult, aversive or unwanted. Reflect on the pain in your experience, both inner and outer (first arrow). Notice if there was any resistance to this pain — not wanting to feel it, or not wanting to be present (second arrow). Reflect on how this felt. Also, did you notice any feelings of unworthiness or shame, or self-attacking thoughts, such as 'I am a failure' or 'I can never get it right'? (third arrow). Reflect on how this felt. Now reflect that most people experience something similar, and while the content may be different, the themes tend to be the same. How does this make you feel?

End the practice by acknowledging that none of this is your fault; it is just part of the human condition. Acknowledge that once you are able to see how resistance to pain creates suffering, a choice opens up to relate differently to your experience.

Informal Daily Life Practice

Practice 5: Gratitude and Appreciation

Set an intention at the start of your day to notice the good things in your life. Think of some examples of good things that you anticipate in the day ahead and set an intention to notice them as they happen. Then reflect on your motivation for doing this; how this will cultivate joy in your mind and enhance your wellbeing. Reflect on how this will benefit you and reverberate out to those around you.

When you notice something good and wholesome, like the sun falling on your skin or a gesture of kindness from a stranger, pause for a moment and appreciate it. Be grateful for it. Then imagine a sphere of energy in your heart centre and breathe into it any joy that arises from these feelings of gratitude and appreciation. As you breathe out, share any feelings of joy with your loved ones and the wider world. Do this for about ten breaths. You can count these breaths on your fingers.

At the end of the day, reflect back on any good things you noticed and appreciated. Reinforce your intention to do the same tomorrow, while recalling your motivation. You might like to journal what you noticed.

If you forgot to appreciate some good moments of your day, think back and bring them to mind now. Set an intention to remember them tomorrow. As you recall them, spend some time appreciating and being grateful for them now. Then imagine the sphere of energy at your heart and breathe into it any joy that arises from the gratitude and appreciation that you are now feeling. As you breathe out, share any feelings of joy with your loved ones and the wider world. Do this for about ten breaths. You can count these breaths on your fingers.

Through practising in this way, the positive energy of gratitude and appreciation will grow stronger within you and it will become a way of life.

Chapter Three

Building the Foundations

Why Mindfulness Is Important

Before we move on to compassion training proper, it is important to point out some important foundations for compassion. These are mindfulness, acceptance and kindness. Normally, in the Mindfulness Association experiential trainings, people would have completed a 4-weekend Mindfulness Course (or an 8-week Mindfulness Based Living Course) before undertaking a 3-weekend Course in Compassion (or an 8-week Compassion Based Living Course). From experience we have found the prior training in mindfulness to be a vital pre-condition for training in compassion.

In the last chapter we identified two aspects of compassion practice. The first entails noticing and turning towards what is difficult or painful. This relates directly to mindfulness. Before we can cultivate a compassionate response to ourselves and others, we need to be attuned to what is present. Often, however, we do not want to be in the present moment because it is uncomfortable and so an imagined future feels far more attractive. Therefore, the first step in compassion training is to have the courage to stay present and to be open to the rich diversity of our unfolding experience.

Modern life provides plenty of ways to escape the present moment. In so doing, we avoid and deny what is difficult in our minds and in our lives. Many of us turn to alcohol as a way of numbing ourselves. Others turn to the endless options for entertainment provided by TV box sets, video games, audiobooks and social media. All of these can be ways of distracting ourselves from what is happening right now in our lives. Moreover, many of us fill every moment of our lives with busyness, so that we never pause long enough to land in the present moment because we are always focusing on what is coming next. We do everything we can to avoid getting in touch with our present moment experience.

If we have spent our lives busily involved in activity and entertainment, then our minds will have developed a very strong habit of distraction. This habit impels us towards worrying about the future, dwelling on the past or daydreaming in the present. Out of touch with our present moment experience, we block the potential for wisdom to arise within us. Wisdom requires space and presence of mind to make itself known. It requires some basic training in mindfulness.

Furthermore, compassion training often involves using our imagination, for example by imagining a safe place or a compassionate being (as we will do in later chapters). It is easy to get lost in our thoughts when we do these imagination-based practices. Our mindfulness practice gives us the stability to stay present, in touch with our direct experience of thoughts, emotions and physical sensations while we are working with our imagination.

Yet mindfulness alone is not enough. As we begin to practise mindfulness and begin to see a lot more of what is going on in our minds, we can easily become discouraged. It is like going into a room and turning up the dimmer switch. The light of awareness gradually reveals what has been there all along — some of which might make us feel very uncomfortable. We might begin to notice dusty files with long lost records of the past, broken pieces of furniture and old photographs of people long forgotten. We might want to forget some of these things and wish we had not seen them. Therefore, we also need to train in kindness so that the energy we radiate within the internal environment of our mind has a warm and friendly quality, rather than a condemning and judging quality.

We also need to train in acceptance; this means coming to terms with what we see in the dusty room of our mind. Not only do we open the door to what is present, but we also welcome what is there and simply allow it to be there. Acceptance is an antidote to our normal habit of denying, resisting and pushing away difficult thoughts, feelings and emotions. It is the doorway to the practice of compassion. As Oliver Cromwell once famously said, 'We need to accept ourselves warts and all'.

One thing we need to acknowledge is the power of non-acceptance. Returning to the analogy above, there are two strong reactions we are likely to encounter when the dimmer switch of mindfulness lights up the messy room of our mind. The first is to shut the door to the room again and pretend not to see what is there by getting lost in distraction. Clearly, if we take this approach nothing will change.

Another reaction might be to work hard at tidying it up. This is our general approach when we find something within us that we do not like. We try to fix it. In trying to do so, however, we use the same methodology that caused the mess in the first place, namely thinking and problem solving. We somehow assume that if we think it through another time, and yet another time, some resolution will miraculously emerge. Einstein is reported to have defined insanity as doing the same thing over and over again and expecting a different outcome! Nevertheless, we can find it irresistible to pick away at our problems again and again. It is like picking at a scab and making it worse.

Once we approach the mess with kindness and allow it to be there as it is, on its own terms, the 'tidying up' happens by itself. If we stop picking at the scab it will heal itself. As a rule of thumb, we could say that acceptance is a skill of allowing what is there to be there and kindness is a skill of befriending what is there. We need both of these skills to bring about healing and change.

Key Mindfulness Skills

Our working definition of mindfulness is 'knowing what is happening, while it is happening, without preference' (Choden and Regan-Addis, 2018). Again, there are two aspects to this definition. The first is *knowing what is happening while it is happening.* This is about being knowingly present. All of us can do this; it is not complicated. At its most simple level, if we can feel our feet on the floor, the weight of our body resting on its seat, and the rising and falling of our body as we breathe, we are being mindful. This is the doorway to presence, which is a natural human capacity. It is most apparent when we do things we love to do, such as walking in nature. However, because of our strong habit of thinking, we very soon forget to be present; we get lost in thinking and we lose touch with the moment.

Therefore, we train in a mindfulness technique. We set an intention to be present and choose a focal support to help us. We might choose the physical sensations of the breath as a support; in which case we direct our attention to the rising and falling of our body as we breathe. This is an anchor that holds our attention in the present moment. After a while it is likely that we will notice that our mind has wandered away from the anchor. We have lost touch with the present moment and got lost in thinking. Nothing wrong here; we have just noticed what is happening. This is a moment of mindfulness. We might spend a moment being curious about where the mind has wandered to so as to familiarise ourselves with its wanderings. Then we bring our attention back once more to the rising and falling of the breath in the body. We have found our way back to presence of mind until we notice that our mind has wandered off once again.

This is the dance of our mindfulness practice: losing it and finding it. We notice we have lost presence of mind and our intention to be present brings us back to finding it again. We do this over and over again. This is why it is called 'practice'.

We bring as much lightness and playfulness as we can to this dance. It is no big deal that we lose awareness; the only issue is finding it again. Each time we notice that the mind has wandered off and we find our way back to presence of mind, we have exercised the muscle of mindfulness. Many repetitions of this process are required to strengthen the muscle of mindfulness. In this way we build a habit of presence and counter the habit of distraction.

Looking more closely at the first aspect of our definition — *knowing what is happening while it is happening* — we might ask ourselves, 'what is happening?' and 'how do we know what is happening?'

What is happening is that thoughts are arising in the mind. Sometimes they are fairly trivial thoughts, such as what we are going to have for dinner. Often they have an emotional charge behind them, such as desire or anger. We might think for example, 'I would like to have pizza for dinner, but I don't have any in the freezer', which may come with an emotion of thwarted desire. We might think, 'I don't have any milk in the fridge for tea because my kids have cleaned out the fridge', which may come with an emotion of frustration and anger. We are more likely to get caught up in the thoughts that arise with a strong emotional charge. These thoughts feel like they *require* thinking about and so we easily lose presence of mind.

The more we practise mindfulness the more we come to see that thoughts arise in the mind *of their own volition*. They just pop into the mind. Reflect back over your last mindfulness practice session: did you choose the thoughts and emotions that arose in your mind? Before you sat down to meditate, did you plan to have a cocktail of different thoughts and emotions arising, like this for example: 'Let me see, maybe I will have a little bit of peace and quiet, then some angry thoughts about my kids who took the milk, followed by anxiety and paranoia about what happened yesterday at work; then a small dose of shame to round it all off!'. Unlikely. Thoughts and emotions arise of their own accord. We call this the *self-arising* nature of thoughts.

But how do we know what is happening in the mind? The great advantage of the human mind is that it is self-aware. It has meta-cognition. This means that we have the capacity to step back and observe what is happening in our mind while it is happening. There is an aspect of mind which we might call the 'observer' that is able to know what thoughts are arising within the mind. If you stop and notice your thinking experience right now, you might get a sense of 'me noticing my thoughts'. The 'me' is the observer and it is able to notice thought activity within the mind. We experience our sense of self as arising within the observing part of the mind.

In mindfulness practice we train the observer to witness the arising thoughts impartially and not to get involved with them. If we are able to do this, then thoughts 'display themselves'. In simple terms they manifest in the mind like a wave rising to its peak, but if we don't add anything to the thought – if we don't react to it or get involved — then the wave subsides again and the thought 'liberates itself'. That means that it loses momentum and subsides. If we are able to witness the self-arising, self-displaying and self-liberation of thoughts, a great sense of freedom arises in the mind. We let the waves of our inner experience well up, rise to a peak and fall again. Through doing this we realise that if we do not give thoughts power by engaging with them they have no power over our mind. This is very liberating when it comes to the negative thoughts that afflict us on a daily basis.

However, this is not what generally happens. The more usual scenario is that when a thought arises, the observer engages with it, thinking happens and we are pulled away from the present moment. Each time we notice this happening we disengage from the thinking process, let the thought go free and bring our attention back to the mindfulness support. So we gradually train the observer to allow thoughts to come and go freely without habitually getting involved with them. We are training the observer to impartially witness thoughts; this means to witness the process of self-arising, self-displaying and self-liberating.

It is easier to observe trivial thoughts impartially. This is because they do not bother our sense of self located within the observer. As we mentioned before, thoughts with a strong emotional charge are more challenging. Before we know it, we have become involved because our sense of self feels it needs to fix the situation in some way. Somehow these types of thought seem to be more sticky, more irresistible, and the observer feels compelled to engage them.

An important part of mindfulness training is not to judge ourselves about this process. This is just how the mind works. The conditioning within our culture and society has instilled in us all a strong habit of thinking. We have been taught that the only way out of a difficulty is to think ourselves out of it. This is not our fault. However, as we become more familiar with how the mind actually works, we are able to take responsibility to train it to refrain from compulsively engaging with thoughts. This allows space for a deeper wisdom gradually to emerge.

Part of this wisdom is the understanding that we need to patiently persist in this training. Every time we get lost in thought we recognise this and come back to the support; we find our way back to presence of mind. We do this over and over again. Gradually, over time the observer refrains from engaging so many of the random thoughts arising in the mind; we remain present for longer periods of time and we are less distracted. Also, when we get distracted, we notice this more quickly and find our way back to presence of mind more easily.

We begin to see that there is a difference between thought and thinking. We cannot control the arising of thoughts any more than we can control the arising of sounds. But we can control whether or not we identify with thoughts and invest energy in them. This is what we mean by 'thinking'. Through mindfulness training we gradually develop wise discernment about which thoughts to invest in and which to leave alone.

Energy Follows Focus

This relates to a key principle in mindfulness training: *energy follows focus*. We give energy and power to the thoughts we focus on. If we follow random, negative thoughts we give them power. If we focus on positive, proactive thoughts we give these power. Similarly, if we put our focus on present moment awareness we strengthen the power of presence within our lives.

This is how habits are formed. If we have spent a lifetime worrying and feeding fearful thoughts, then we will have placed our focus and fed energy into a strong habit of anxiety. This means that anxious thoughts are more likely to arise in the mind and when they do the observer is habitually inclined to engage with them. This becomes a vicious circle. We spend a lot of time worrying and we end up becoming an anxious person.

Through mindfulness practice we shift our focus from compulsive engagement with thinking to present moment awareness, and we gradually train the observer to refrain from engaging anxious thoughts. The less these thoughts are engaged, the less energy is invested in this habit. Gradually over time less anxious thoughts arise in the mind and when they do the observer is less inclined to identify with them. The same is true for other types of thoughts, such as angry or sad thoughts.

Our teacher, Rob Nairn, describes us human beings as 'ramshackle collections of habitual patterns', and our mindfulness practice certainly reveals this to be true. However, our mindfulness practice gives us the skills to refrain from perpetuating negative, unskilful habits, like rumination, worry and persistent irritation. Instead we begin to cultivate skilful, life-enhancing habits. This is important when it comes to compassion training because a key focus is cultivating qualities such as loving kindness, joy, and equanimity. But we can only do this once we have found a way to uproot the negative habits, and mindfulness is the key method for doing this.

Without Preference

We will now explore the second aspect of our working definition of mindfulness: *without preference*. This phrase needs some unpacking. It does not mean that we should not make any choices, which is implied by the term 'preference'. It means that we should be aware of our habitual, knee-jerk likes and dislikes and not immediately buy into them, but instead pause and choose what response we want to make. So, instead of reacting automatically and habitually, we respond based on the emerging awareness and wisdom that comes from mindfulness practice. This is another way of describing the principle of *energy follows focus* that we touched on above.

The key point here is that we need to train the *attitude* of the observer. This is something we begin in mindfulness training. The first stage is to clearly identify the dysfunctional observer within ourselves: that part of us that is addicted to its habits of like and dislike even if they do not serve us. We like to feel calm and not anxious; we like to feel clear and not fuzzy headed etc. It is also that part of us that has distinctive preferences for how life should go in the world outside: for example, what kind of people we like to spend time with and who we definitely want to avoid. We need to see these reactions clearly and choose whether to invest energy in them or not. This is the role of mindfulness training.

The next step is to consciously cultivate a compassionate observer within ourselves. This means that we begin to cultivate certain qualities within the observer based on a value system we choose, namely wishing not to harm ourselves and others and wishing to benefit ourselves and others wherever we can.

This is the value system of compassion. As the Dalai Lama once famously said, 'Do your best to benefit other living beings, and if you cannot benefit them, then at least do not do them any harm'. This is the function of compassion training. But what is so important — and why we are explaining mindfulness in some detail in this chapter — is that we cannot proceed to this step unless we have the stability that comes from sustained mindfulness practice.

In Chapter 8 we will focus on how to cultivate a compassionate observer. Two very important mindfulness skills that lay the foundations for doing so are acceptance and kindness. In our approach to mindfulness training these are two key elements of the attitude we learn to cultivate within the observer.

We can unpack the *without preference* part of the mindfulness definition some more by saying that we are training to be accepting and kind while at the same time patiently working on the mindfulness method of noticing distraction and returning to the focal support. Moreover, we are accepting and kind *both* towards our experience — the endless thoughts and feelings that arise within us — and also towards the dysfunctional observer within us that is always falling prey to the same reactions again and again.

Once we have some training in cultivating this attitude of acceptance and kindness, we can build on this further by doing the compassion training that is the focus of this book. But right now, let's look a little more at acceptance and kindness.

Acceptance

Acceptance opens the door to compassion. As long as we are denying, resisting and fighting with our inner experience, this door remains firmly shut. But once we develop the courage to notice uncomfortable or troublesome feelings and open our hearts to them, this door gradually begins to open. Along with courage, it is important is to be curious about what we find. When there is both courage and curiosity then genuine acceptance arises, and this creates the conditions for genuine compassion.

We can use our imagination as a way to facilitate the process of acceptance. The human imagination is very powerful. Choden appreciated this fact when he was about to swim in a murky pool in South Africa and imagined that there might be crocodiles lurking beneath the surface. Even though people reassured him that crocodiles have never been spotted in this pool, the very fact that he was in the wilds of Africa inspired irrational fantasies that no reasoning could dispel! The body responds to our imagination by feeling terror even if there is no logical reason for feeling that way.

Conversely, we can use our imagination in a helpful way. One way of doing so is by using the Rumi poem, *The Guest House* (Rumi, Coleman, 2003) as a visual metaphor for the process of acceptance. In this poem the human experience is compared to that of a guest house. New guests are arriving and old ones are leaving in a constant succession. Some of the guests might be the type we naturally prefer, such as joy, wellbeing and even-mindedness. Other guests might be the type we would rather not accommodate, such as depression, malice, sorrow or shame. Regardless of the type of guest that arrives at our door, the poem exhorts us to welcome them all and be grateful for their arrival. The invitation to 'meet them at the door laughing' comes from the recognition that even the most troublesome guests can turn out to be the ones that we learn the most from in the long run.

The actual practice of acceptance can be described as a series of steps: Recognising, Allowing, Intimate attention and Non-identification (popularised as the RAIN acronym). This practice has been discussed in detail in our MBLC book (Choden and Regan-Addis, 2018) and by other mindfulness teachers like Tara Brach. However, we will touch on it briefly here because it is an important foundation for compassion practice.

Recognising — The first step in accepting a difficult emotion or issue is simply to acknowledge it. The mind is tricky and it can subtly tune out of such emotions or issues by getting lost in daydreaming or planning. If we are not even aware of a difficult emotion or troubling thought then there is no chance of accepting it. Whilst if we acknowledge it then we step out of denial and the door to acceptance opens. This first step is to imagine the emotion or issue to be like a guest knocking on the door of our internal guest house and us opening the door to see who is there. All this step requires is simple acknowledgment, such as saying to the guest, 'Hello anxiety, or hello frustration, or hello low mood'. This is like acknowledging the *self-arising* nature of experience. All we are required to do is simply to notice it and give it space to express itself, which leads to the next step.

Allowing — The second step is to allow the issue or emotion to be present in our experience. Here we imagine welcoming the guest into our guest house and inviting it to make itself comfortable. All the doors of the guest house are open and it can leave whenever it chooses, but we do not try to force it out. This stage is powerful because we are placing ourselves in alignment to the present moment situation of how we are feeling rather than being in opposition to it. If we resist how we are feeling, the energy of resistance acts as a glue that paradoxically binds us to the difficult emotional state; but if we allow the situation to unfold in its own way then the inexorable process of change will provide the resolution that we are seeking.

This is another way of expressing the principle we discussed above of training the observer impartially to observe what is happening in the mind. It creates the conditions for the process of *self-display*: the guest is given space and freedom to express itself without us blocking or suppressing it. Here we might imagine that it is sharing something about itself and we are open and curious about what it has to say, without interfering in any way. If we are able to do this then the difficulties surrounding an issue often resolve themselves and some new perspective emerges of its own accord. We understand something new about the guest, who is then happy to leave the guest house of its own accord.

In Buddhist texts they say it is like a snake that has become all tangled up in a knot; we just need to leave it alone and it will disentangle itself. If we interfere and try to disentangle it ourselves then we end up getting bitten.

In most cases the first two stages of RAIN are sufficient. However, sometimes we experience what Rob Nairn calls the 'elastic band syndrome' in which the mind cannot leave the issue alone. Every time we draw our attention away the force of habit pulls us back like an elastic band. The observer repeatedly engages with the arising issue or emotion and cannot stop picking away at it. It is like we are trying to disentangle the snake without letting this happen by itself. In this way we interfere with the process of self-display and we block the self-liberation. When this happens we need to use the next stage of the RAIN practice.

Intimate Attention — In this stage we make the presenting issue or emotion the focus of our mindfulness practice rather than using a neutral support such as sound or breath. Here we might imagine that we are sitting down for a good ole cup of tea and a chat with the guest. We are open to all that it has to say about itself, and we do so with an attitude of kindness and curiosity, without interrupting the guest or trying to fix or advise it in any way. We use this stage of RAIN to provide an open space for the guest to speak its truth and tell its tale. This is a way of creating the right conditions for self-display to happen.

We do this by first attending to the physical sensations in our body that relate to this emotion or issue. We ask ourselves where do we feel the sensations in our body and how do they feel from the inside? Secondly, we notice any emotions that are associated with the issue. There may be just one or several layers of emotions to notice. We might ask ourselves, does this guest come with an emotion attached to it? Thirdly, we notice the thoughts that we get caught up in that are associated with the issue. Finally, we notice how we are relating to the issue. Are we taking it to be solid and real — some permanent reflection of who we are? We inquire about how we are relating to the guest. Do we buy into its tale of woe? Do we believe it reflects badly on us? And finally, do we think that *we are the guest*?

Non-identification — In the final step of RAIN we zoom out of the issue and recognise that it is just one aspect of a much bigger experience. The key insight here is that the guest does not define us — it is not who we are — it is just something moving through us. We are the guest house and not the guest. We realise that we do not have to take the issue quite so seriously. In our imagination we see that this is just one guest amongst many, all of whom come and go from our guest house over time. The guest is free to roam about and stay in the guest house as long as it would like to. We might even imagine giving the guest a comfortable room with a nice view and inviting it to stay for as long as it wants. Sometimes the guest will then leave amicably as a friend. At other times is will take up the invitation to stay and make the room its home. It is important that we do not have an agenda to get rid of our guest. We gradually learn, by using our imagination in this way, to relate to our guests in a kind and accepting way, as any good guest house owner should! In so doing, we create the conditions for *self-liberation* — for the emotional issue to arise, express itself and change in its own time and in its own way.

The stages of acceptance described in the RAIN practice are very important foundations for doing the compassion practices described in the rest of the book.

Kindness

In the RAIN practice we are learning to welcome and accept the guests that arrive at the internal guest house of our mind. We are learning the skill of *allowing*. In our kindness practice we are cultivating kindness towards all the guests that arrive at our guest house as well as to our self as the proprietor of this crazy guest house. This is self-kindness. We then extend this kindness to others and recognise that everyone else is in the same situation; everyone else is a proprietor of their own guest house with a wide variety of unruly guests coming and going. This is kindness for others. Through kindness practice we are learning the skill of *befriending*.

Kindness is the basic building block for the second aspect of compassion, namely cultivating our inner resources to respond skilfully to suffering. Therefore, it is important to become acquainted with what kindness actually feels like. For this reason we start with the *Felt Sense of Kindness* practice. This practice is a daily life practice that is adapted from the *Memories of Kindness* practice that is used in our mindfulness training (Choden and Regan-Addis, 2018).

Felt sense is much more important than an idea of kindness. People can have many ideas about what kindness means but knowing what it feels like for oneself is the most important thing. Then we can start to cultivate it. This relates to the principle of *energy follows focus*. If we tune into the feeling of kindness in our self and give it energy, then kindness grows.

Like compassion, kindness flows in different directions: from self to others, from others to self and from self to self. In the *Felt Sense of Kindness* practice we will learn to become directly acquainted with the flow of kindness in these different directions. Through paying attention to how kindness flows in our lives and by actively cultivating it, a habit of kindness begins to grow. From time to time we might notice blocks to kindness such as going numb or being unable to feel anything.

When this happens we bring to mind one of the key principles underlying compassion training — that the blocks are part of the path (see Chapter 1) — and work with these blocks and obstacles by using the RAIN method.

Body Like a Mountain

The main formal sitting practice for this chapter derives from a Zen Buddhist practice called, *Body Like a Mountain, Breath Like the Wind and Mind Like the Clear Blue Sky*. We have added another element to it, *Heart Like the Sun*. This practice contains within it everything we have discussed in this chapter. *Body Like a Mountain* refers to the sense of stability that comes from our meditation posture and feeling of being grounded that is so important in mindfulness practice. This quality is especially important when we come to engendering the Compassionate Self in Chapter 8. *Breath Like the Wind*, or a gentle breeze, refers to the focal support of breathing in mindfulness practice. It is the anchor that ties our mind to the present moment. *Mind Like the Clear Blue Sky* refers to the process of acceptance. Once we have welcomed all the guests that show up in our minds, the natural spaciousness of the mind becomes available to us. Simply put, we feel more head space. It is only when we fight and resist the guests that this space shuts down. *Heart Like the Sun* refers to the quality of kindness that we nurture as we train in mindfulness and compassion. It emanates warmth like sunshine.

Practice Section

Formal Sitting Practice

Practice 6: Body Like a Mountain (20 – 30 minutes)
Begin by sitting in a relaxed and comfortable posture on a cushion or chair. Feel the weight of your body on your seat while sitting dignified, upright and alert. Then pay attention to

the rising and falling of your body as you breathe. To help settle your mind, try deepening your in-breath a little and lengthening your out-breath. See if you can regulate your breathing so that your in-breath and out-breath are of a similar length and rhythm. You might like to count to three or four on the in-breath and a similar count on the out-breath. If your mind is flighty and full of thoughts try placing one hand on your abdomen, feeling the movement of your body as you breathe. When your mind begins to settle a little, let go of counting and allow your breathing to find its natural rhythm.

Now deepen the sense of grounding by imagining your body to be like a mountain, stable and immovable, rooted on the vast Earth beneath you. Imagine drawing a sense of strength and stability from this image: body like a mountain rooted on the vast Earth beneath you. What is more important than the image of a mountain is the felt sense of stability and strength — really feeling that you are like a mighty mountain and drawing on the vast Earth beneath you that is supporting you and giving you strength. And, just like the vast Earth holds your body, so does your body hold your mind. *Body Like a Mountain.*

Now imagine your breath to be like the wind or a gentle breeze caressing the mountain. Just like the wind, the breath has a life of its own. You are being breathed. Simply let your attention flow with the natural rhythm of your breathing, while maintaining the image of your body being like a mountain. Connect with the naturalness of your breath coming and going just like the wind is a natural expression of the elements. When your attention drifts off and gets lost in thought, simply notice this, and return your attention to your breathing: *Body Like a Mountain, Breath Like the Wind...*

Now imagine your mind to be like the limitless blue sky. Many clouds can appear in it; there can be many storms and flashes of lighting and torrential rain, but none of this affects the clear blue sky which is always limitless and open. Similarly, when you simply notice the arising of thoughts, emotions and mind states, and just allow them to come and go, then you stay in touch with the clear blue sky. Just say Yes to whatever arises in your experience; and even if a strong No resounds from within you, say *Yes to this too. Body Like a Mountain, Breath Like the Wind, Mind Like the Clear Blue Sky...*

Now imagine that there is a coloured sphere of energy in the centre of your chest. As you breathe in, imagine that this sphere of energy glows like sunshine, and as you breathe out imagine that a warm energy of kindness fills up your body and mind bringing you healing and wellbeing; then when you breathe in again it glows brighter still and when you breathe out this time the energy of kindness streams out to other people and animals in your immediate environment bringing them healing, kindness and wellbeing. In this way alternate between self-kindness and kindness to others. *Body Like a Mountain, Breath Like the Wind, Mind Like the Clear Blue Sky, Heart Like the Sun...*

To conclude the practice, rest without any specific focus, not trying to meditate any longer, just resting loosely.

Informal Daily Life Practice

Practice 7: Felt Sense of Kindness

As you go about your daily life, see if you can pay attention to small acts of kindness that other people do for you. For example, a stranger might smile at you or a shop attendant might be very helpful and warm. Notice how this feels and notice where you feel it in your body. Once again imagine (or just feel) that there is a sphere of energy in your heart. It can be any colour you associate with kindness. When you notice and appreciate the act of kindness imagine breathing it into the sphere of energy in your heart, feeling it grow brighter and stronger. As you breathe out, share any feelings of kindness with your loved ones and the wider world. Try to find a natural flow to this process that is simple and easy and works for you.

Next, notice small acts of kindness that you do for others or intentionally perform random acts of kindness for others. Notice how this feels and notice where you feel it in your body. Once again imagine breathing the feeling of kindness into the sphere of energy in your heart centre, imagining that it grows brighter and stronger. As you breathe out, share any feelings of kindness with your loved ones and the wider world.

Next, notice small acts of kindness that you do for yourself or intentionally perform little acts of kindness for yourself. Notice how this feels and notice where you feel it in your body. Once again imagine breathing the feeling of kindness into the sphere of energy in your heart centre, imagining that it grows brighter and stronger. As you breathe out, share any feelings of kindness with your loved ones and the wider world.

When you go to bed at night, recall any acts of kindness from the day that has just passed. Once again imagine breathing the feeling of kindness into the sphere of energy in your heart centre, imagining that it grows brighter and stronger. As you breathe out, share any feelings of kindness with your loved ones and the wider world. Then make the intention to notice acts of kindness tomorrow when you wake up.

Chapter Four

Compassionate Mess

Ascent to Perfection

When many people embark on the path of compassion they nurse a secret hope that they will ascend to a spiritual high ground where they are above all the messiness of life. They bring to mind great examples of compassion — like Mother Theresa, Ghandi and the Dalai Lama — and try to emulate them. They might even start wearing white (or indeed maroon) robes, light scented candles and feel increasingly pure and holy. Underlying all this is a subtle but powerful wish to become perfect; to become the best, most exalted, version of our self, leaving behind all the shadowy and dark aspects of our personality as we ascend to the spiritual heights where the great beings dwell.

We live in a culture in which there are many examples of 'perfection' and where there is a subliminal message pervading mainstream media that happiness lies in the quest to become perfect, for example aspiring to have perfect bodies like models in fashion magazines or yearning for a perfect life in all its aspects. The 'American dream' is a good example of the drive to perfection. It is selling a perfect marriage and happy family, living in an eco-perfect house in the appropriate middle-class neighbourhood. We have examples of perfection in every human endeavour from business to sport, politics to art. The overall message is that happiness and fulfilment depend on us following the path 'upwards', such as moving up the corporate ladder in business.

This way of thinking can also affect our spiritual pursuits. Many religious paths can also have a powerful message of self-improvement, and the practices are often focused on purifying negative tendencies and acquiring positive qualities. In itself this is not a problem. It is the mind set or motivation that drives it. If we subtly disown the negative and focus just on becoming good and holy and positive, there is the very real danger of what is described as a 'spiritual bypass'. We avoid all the stuff that really needs to be addressed in ourselves and focus instead on becoming better versions of our self. Choden is very aware of this from his experience of living as a monk. It is so easy to waft upwards to the 'higher realms' wearing his maroon robes, and many people project onto monks the idea that they are somehow above it all and dwell on a higher plane of awareness. Luckily, in Choden's case, he has teachers and friends who regularly bring him down to Earth!

The tragedy in the self-improvement project is that so much energy is expended in keeping up the pretence of perfection; and there is always so much shame when it comes to falling short. We see ourselves not having a perfect body, partner, car, job etc., and to top it all, we also have an imperfect mindfulness and compassion practice! At a deeper level, this quest to become perfect comes down to the yearning to be loved and accepted. We think that only by being the best version of ourself will we be loved and included. The great, unspoken fear is that if we are seen as imperfect or unworthy we will be cast out of our group. From an evolutionary perspective this is disastrous because our very survival is then threatened.

This 'perfection complex' was acknowledged a long time ago in the Buddhist tradition. It was seen as a major pitfall on the path of genuine wisdom and compassion. There is a wonderful story that speaks to the aspiration towards spiritual perfection and the subsequent descent into ashes.

The Story of Chenrezig

In the Tibetan Buddhist tradition the archetype of compassion is the bodhisattva Chenrezig. A bodhisattva is someone who forsakes the bliss and peace of Nirvana to continually reincarnate to help living beings wake up to the truth of their true identity.

According to the myth surrounding Chenrezig, Amitabha, the Buddha of limitless light, realised that he needed an emanation of his compassionate activity to help him free beings who were sunk deep in interminable confusion and suffering. He emanated a ray of light from his forehead and Chenrezig miraculously appeared from this light. Chenrezig then knelt down in front of his creator, Amitabha, and took the bodhisattva vow: that he would work tirelessly for the benefit of all living beings and would not rest in the peace of Nirvana until all beings were free of suffering. He then added a radical endnote to this vow: that if he should forsake this commitment, 'may he shatter into a thousand pieces'. Clearly, Chenrezig meant business!

When Chenrezig began his work of rescuing beings from the limitless pit of samara (the realm of conditioned existence that all of us are in) his heart was so struck by the deep confusion and pain afflicting so many living beings that he wept tears of great sorrow. From the tears that fell from his left eye, the bodhisattva White Tara appeared and from the tears that fell from his right eye, the bodhisattva Green Tara appeared. Both forms of Tara are feminine expressions of compassionate activity. Green Tara is a fierce and quick-acting bodhisattva connected with overcoming fear and obstacles, whereas White Tara is a peaceful bodhisattva connected to promoting health and longevity.

Chenrezig now had two allies to assist him with his compassionate quest. For countless aeons (many thousands of years) he and his two allies worked tirelessly to wake beings up from their sleep of confusion and to point out to them the true nature of their minds, whilst also rescuing them from all manner of dangers and disasters like any good parent would do looking after their children.

After working tirelessly for many thousands of years, Chenrezig decided one day to climb to the top of the highest mountain in the universe, Mount Meru, and look down on the different realms of existence. Basically, he wanted to see how his work was going. To his great dismay, despite all of his work over countless eons, the number of beings sunk in misery and suffering was innumerable, just like when he started his quest.

Like any reasonable bodhisattva, he realised that his mission was going nowhere. When he began, there were countless number of beings sunk in suffering, and now thousands of years later there were still as many. He lost heart and thought, 'what is the point, where is this going?' and then decided to retire to the peace of Nirvana. At that moment he shattered into a thousand pieces because he had broken his vow to Amitabha and the fragments of his sublime form fell down to the foot of Mount Meru scattering on the plain below.

This stirred Amitabha from his meditative equipoise. He looked down from his heavenly realm and saw that his creation was in pieces and in great agony. And then through the power of his enlightened mind he recreated Chenrezig from the shattered fragments into a 1000-armed and 11-headed version. He was now even more powerful and effective than before. Each of his 1000 hands had an eye from which he could look out and perceive the suffering of beings, and each of his 11 heads looked out in different directions, surveying with compassion the different realms of samsara. Something much more magnificent had emerged from the shattered remains of his former self. Once again in the presence of Amitabha, he took his vow to free beings from suffering and not to rest in the peace of Nirvana until his job was completed. Perhaps this time he did not include the fatal endnote, who is to know!

Compassion as Descent

This story describes the process whereby our heart breaks open to give birth to true compassion. First, we are inspired by lofty ideas. We want to scale the heights and do great things in the world. In the case of Chenrezig it was a wish to liberate all beings from suffering and bring them to Enlightenment — what could be more exalted than this! Then there is the dismay and despair as it dawns on us that our efforts are not yielding the fruit we had hoped for. This then begins a process of agonising descent as we tumble down from the lofty peak of our idealism and crash back down to earth.

Many of us are like this. We might be inspired by a compassionate zeal to become a nurse or social worker or clinical psychologist. We want to really make a difference in the world, and then reality kicks in. Perhaps we experience lack of adequate staffing and heavy workloads or institutional structures that lack a compassionate ethos. We give out too much and there is not enough taking care of ourselves. Consequently we hit the wall and crash — just like Chenrezig did. All our dreams turn to ashes. The huge prevalence of burn out in the modern workplace is a sad example of this process. In the caring professions this is being called 'compassion burnout'.

All seems lost. But then something is touched within us that initiates a process of renewal. Out of the anguish and the despair and chaos something much more powerful and genuine can be born. But this depends on whether the right conditions are in place and how we respond to the situation we are in. This brings us to the second part of the Chenrezig story — the lotus flower emerging from the mud — which we will come to shortly.

The real cost of the process of descent is that the bubble of perfectionism is burst. We cannot sustain the effort of climbing the ladder upwards any longer, whether it be the corporate ladder or the compassionate ladder, or the stairway to heaven immortalised in the famous song by Led Zeppelin! We cannot maintain the pretence anymore. We might come to see that we have been nurturing an ego ideal of being a good person or a kind person or a person who always comes to the rescue of others. This is what hits the wall. If we are honest, we are often compassionate because we want to be liked and when we think that people like what we are doing we may feel good and then confuse this with compassion. Just like in the story of Chenrezig, compassion is not necessarily going to give us what we want; we might not get the satisfaction of climbing to the highest peak and surveying our work with pride.

As the story of Chenrezig shows us, what is called for is the willingness to drop down into our unpredictable, messy humanity that normally we prefer to sanitise or avoid. When we begin to do this our inner voices of conditioning might start to cry out: 'Don't go there, you may lose control; stay in your familiar prison of trying to be good and kind and nice, and work on your self-improvement project'. But the call of compassion is the willingness to continue the descent and not heed the voices of conditioning. In reality it requires a lot of courage and skill and support to embark on this journey. We need to have the two aspects of compassion fully honed and developed within us.

For many people, this process of descent is not a choice. Life hits them hard in some way and they take a fall. This can take many forms: the sudden death of a loved one, discovering that one has a life-threatening illness, depression, losing one's job or facing economic insecurity. Life deals us a heavy and unexpected blow. There is the scary realisation that we cannot go back to the way that things were before, but the way forward is not at all clear.

In the writing of the mystical Christians this process of descent is described as the dark night of the soul. We fall from certainty and conviction into unknowing and confusion. The way forward is not clear and yet there is no way of going back. It is like a descent into the underworld where life as we know it turns to ashes and all seems bleak. St John of the Cross describes the dark night as a time when everything we do in life loses its lustre. Our spiritual compass has gone off course and life has lost its meaning. This can indeed be a very troubling time, but all the great saints of the past have agreed that if we can find our way through the dark night it can be a highly creative time, in which there is a significant shift and reorientation at the very core of our being.

Compassionate Mess

The term 'compassionate mess' was famously coined by Rob Nairn in one of our early compassion retreats. It resonated with many of us and over time it has become a core theme in our compassion training. Rob was pointing to exactly the process we have been describing in the paragraphs above. Once we recognise that the human condition is not one of perfection, we can begin to recognise that our inner environment is a bit (or a lot) of a neurotic mess. We can own the fact that we are a compassionate mess. What a relief!

In some of our early retreats Rob would begin by insulting his audience and saying things like, 'Face it, you are all a bunch of neurotic messes, and what is more I am the biggest mess of you all! So how about we just mess around together and stop pretending!' The effect was huge. Instead of feeling indignant and taken aback, there was a palpable sense of relief in the room. People could let themselves off the hook of trying to be good and perfect and just accept and befriend the wonderfully quirky and unique person that they really were. We would notice people furtively looking around and thinking, 'Well maybe these people are like me; they are also insecure and vulnerable and longing to be loved and accepted for who they are, not for who they think they should be'. It was always a poignant moment.

At one memorable retreat in 2009, the Mindfulness Association had recently been formed and we were in the process of setting up structured trainings that continue to this day. We had just launched the first cycle of compassion training and people who had successfully completed the three training weekends were awarded a certificate of completion at the end of this cycle. There was a little ceremony in which we acknowledged each participant, they shared a little about their journey and then Rob handed them the certificate. Just before the ceremony began, Rob had this to say:

'Maybe you are going to get 2 certificates at the end of this course. One will be a certificate of completion, the other a certificate of authority. This second one will say that you are allowed to be human — to be imperfect, dysfunctional and neurotic. So, if nothing else, by the end of this course, you will be happily imperfect, dysfunctional and neurotic. Join the human race! If that is what emerges then I for one will be blissfully happy. My life will have been worthwhile and I will be able to retire. I know I'm given to exaggeration but right now I'm not exaggerating: if you can arrive at that point your life will transform. There is no doubt about it. This is because you will let yourself off a very painful hook. You will finally settle down, and instead of dangling, you will land on your bottom. And it is much more comfortable to sit on your bottom than to dangle on a hook! And then there's a chance of being happy and bringing happiness to others. So we are taking compassion from the level of interesting aspiration to really nitty-gritty reality. And you may well discover that it is something that you can actualise in your own life, and then bring to others — and still you are not required to be perfect. You can be a compassionate mess. You can go forth into the world as a compassionate mess. We may even develop different categories: the neurotic compassionate, the dysfunctional compassionate, the anxious compassionate, and so forth — there is a place for each one of you and you will find it!' (Nairn, 2009.)

The Lotus Flower Growing Out of the Mud

We now return to the story of Chenrezig. The first part was about ascent and fall and shattering into a thousand pieces. The key point was that he had to go through this process to achieve his full compassionate potential. The same is for all of us. The more painful the experiences that life throws at us, the more potential arises for the development of compassion. On the path of compassion we don't ask for the hard times; however life often obliges us by providing them. Experiences that are difficult and painful become opportunities for learning and personal growth, rather than a source of misery to be avoided. We begin to approach the inevitable pain of life with open curiosity, rather than aversion.

The second part of the story relates to the origin of Chenrezig and it is about descent and emergence. The metaphor used to describe this process is that of a lotus flower growing out of the mud at the bottom of a lake. The lotus flower is a Buddhist symbol for the mind that awakens its birth-right of wisdom and compassion. It is a powerful image because the flower grows out of the mud and yet when it blooms on the surface of the lake its white petals are completely pure and untainted.

The seed of the lotus flower is covered over by the mud at the bottom of the lake. The lotus seed is a metaphor for our compassionate potential. Only by descending to the bottom of the lake and befriending the mud will we uncover this seed and allow it to germinate. Once again, we cannot access the qualities of compassion by ascending upwards into the heavens where the great saints dwell. Our perfectionist mentality will not serve us here. It needs to crash and fall and shatter into a thousand pieces.

The key point about this story is that the lotus flower needs the mud in order to grow. The mud is the manure without which it will shrivel and die. Similarly, we need to turn towards our painful experiences — our own inner mud — in order for our compassionate potential to grow and mature. The mud is our messy, flawed, imperfect humanity that Rob Nairn encouraged us to drop into. It symbolises our dark side; all those difficult, troublesome emotions that afflict us on a daily basis like anger, desire, jealousy and pride. It also represents painful, habitual patterns such as shame and unworthiness, loneliness and insecurity. It is all those parts of us we would prefer that other people did not know about us, and furthermore it is those parts of us that not even we want to know about.

Therefore, approaching and befriending our mud requires courage and skill. This is the first aspect of compassion. We do not want to throw ourselves headlong down into it and drown in it. It needs to be a gradual process. For this reason we need gradually to build our capacity to contain the mud and to support the process of the growth of the seedling of compassion within us. This is the second aspect of compassion.

From that seed a shoot will sprout and gradually grow upwards towards the surface of the lake. This symbolises our gradual emergence as a wise and compassionate human being. Initially we will not recognise this process because it is happening beneath the surface of the lake. The water represents different levels of unconsciousness and the surface is the threshold of full conscious awareness.

People sometimes tell us that the process is hard going and all they can see is more and more mud — and it is smelly and foul! We find that compassion training is where things can get tough and where we are really up against the difficult and painful parts of ourselves. But, to use the colloquial phrase, we often do not 'see the wood for the trees'.

Yet, if we are patient and hold faith with the process — and this can take months and even years — the shoot will break the surface of the lake and gracefully unfurl to become a beautiful lotus flower. At this point it is visible to the world and we will feel its presence within ourselves. An example of this is Nelson

Mandela. For many years he was locked up on Robben Island. To many in South Africa he was seen as a terrorist and the embodiment of evil. Yet, when you read his autobiography you could tell that he was working with his mud. It was not easy and it took a long time — 27 years in his case. His story read like that of a great bodhisattva. When he was finally freed from prison this was like the moment when his lotus flower unfurled on the surface of the lake. All the world could see what a great man he was, even those who had previously thought ill of him.

It is important not to get caught up in striving here. We can't make the seed germinate in the mud through an effort of will, nor can we hurry up the process of the seedling growing into a lotus flower, and nor can we make the bud unfurl as it breaks the surface of the lake. Interfering with the process of the lotus flower's growth could damage it. Similarly, we cannot force compassion to blossom in our hearts and minds, but we can create the *conditions* for it to arise and grow in its own way and in its own time. Patience is required as there are unlikely to be significant results overnight. The chapters that follow provide us with the skills and capability to do exactly this.

Applying this process to our own experience, we find the seed of compassion in our heart. Then we fertilise the seed by repeatedly turning towards what is difficult and painful in our experience, rather than turning away. We let go of our storylines and simply feel our feelings. There is no exemption certificate from feeling our difficult feelings, such as anger, desire, sadness and jealousy. This is our inner mud. We need to own it fully because it creates the conditions for the germination of the seedling of compassion in our heart.

We nurture this seedling by remembering our compassionate motivation. This generates the courage and fortitude to continue on the path. We shine the energy of mindful acceptance and loving kindness on the seedling and this allows it to grow into a flower bud. Whenever more mud presents itself in our life, we turn towards it again and again, knowing that it will support the growth of the flower bud. And then one day the bud will break the surface of the lake and unfurl into a beautiful lotus flower as our compassionate potential matures and we become a force for good in the world.

Openness Practice

In the practice section below, the formal practice we offer as a way of working with the mud of our experience is the *Openness Practice*. This practice was developed by Akong Rinpoche, the founder of Samye Ling Tibetan Centre in Scotland. It was published in his book *Taming the Tiger* (Rinpoche, 1994) and is part of the therapy programme he developed to help people lay the groundwork for entering more deeply into the path of meditation. Through working with Westerners for many years he came to see that many of us need strong affirmation that at the core of our being we are fundamentally sane and well. This practice helps prepare the way for this viewpoint by showing us that all our experience — indeed all our emotions, struggles and issues — are the raw material for the development of compassion.

Embodiment

The key theme of this chapter is that genuine compassion requires that we descend into the mud of our experience and, in the words of Rob Nairn, go forth into the world as a compassionate mess. Then the lotus flower of compassion can take birth in our hearts and minds.

If we look more closely at what descent really entails, it means being willing to drop into and feel what is happening in our bodies. Our bodies hold so much of our past. They hold memories, hurts and traumas. Therefore, the real meaning of the lotus and mud metaphor is to descend into our *embodied experience* — to open up to and to feel all of who we are. This is not easy. The reason that many of us live in our heads is because our bodies are painful to inhabit. This might be physical pain or emotional pain or a combination of both. Therefore, it takes courage to live fully in our body.

We also do not want to just drop headlong into the traumas or wounding held in our bodies, just like we do not want to throw ourselves into the mud at the bottom of the lake. This needs to be approached in a gradual, sensitive way. We need many conditions in place to support the process of genuine embodiment. In many ways this is what this book is all about — offering us the skills and methods to do just that.

It also takes time and persistent work to go against a lifetime habit of taking flight into our heads and living a life lost in thought and distraction. As the author, James Joyce, once famously said in his novel, *The Dubliners*: 'Mr. Duffy lived a short distance from his body'.

Furthermore, our modern culture conspires to lead us ever further away from the living, breathing world of our bodies through the pervasive addiction of social media. These days many of us prefer to live in virtual reality than to live in the real world. We could say that these days we live a *far* distance from our bodies!

All of the compassion practices offered in this book include an element of embodiment, where we focus on whatever physical sensations are present in the body. These practices help us to drop our centre of gravity more fully into our body as we learn to trust and feel safe living in a more embodied way.

There are many practical advantages to staying in touch with our bodies. One such advantage is that our body is always present. The mind is often absent, worrying about the future, dwelling in the past or analysing in the present. The body is always right here and now; it is an anchor for us to return to every time the mind takes flight from the present moment and gets lost in thought.

If we revisit the first part of our working definition of compassion, 'Sensitivity to the suffering of ourselves and others', we can ask ourselves, how do we notice suffering? We feel it. We feel physical pain in the body. We feel emotional pain in the body. Think of the clenching of our fist or the tightening of our jaw when we feel anger; or the heaviness of our shoulders and prickling in our eyes when we feel sad; or the butterflies in our stomach or queasiness when we feel anxious. Each of us experiences these emotions differently, but each of us will recognise tell-tale signs of strong emotions being expressed through our bodies.

If we are closely in tune with how our body normally feels, when a difficulty or challenge arises and the emotional feeling tone in our body changes, we are much more likely to recognise this shift. In this way, the body acts as a barometer of how we feel. The body gives us early warning signs of changes in our emotional state. This helps us to recognise that we are experiencing a difficulty or challenge, which is the important first step in making the compassionate choice of turning towards it. If we live continually in our heads we will be out of touch with the movement of emotion in our bodies until it is too late and we lose our temper or burst into floods of tears.

Since our bodies hold our emotions, a compassionate approach is to befriend the body as a way of tending to these emotions. Then we can respond to the physical sensations that are linked to difficult emotions with kindly curiosity. This creates conditions for insights to arise about our emotional patterning. For this to happen we need to learn to trust our bodies and develop the body as a safe container within which to experience our emotions. We will look at creating conditions of safeness in Chapter 6, but in the meantime we can attend to what is happening in the body during each of our compassion practices.

It is a great act of self-compassion to work on feeling comfortable within our own skins because we are always in our body as we move about our world. For some of us our bodies are working pretty well, at least for the time being. But for others of us, our bodies will have limitations, possibly pain, weakness or disability. Still, we can rejoice in the parts of our bodies that are working well, since after all we are alive! As Jon Kabat-Zinn once famously commented, 'If you are breathing there is more right with you than wrong with you'. Then we can bring compassion to the suffering within our body and gradually feel more at ease within this skin of ours. For those in chronic pain, this is easier said than done, but with practise even those in chronic pain can come to experience the 10% of original pain and be relieved of the 90%, which comes from the resistance to pain.

Some people may like how their bodies look and feel. But many people dislike their bodies because they compare themselves unrealistically with fashion icons and sporting heroes. A lot of suffering comes from feeling aversion to our bodies. After all, as Rob Nairn often said, 'We don't have a spare body hanging up in the wardrobe to change into'. We are stuck with this one and so it is both prudent and kind to accept the body we were born into and learn to love and honour it because it is the container for the life we live.

Compassionate Body Scan

In order for us to befriend the physical body we will offer an adapted version of the body scan practice in the practice section of this chapter. In the compassionate body scan we move our focus up and down the body, just like we do in the normal body scan practice, but the difference is that we imagine that our attention is like a glow of kindness. As we move our attention through the different body parts we feel the feelings that are present whilst imagining that these feelings are illuminated and held by a glow of kindness. In those parts of the body that feel well, we allow the kindness to transform into an energy of joy that resonates with appreciation and gratitude for feeling healthy and well. In the parts of the body that feel painful, we allow the kindness to transform into compassion and imagine breathing an energy of compassion into and out of that part of the body. The breathing in and out has a soothing quality, but we are mindful not to try to change or get rid of the pain. If the pain changes, it changes; if it doesn't, it doesn't. We aspire to cultivate an attitude that whatever happens is fine.

Practice Section

Formal Sitting Practice

Practice 8: Openness (20 minutes)

In this practice we cultivate the attitude of being open to others. By accepting and acknowledging all of our thoughts, feelings and sensations, no matter how destructive or disturbing, our natural experience becomes the raw material for the development of compassion. We discover all our thoughts, feelings and emotions can be transformed rather than suppressed, got rid of, or held back. All our experience is equally and immediately valuable in the development of compassion, both towards oneself and to others.

Find a comfortable and upright position either sitting or lying. Settle the mind and become aware of the natural rhythm of your breathing. Let your mind wander freely through the body, alert to prominent sensations. Ask yourself what sort of mood you are in, what is the predominant emotional feeling and whether there is any particular physical sensation connected with this. Next, turn your attention to your thoughts: are they fast, jumpy or slow and even? Lightly note your whole experience with an attitude of curiosity.

Next, visualise in front of you, at a comfortable distance in the space, a completely open sky — either a clear blue daytime sky or a night sky filled with stars. In the centre of this luminous space, imagine a doorway or gateway opening outwards away from you. Focus only on the out-breath. As you breathe out, think that everything inside you — all your thoughts, feelings and experience in the moment — leaves and passes through the gateway into space. Imagine that this continuous flow of thoughts, emotions and sensations, whatever their original form, changes into a beautiful golden energy of universal compassion.

Onwards and outwards the energy shines through the gateway in all directions, bringing to all beings everywhere, whether human or animal, whatever it is that they most need and most want in a beneficial way. When the energy reaches those who are in pain, they are relieved of that pain, while for those who are hungry, the golden energy brings food. Whatever is lacking or needed arrives spontaneously with the energy. So you are not denying or suppressing your own pain and negative emotions here, rather you are acknowledging them as the vital raw materials for the development of true compassion.

If you are aware of any particular suffering of your own, as you breathe it through the gate and it transforms into the golden energy, think of others who are suffering in a similar way to you and send the energy first to them. In this way, through empathy, your own suffering can become useful. It can become like medicine for those who suffer in the way you do.

Finally, the golden energy fills the whole universe and touches every single being with its compassion and this includes yourself. Allow yourself to feel the golden energy finally coming to you, bringing whatever you most want and need.

At the end of this practice, rest for a little while, allowing your thoughts to come and go freely without any restriction, feel the absence of any conflict, or even the distinction between the spaces outside and inside of you. This is openness. (Akong Rinpoche, 1994.)

Practice 9: Compassionate Body Scan (20 – 30 minutes)
Find a comfortable place to lie down remembering that your intention is to foster kindness and wakefulness and not to fall

asleep. If you like you can do the exercise sitting upright too. Ensure that you will not be disturbed for the duration of the practice and that you will be warm enough; cover yourself with a blanket if necessary.

Close your eyes and focus for a while on the rising and falling of the diaphragm as you breathe, and then become aware of the movement of the breath throughout the body. Feel the sense of release and letting go, as each out-breath leaves the body. Then take a few moments to become aware of your body as a whole: the outline of the body, the weight of your body and the sense of gravity bearing down upon it. Notice the points where your body is in contact with the surface it rests upon. Now place your hand on your heart as a reminder to be kind to yourself. Take three deep, relaxing breaths and then place your arms by your side.

Imagine that your attention is infused with warm glow of kindness and then bring your attention to the big toes of both of your feet exploring the sensations that you find here. You are not trying to make anything happen, just feeling what you are feeling. Gradually broaden your awareness to include your other toes, the soles of your feet, and the other parts of your feet. Simply feel the sensations as they are and soften around them. Bring a sense of gratitude to your feet: they work so hard for us yet we pay them so little attention. Then imagine that you are breathing into both your feet on the in-breath and breathing out from this part of the body, into the space surrounding it, on the out-breath.

Gradually move the warm glow of your attention up your body to your ankles, calves, knees and thighs, simply experiencing the sensations you encounter; always being sure that your attention is tender and saturated with gratitude and respect for each part of your body. Now let the soft glow of your attention move up to your buttocks and notice if you are holding any tension in this part of the body; and if so soften around it with your awareness. Then imagine that you are breathing into this part of the body on the in-breath and breathing out from this part of the body, into the space surrounding it, on the out-breath. As you breathe in imagine that you are holding the entirety of the lower part of your body within your awareness and as you breathe out, imagine that you release this part of your body from your awareness.

If you notice any areas of pain, discomfort or tension try breathing into these areas of your body, softening as you breathe in and releasing as you breathe out. You can imagine that you breathe in a warm glow of kindness on the in-breath, but don't do this with an agenda of trying to make the difficulty go away.

When you notice that your mind has drifted off into thinking or dreaming or planning, as it will do very often, simply notice this and return to the sensations in your body — no judgement, no sense of getting it wrong, as this is just what the mind does. And then gradually move your soft attention to your abdomen, lower and upper back, shoulders, rib-cage and chest. Every now and again, pause and bring a sense of gratitude and tenderness to the part of the body you are holding in awareness, reflecting on what it does for you and how so often you may take it for granted.

Now bring kind awareness to your spine, gently curving through your body, and the point at which it meets the skull. Have a sense of the solid frame of your body. And then once again, imagine that you are breathing into your torso on the in-breath and breathing out from this part of the body, into the space surrounding it, on the out-breath.

Then bring your awareness down your arms and into your hands, fingers, and finger-tips. Notice the warmth and energy that is stored in the palms of your hands. Notice what the hands feel like at rest. Every now and again, pause and bring a sense of gratitude and tenderness to the arms and hands, reflecting on all they do for you and how so often you may take them for granted. Now imagine that you are breathing into your arms and hands on the in-breath and breathing out from this part of the body into the space surrounding it on the out-breath.

Then gradually bring the soft glow of awareness to your head, neck, throat and face, noting any tension held in the muscles around the forehead, around the eyes, the jaw and the mouth. Notice any sensitivity of your face to the temperature of the air in the room. Allow your face to soften.

Now sweep your attention from your head back down to your feet again, but more quickly this time, and then bring your attention back to your breathing. Pay attention to the movement of the breath in your body as a whole — as if your whole body is breathing and held in the warm glow of your awareness. When you are about to finish the practice, place your hand on your heart again as a final gesture of kindness. Then slowly start moving your body, rolling over onto one side and then gradually getting up. Make sure not to jar yourself back into ordinary awareness too quickly.

Informal Daily Life Practice

Continue doing Practice 5 (Gratitude and Appreciation) and Practice 7 (Felt Sense of Kindness) but with a specific focus on how the cultivation of appreciation, gratitude and kindness feel in your body as you do them.

Chapter Five

It's Not Our Fault

The Evolutionary Model

In this chapter we will shift perspective and look at the 'mess' and the 'mud' of our lives through the lens of Evolutionary Psychology. We will draw on the work of Professor Paul Gilbert and his model of *Compassionate Mind Training.*

Paul has been a great friend and supporter of the Mindfulness Association and we owe a debt of gratitude to him for the shape and direction of our compassion training. Along with Rob Nairn, he was one of its pioneers. Through their influence this training has the distinctive approach of fusing the bodhisattva vision of Mahayana Buddhism with the science-based approach of Evolutionary Psychology.

The Flow of Life

The evolutionary perspective on compassion places our personal experience within the vast sweep of life on this planet. We come to see that we chose so little of our present life conditions. We just find ourselves in the flow of this life and so much of how we think, feel and behave is *not of our choosing and not our fault.* These are key insights of the Evolutionary Model.

The concept of *not our fault* has become the cornerstone of *Compassion Focused Therapy* developed by Paul Gilbert. It is a way of helping people see that what goes through their minds is not personal. Many people think that their dysfunctional thoughts and emotions are unique to them. They think that they are a mess and everyone else is fine. This can be the basis for the destructive force of self-criticism and shame.

Through this approach we realise that *everyone* is in the same situation. Maybe others do not feel and experience exactly what we feel, but the broad strokes of experience are the same. This helps to build the bridge of common humanity with others and it is a way of finding release from the awful prison of shame. In Chapter 2 we described shame as the 'third arrow'; it is the killer blow that strikes at our very identity and sense of self-worth. When we shame ourselves we feel flawed and worthless and we condemn ourselves to a life of hiding — from other people and from ourselves.

Reflecting on the flow of life has two dimensions. The first is an intellectual one through which we come to understand the complex processes that have shaped us as human beings. There is a great deal of scholarship and research in this area. Through the powers of reasoning we can begin to understand the evolutionary bind we find ourselves in. However, we need to go further and develop a *felt sense* of how this evolutionary bind impacts our lives and can plunge us into the depths of despair and suffering if we let it run unchecked.

This is the second dimension. It is emotional rather than intellectual. Here, we let ourselves feel the fragility and vulnerability and poignancy of being part of life on this planet. We will do this by meditating on the *Flow of Life* practice at the end of this chapter. This practice calls upon us to feel from the very core of our being how we just find ourselves in this flow of life that is shaped by powerful forces beyond our control. When the immensity of the great evolutionary drama touches our heart and we realise that all living beings are caught up in it, through no choice of their own, this is a wakeup call to cultivate our evolved capacity for self-awareness and compassion.

It can be helpful to see the flow of life in terms of three archetypal stories: the long story, the middle story and the short story.

Long Story: Gene-built Life

We are a human being and the history of our species stretches back millions of years. We are built by the genes that we inherited from our parents, and their parents stretching back into the depths of time. Our genes interact with our environment in unique and unpredictable ways, and some genes will get turned on or off depending on the environment in which we grow up. It is like being in a genetic lottery.

We are designed to be short-lived because our main evolutionary function is to pass on our genes to the next generation and to survive long enough to do this. Living long, happy and fulfilling lives is not the priority of the genes that built us. We have evolved to survive and procreate, not necessarily to be happy. This is something we need to work on.

As we grow up we find that there are powerful drives and goals that we share with other people and with other animals: to live and stay healthy, to be part of social groups and find our niche within them, to meet a partner and settle down and maybe have a family. We find that there are rituals we share with others, like dating rituals and rituals to gain entrance to groups. These are common to many other animals too and are like archetypal scripts that are hard-wired into us.

Furthermore, we feel strong emotions, none of which we chose or designed, which direct us towards those goals. Many of these emotions can feel very unpleasant, like strong anger and anxiety, but they have an evolutionary function to keep us out of danger, to fight when we need to fight and to run when we need to run. We have a sophisticated brain that can do extraordinary things like build computers and high-rise buildings and design fancy systems for running complex societies. But this very same brain can generate a living hell within us as the old and new brain circuitry get caught in self-perpetuating loops that can damage our mental health. We will come to this shortly.

We designed none of this; we just find ourselves in this situation. They key point of the long story is that so much of who we are and what we have become has nothing to do with any personal agency on our part. And yet most of us take it all so personally and blame ourselves for the complex and difficult life situations we find ourselves in.

Furthermore, evolution has not necessarily done a good job; it has just happened the way it has happened — one evolutionary adaption building on the previous one. It works on the basis of compromises and it can never go back to the starting point and wipe the slate clean. It is not like we can go back to ground zero and build a human being perfectly adapted to this modern world. Instead, we carry the ancient world within us. For example, humans evolved to walk upright which has an evolutionary advantage because our hands are free and we can use them to craft tools and wield weapons on unsuspecting prey. But this has resulted in the women of our species having narrower hips making childbirth difficult.

Middle Story: Social Conditioning

Human beings are tribal creatures. We function best in communities and collectives. Over the millennia these have constellated into cultures and societies each with their own rules and traditions. The key point here is that our genetic inheritance, along with our inbuilt evolutionary drives and emotions, are channelled through the particular culture and society we are born into. This has a huge impact on how our genes are expressed, and the kind of people we grow up to be. All too often, however, culture and society are just as dysfunctional as the minds that begot them. Paul Gilbert loves to recount the story of how in Roman times people would go to the gladiatorial games each Saturday, in the same way that people today might go to watch football or rugby. To the Romans, it seemed perfectly normal at that time to watch people kill each other for the sake of entertainment. Looking back now through the lens of modern culture, this seems utterly abhorrent.

Human beings have a disturbing tendency to tune out of suffering when cultural norms legitimise it and when it does not directly affect our kith and kin. Once again this is not our choice and not our fault. We did not choose the culture and social era we were born into; but the important point is that once we wake up to the cultural and societal biases that are shaping us there is an ethical imperative to cultivate mindful awareness and compassion. It is not our fault but it becomes our responsibility once we become aware of it.

Short Story: Family and Upbringing

Normally we see family and upbringing as the determining factor in shaping the person we grow up to be. Many psychological therapies focus a great deal on family dynamics since these are regarded as the driving force behind inner conflicts and issues; they are seen as determining whether we grow up to be happy and well-adjusted or unhappy and emotionally conflicted. But from the evolutionary perspective the long and middle stories are just as important.

Once again, we have little or no choice as to whether we are born into a poor family or a rich one, a stable or dysfunctional one, a family where abuse is rife or one that is nurturing. And yet this will have a huge impact on the person we grow up to be. This is the tragic lottery of life. For those of us who have grown up in dysfunctional or abusive families, we know the massive impact that this has had on everything in our lives: our self-worth, our ability to form loving bonds and trust others, and so forth. So much depends on the early life conditions in which we grew up. Through advances in neuroscience we know that the wiring of the brain, and whether certain genes are turned on or off, depend on whether our childhood rearing was stable and nurturing or dysfunctional and isolating. This seems so tragic and unfair and yet it is the stark reality of life.

Furthermore, the short story is strongly tempered by the middle story of culture and social conditioning and the long story of gene-built life on this planet. We just find ourselves in the flow of this life and the way we are is not our fault. Simply acknowledging this fact is a big relief.

We realise that others are in the same boat too. Some of them might have a seemingly better life situation than ours, and others a worse situation, but the bottom line is that all of us just find ourselves in this life through no choice of our own and all of us are muddling through to the best of our ability. All life is transient, fragile and vulnerable to so many things like natural disasters, pandemics, accidents and untimely death.

As we begin to see more clearly the evolutionary bind that we find ourselves in, self-compassion naturally arises and we are then in a position to cultivate the conditions for greater self-awareness and freedom. In the words of the evolutionist, Robert Wright, 'we can initiate a silent rebellion against our overlord, the process of natural selection' (Wright, 2017). Moreover, when we see how those around us are caught in this self-same evolutionary bind, our compassion for them naturally arises too.

The Evolved Brain

With the flow of life as a context, we will now explore some features of the evolved brain — how it evolved for survival rather than for happiness and contentment and how it is adapted for a hunter gatherer lifestyle rather than for the speedy technological environment of the twenty-first century.

When we refer to the 'old brain' and 'new brain' in the paragraphs below we are not referring to specific regions of the brain that have distinct functions. Neuroscience is a rapidly changing field of research. Models of the brain that imply that the brain has evolved in strata with new layers sedimenting over old ones have become outmoded as current research shows the brain systems operate in complex and highly interactive ways.

Instead, when we use the term 'old brain' we are referring to ancient brain systems that we can observe in animals *as well as in human beings.* For example, we can observe emotions such as anger, anxiety, love and joy in animals as diverse as rats, horses, giraffes and monkeys — and we can detect them in ourselves too. We can also notice behaviours in animals that are similar to humans. We observe them fighting and challenging each other for status and social position, having sexual relationships, caring for their children, answering distress calls, and clinging to each other when frightened. We can also recognise these self-same behaviours in ourselves. That is why nature programmes are so fascinating to watch. We see our own behaviours mirrored in other animals in fascinating ways.

When we refer to the 'new brain' we are referring to capacities that evolved much later and which current research indicates as pertaining *primarily to human beings.* Through the development of the cerebral cortex we became able to think, reason and plan in complex ways that other animals cannot do. We have a type of consciousness and sense of self that other animals do not seem to have.

This distinction is important for the evolutionary model for two reasons. Firstly, because it identifies the key evolutionary dysfunction that causes so much suffering: animal-like passions of old brain systems being inflamed by the sophisticated thinking of the new brain. Secondly, it shows the route out of suffering by enlisting the power of self-awareness and imagination in the new brain and linking it to those parts of the old brain associated with our mammalian heritage of caring and affiliation. This is the basis for training in compassion.

The Old Brain

The first major characteristic of the old brain is reacting to threats, in which we attack if we are angry, run away, submit, or freeze if we are anxious, and recoil if we are disgusted by something.

For example, if we feel threatened by someone disagreeing with us, a common reaction is to fight back. This might involve a stand-up row with the person or firing off an angry email. We can see this reflected in the animal world too when animals fight with each other over scarce resources such as food or territory.

Another reaction to feeling threatened is to avoid or run away from a difficult life situation. This might entail us leaving a relationship or failing to respond to an email or social media post. This is a common reaction in the animal world too and we can notice animals running away from predators; for instance birds flying off when a cat or dog is stalking about.

There is also the reaction of submitting to those who are more powerful than us when we feel threatened by them. This often happens in work situations when there is a bullying culture in the management. In these situations we can find ourselves submitting to unreasonable demands as we do our best not to rock the boat. We also see pack animals exhibiting similar behaviours when they bow or roll on their backs to signal their submission to an animal higher up the pecking order.

We can observe the freeze response in animals when serious injury or death is imminent: a rabbit freezing when it sees the headlights of an approaching car perhaps. Similarly, we can notice the freeze response in human beings when they encounter a traumatic event. This is the root of psychological conditions like PTSD (post-traumatic stress disorder) when the emotion and associated memory become frozen in our nervous system and inhibit our functioning in the world.

We feel disgust in ourselves when we encounter something distasteful or revolting. There is the immediate reaction of recoiling and moving away. Similarly, we can notice this reaction in animals too because it is an important evolutionary protection against ingesting poisonous substances.

These reactions of fight, flight, and freeze and the associated emotions of anger, anxiety and disgust are hard-wired into the sympathetic nervous system of our animal cousins and we can see them operating in ourselves as human beings too.

The second major characteristic of the old brain is the drive to obtain the resources we need to survive in the world. This involves activities such as gathering food, finding a place to live, attracting partners, and starting a family. This is the impetus that gets us out of bed in the morning to do the things we need to do to ensure the survival and flourishing of ourselves and our loved ones. Furthermore, it is the drive to rise up the social ladder by acquiring material wealth and status so that we can impress prospective partners with our dashing clothes! It is underpinned by feelings of excitement and vitality.

Again, we see our animal cousins engaging continuously in the gathering of food to feed themselves and their young. We see them building nests or dens and engaging in mating rituals with spectacular displays to attract mates. Where animals live in groups, we see a constant drive to move up the pecking order; for example in packs of dogs or troops of primates. In essence we are just the same as animals when it comes to our basic drives and motivations; it is just the behaviours that are different.

The third major characteristic of the old brain is an impulse towards resting, digesting and connection. This is only possible when our needs are met and threats are absent. This creates the conditions for feeling safe and for being soothed and supported by those around us. It can involve being part of a family as well as friendships and alliances. This characteristic is most advanced in mammals where their young are cared for, soothed, groomed, played with, trained and socialised by their parents and others in their kin group.

As human beings we go to great lengths to care for and bring up our children over many years and there is often a reciprocal life-long connection of love and care between parents and children. Again, this involves a process of mutual soothing so as to create feelings of safeness. Research shows that relaxed time spent in meaningful friendships is so important for our health and wellbeing. This reciprocal network of support is extended to include the strategic cultivation of alliances in our workplace, communities, politics and the wider world.

This characteristic has evolved to support groups in the same species to work together to improve their chances of survival.

Our human ancestors would not have survived on their own. Being cast out of the group in the distant past would have meant certain death. We needed to be part of a tribe or kin group that worked together to support each other.

These three characteristics of threat, drive and connection are archetypal life patterns that evolved to ensure our survival. They are hard-wired in the neural circuitry of our brain over millions of years of evolution. They are in us all. They are automatic and intertwined with each other. We see them constantly playing out in our families, communities, and workplaces as well as being depicted in movies and novels. They are so ingrained within us that often we fail to recognise their power and how they condition our lives.

In Buddhism the threat and drive characteristics are understood in terms of aversion and grasping. If we do not like things there is an automatic move towards aversion, whereas if we like things we tend to grasp for them. One of the main reasons for practising meditation is to learn not to feed our ingrained habits of grasping and aversion so that we are not driven by them. Interestingly, the precondition for working with grasping and aversion is first to settle the mind in a state of calm abiding, which is analogous to cultivating the soothing-affiliation system (described below). Only once we are abiding in this system can we begin to tame our grasping and aversion. Therefore, recent insights in Evolutionary Psychology and neuroscience were predated and confirmed by the more intuitive approach of the great wisdom traditions of the East.

Emotional Regulation Systems

Neuroscience research shows that these three archetypal life patterns are expressed through three emotional regulation systems. These are set out in the diagram and table below.

Image 1. Interactions between the three types of emotional regulation systems. (Compassion Focused Therapy — Prof. Paul Gilbert.)

All three of these systems are essential for our survival. For example, if we were about to step out in front of an approaching bus, our threat system would automatically kick in and we would find ourselves taking an involuntary step backwards before we consciously realised what was happening. We need the drive system to motivate us to get what we need in order to survive. We also need to feel safe and supported in order to thrive and survive. However, these emotional systems need to be in balance with each other for us to flourish in our lives; but in modern life this is seldom the case.

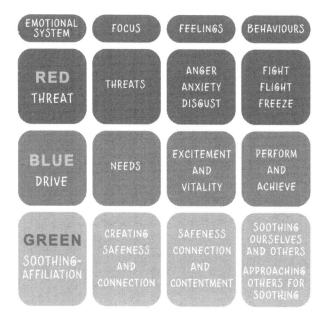

Image 2. Three emotional regulation systems. (Compassion Focused Therapy — Prof. Paul Gilbert.)

The New Brain

About 2 million years ago, a new brain capacity evolved in human beings centred around the cerebral cortex. This new capacity enabled us to imagine, reason and plan. It gave rise to a specific type of self-awareness called meta-cognition whereby we can know what we are thinking while we are thinking it. This in turn gave rise to a sense of self that other animals do not have — or at least not to the same extent.

We can think about the future and the kind of person we want to be, how we want to feel and the life we want to create for ourselves; whereas we believe that animals live primarily from day to day. We can also look back with regret and ruminate about unhappy things. Animals tend not to do this, so far as we can understand them.

The human imagination has great power. Try closing your eyes now and imagining your favourite meal. Bring to mind how it looks, smells and tastes, and how it feels in your mouth. You may notice that there is a physiological response. The body responds by causing the mouth to salivate.

Likewise, if we imagine a threatening situation, the body responds by triggering the sympathetic nervous system and firing up our fight or flight response. Adrenaline is released and blood goes to our muscles, and very quickly we will feel speedy and stressed. Similarly, if we imagine all the things we want to achieve, the drive system will fire up releasing the hormone dopamine. This will result in feelings of excitement and anticipation.

The key point is that the brain does not know the difference between what is real and what is imagined. The very real threat of living in a stone age world inhabited by lions and tigers where our children might get eaten any moment is felt in the brain and body in a similar way to the imagined threats that abound in our modern world, such as being looked down upon or ridiculed if we don't have the latest smart phone, plastic surgery or book on compassion!

When a zebra is chased by a lion and luckily escapes, it will shake its body for a couple of minutes to burn off the adrenaline of the chase and then will calmly go back to grazing. If we humans were to be chased by a lion, we would ruminate endlessly over what might have happened if we had been mauled and we would worry constantly about it happening again. Zebras don't do this, but humans do.

It is wonderful that we have this ability to imagine, reason and plan. It has kept us safe from lions and many other threats to the survival of humankind over the millennia. It has given rise to the emergence of civilisation. We have made great advances in science, medicine and human rights that have enabled us to flourish on this Earth. Human beings have also created extraordinary works of art and literature. This is the blessing of the new brain.

But we can also think about conflicts and plan revenge. We can use our intelligence to work out how to build weapons of mass destruction to use against each other. Unfortunately, our new brain capacities can be hijacked and directed by old brain passions. Furthermore, our sophisticated capacity for thinking and imagining can inflame the powerful emotions in the old brain. We can imagine all manner of threatening scenarios and the old brain threat system reacts as if the threat is real. We then get caught in a vicious cycle where the two inflame and feed on one another.

A common example of this vicious cycle is rumination. We might start feeling anxious about something that we said or did in the recent past. These feelings fuel our thinking and before long we find ourselves dwelling on what happened, imagining a different scenario where we spoke or acted differently. Our thinking mind comes up with all kinds of different angles and solutions, but the problem is that the incident is in the past and the past cannot be changed. All the thinking serves to do is to inflame our anxious feelings which then triggers more thinking. Before long our mood drops and we feel depressed and forlorn.

This is the evolutionary bind we find ourselves in: worrying constantly about imagined threats; driven to achieve unrealistic goals; and chronically stressed and exhausted. As we have said many times before, it's all a big mess!

It's Not Our Fault

We live in world that over-stimulates the threat system. We receive constant messages from the media that we are not good enough. We listen to 24/7 newscasts of every terrible thing that is happening around the world. We hear all the bad economic news, such as people losing their jobs and homes. We read judgmental magazine articles and watch TV programmes that are looking for weaknesses and humiliating people, such as reality TV shows. This culture of perfectionism, judgement and humiliation has permeated our communities and workplaces. We live in an unfair society in which a few own the majority of the wealth and the majority are working in insecure, low paid jobs with a diminishing welfare safety net to fall back on. As a result, many of us don't feel safe in the world and our threat system goes into overdrive. We did not choose this and it is not our fault.

We live in a world that over-stimulates the drive system. Modern capitalism goads us to achieve success and power and accumulate money to buy lots of things to show off our status. It has promoted an individualistic dog-eat-dog mentality, which views greed, dishonesty and trampling over others as necessary evils to get to the top of the pile. In most families, both parents are working and juggling their demanding jobs with childcare and a million and one other things that need to be done to live up to the cultural norms of our society. The marketing industry has grown in sophistication over the last fifty years and knows exactly how to press our buttons to get us to buy the product it is promoting. As a result, for most of us the drive system is in chronic overdrive.

Furthermore, failing to achieve what we think we must achieve activates the threat system even more and so we find ourselves in a vicious circle of threat and drive.

Finally, there is little in our culture and society that values taking time out to unwind with friends and family. Any downtime is crowded out by a host of demands from our never-ending to-do lists and the daily stresses of modern life. Therefore, spending time in the soothing-affiliation system is down valued.

The soothing system is further compromised if we experienced a lack of love, care and support early in life. This emotional system requires such early life modelling to come fully online.

We first need to experience soothing and care from others before we can provide this to ourselves. Many of us, however, grow up in challenging family environments and experience disrupted early life attachments. Consequently, the soothing system remains undeveloped and we live our lives hooked on drive and threat. A common symptom of this malaise is being unable to turn off the endless stream of stressful thoughts that circle around in our heads.

For most of us the drive and threat systems are hugely over-stimulated and the soothing-affiliation system is very undeveloped. We spend our days anxious, worried, fearful, overworked and stressed. This prevents us from prioritising caring for ourselves, our loved ones and wider society. It leaves little time for relaxation or for spending quality time with our loved ones.

Burnout

An over-stimulated threat system gives rise to stress, which is a good short term coping strategy. There is nothing wrong with stress, but we need to take enough time out to recover and regenerate. When we make an emergency out of every situation, the body reacts by producing more adrenaline and this stops us from feeling tired, so we keep going without realising what a large amount of energy we are demanding of our bodies. This can result in ongoing chronic stress, and if we are not careful it can lead to burnout.

Burnout has become a modern epidemic and it is increasing at an alarming rate. It is an expression of the three circles being chronically out of balance and us not heeding the warning signs of this lack of balance. It starts with an overactive threat and drive system in which we are constantly trying to meet the demands of life, which are often complex and multifaceted. An early warning sign of burnout is ignoring our basic needs, such as forgetting to take lunch and working non-stop. It can then be aggravated by things like workplace stressors, deadlines, and demanding bosses.

Another key indicator is feeling disconnected from others and a breakdown in the sense of community resulting in feelings of emptiness and lack of meaning. This is indicative of the soothing-affiliation system taking a nosedive. All three combine to plunge us into chronic stress, withdrawal, depression and burnout. People take a long time to recover from burnout and so paying attention to the warning signs is important. One way of doing this is to regularly monitor our three emotional systems and to work on bringing them into balance.

Out of the Red and Into the Green

How do we re-balance our emotional systems? The simple answer is to stimulate the soothing-affiliation system. In Compassionate Focused Therapy there is a simple slogan: get out of the red (threat system) and into the green (soothing system). Much of this book is about how to do this. In order to train our hearts and minds in compassion we need first to cultivate the soothing-affiliation system.

A useful starting point is to pay attention to what triggers our three emotional regulation systems and to become aware of how much time we spend in each of the three circles. At the end of this chapter we will have the chance to do the *Three Circles Exercise*, which enables us to explore the operation of these three systems: threat, drive, and soothing within our own life experience. Seeing how these systems operate within us, is the first step in beginning to re-balance them.

Through doing this exercise most of us will find that we need to strengthen the capacity of the soothing-affiliation system, and in so doing the threat and drive systems will naturally come more into balance. It is important to acknowledge that we have started doing this already. Our mindfulness practice stimulates the soothing system. The deep rhythmical breathing we use to settle the mind, and the body focus of grounding, which we use at the start of every practice, stimulates our soothing system.

It is important, however, to pay attention to the threat and drive systems and how they get activated in our lives. To offset the over-stimulated drive system, we need to revisit our basic life values and see if we can place less priority on achieving and focus more on downtime and appreciating our relationships with key people in our lives. To offset an overactive threat system, it is important to try to simplify our lifestyle and remove some of the stressors wherever this is possible.

It is a sad truth of how we have evolved that the threat and the drive systems need little encouragement and escalate of their own accord, but the soothing-affiliation system needs consistent, patient cultivation.

Practice Section

Formal Sitting Practice

Practice 10: Flow of Life (20 minutes)
This practice is best done by listening to a guided audio and by playing some background music that evokes a poignant heart-opening feeling.

Begin by sitting in a relaxed and comfortable posture on a cushion or chair; or lie down if you like. Then pay attention to the rising and falling of your body as you breathe. To help settle your mind, try deepening your in-breath a little and lengthening your out-breath. See if you can regulate your breathing so that your in-breath and out-breath are of a similar length and rhythm. You might like to count to three or four on the in-breath and a similar count on the out-breath. When your mind begins to settle, let go of counting and let your breathing find its natural rhythm.

Reflect that you did not design your body the way it is — you just find yourself in the flow of this life. Reflect that the form of your body has evolved over millions of years from single cell organisms in the sea, to complex organisms that fed on one another to survive, to the first amphibians who emerged from the ocean to reptiles who crawled upon the earth, to mammals who learned to care and nurture their young, until finally us humans who learned to stand and walk upright.

Reflect that the particular form of your body has emerged from the genes of your parents and then their parents stretching back into the distant past. You did not choose to be tall or short, left-handed or right-handed — your genes designed you in this way. Also, you did not plan on getting sick or growing old or dying, this is just the way life is. You just find yourself in this inexorable flow of life whether you like it or not.

You did not design your brain with its complex and contradictory drives. Like many other animals you seek rank and status, to be part of groups, to seek out a partner, to love and be loved, and maybe to have a family and children. You did not choose your drives, the quest for power and status, or competing for rank and position — this all comes with the deal of being alive.

You did not choose to have powerful emotions surging through you like anger and anxiety and desire. Like many other animals you are at the mercy of these powerful emotions because they are part and parcel of the evolutionary drive for survival and procreation. We find ourselves competing for resources, with the arising of jealousy and hatred, and coalescing into groups and tribes as we humans act out archetypal dramas of dominance and conquest causing terrible harm to fellow humans and other life forms.

You did not design this human cerebral cortex that can reflect and plan and imagine. Furthermore, you did not bargain on this sophisticated brain being hijacked by animal passions of desire and rage — stirring it all up with incessant thinking. You did not choose this brain that can ruminate and dwell and endlessly worry, thus driving you to distraction!

You did not choose to be born, nor did you choose the genes that built you. You did not choose your basic temperaments — some people are shy and anxious, withdrawn and passive, while others are more assertive and outgoing. Some people will be bright and discover that they have talents in sport or music; others less so. You did not choose to be born into a loving, neglectful, or abusive family, into a Christian, Muslim or Atheist family, or into a rich or poor family. You did not choose to be born in your particular town in this time in history.

Yet all these will have a profound effect on how you experience yourself and the life that you live. So much of what goes on in your mind, and even your core values, beliefs, likes and dislikes have been built for you not by you. It is the same for others too. We are all built in basically the same way, and we choose so little of it. We just find ourselves here in the flow of this life.

We become aware that we exist as a feeling self around two to three years old. As we grow up our brains quickly mature and we become capable of understanding new things. As we enter adolescence we find that hormones are changing our bodies, desires and interests. We choose none of this, it just happens inside us. Emotions intensify; we become more easily shamed and sensitive about our bodies; we become more interested in winning the approval and acceptance of our peers; we find ourselves interested in music and clothes. Later we may want to find partners, have children and create a family. All of us want to be valued, appreciated and accepted rather than devalued, criticised, and rejected.

Just realise how much of who we are now we did not choose. We did not choose the difficult patterns that were scripted by early childhood traumas and struggles. It is not our fault that we are anxious or depressed or prone to fits of rage and feelings of abandonment. It is not our fault that we find it hard to form loving bonds. So much of this was shaped by the conditions in which we grew up. How our bodies look, how our emotions play out, the thoughts and dramas that unfold in our minds are not of our choosing and not our fault.

We just find ourselves in this life, in this place, in this mental or emotional state due to so many factors beyond our control.

Seeing things from this perspective, can we begin to let ourselves off the painful hook of blame and shame? Can we drop into a place of not taking it all so personally? Then and only then we can begin to take responsibility for this unique life of ours. All other living beings are in the same boat too. Each of them just finds themselves in the flow of this life shaped by powerful forces beyond their control.

Now imagine that each of these countless living beings has a spark of compassion in their hearts. As we breathe out this spark is fanned and turns into a flame, and the more we breathe out with an understanding of that we are all caught up in and with a wish to reach out and connect to others, the more this flame strengthens and grows — until finally the whole world is aglow with the energy of compassion that stretches out in all directions.

Now spend some time resting and absorbing the feeling of the practice — giving yourself a little time to process it — before getting up.

Practice 11: Three Circle Exercise (10 – 15 minutes)

Find a large piece of paper and write three words: threat, drive and soothing-affiliation systems spaced apart across the page.

Let's begin with the threat system. Think about the things in your daily life right now that can trigger your threat system. It may be small things, such as needing to get to work on time, concerns about the traffic, completing a piece of work; or it might be more serious things, such as facing a divorce or a worrying about a health problem. Write these things around the word 'threat' on your page. Think about how much of your time is spent in this emotional system and how often these worries and concerns ripple through you. Over the next few days more things might occur to you, so you can write them down too.

Now pause for a bit and then focus on the things in your life that give you a sense of pleasure and enjoyment; things you feel excited about and look forward to; positive things that make you want to get out of bed each day. This could be something you want to achieve or it might be the thought of going on a holiday. It might be looking forward to coming home to a nice meal, going to the movies, or doing a satisfying piece of work. The key thing is the experience of feeling energised by whatever it is that you think of. Keep in mind though that some of these energisers can be threat focused. For example, you may want to achieve something not through enjoyment of the thing in itself, but because you are frightened that if you do not do so people will berate you. How much time do you spend in the drive system? Write these things around the word 'drive' on your page.

Now pause for a bit and then focus on the things in your life that give you a sense of slowing down, of being content and feeling a sense of wellbeing; not wanting to achieve anything or go anywhere because you are content with the way things are right now. What activities or relationships foster this sense of feeling safe, connected and content? How much time do you spend in the soothing-affiliation system? Write these things around the word 'Soothing-affiliation' on your page.

When you have completed this task, stand back and think about which system you spend most of your time in and draw a circle around each of the three groupings of words on your page. The size of the circles corresponds to where most of your time and energies are applied. So if most of your time is spent worrying and ruminating, then draw a big circle for threat; while if you spend very little time feeling safe and content, then draw a small circle for the soothing system. It's not unusual for people to realise that it's the threat or drive system that has the biggest circle. Some people even start to feel a bit anxious if they spend too much time in the soothing system!

Try to do this exercise from time to time and notice if there are any changes to the size of your three circles and the things you write in them.

Chapter Six

Creating Conditions of Safeness

Stimulating the Soothing System

In the last chapter we explored Professor Paul Gilbert's model of the three emotional regulation systems: threat, drive and soothing-affiliation. An important learning from this model is that we cannot resolve the intensity and over-activation of the threat and drive systems while locked into those systems. This is like trying to resolve the problem of thinking too much by trying to think our way out of it! This applies especially to the threat system where it is so easy to get locked into a civil war within this system: anger fighting anxiety, or anxiety fearing sadness, and the self-critic condemning them all!

The key training is to step into a different emotional system and place our focus here — namely the soothing-affiliation system. Hence the simple instruction we mentioned in the last chapter: 'go from the red into the green'. When we step out of the red zone of the threat system into the green zone of the soothing-affiliation system, our inner emotional world naturally calms down. The threat and drive systems are down-regulated because we are placing our focus elsewhere.

In this chapter we will explore how to stimulate the soothing-affiliation system in order to create conditions of safeness within ourselves. This is crucial for the emergence of compassion. We will do this in an embodied way so as to create a felt sense of safeness within this body of ours. Then our body becomes a safe container for any difficult feelings we may experience. This won't happen overnight, it will take a lot of time and practise. In this chapter we will focus on imagination-based practices and in the next chapter we will focus on mindfulness-based practices.

Revisiting Energy Follows Focus

In the last chapter we explored the evolutionary glitch of how our 'new brain' can cause us to think in ways that stimulate the threat and drive systems that are part of our 'old brain'. Once these are activated, they fuel more intense thinking in the cerebral cortex and we get caught in a vicious cycle. Thoughts arise in the mind with great force and energy, such as angry thoughts and anxious thoughts, and they feel sticky and irresistible. We find ourselves compelled to think more and more about terrible things that could happen or about all the things we want and must have right now! Our thinking is under the power of the threat and drive systems — and so the vicious cycle continues.

We all know what this feels like. Each one of us gets locked into cycles of rumination and we instinctively know that it does not serve us and yet we continue to feed it. Once we understand the dynamics at play — how the old and new brain systems get locked into self-destructive loops — then there is the opportunity to choose a different response. Also, once we know about the soothing-affiliation system and that cultivating it frees us from this vicious cycle, then we feel motivated to nurture this emotional system. This is like a doctor telling us that certain food and activities increase our blood pressure and others decrease it. Armed with that knowledge we immediately feel inspired to change our diet and lifestyle. Working with our emotions is just the same.

When we discussed the principle of *energy follows focus* in Chapter 3, we learnt that when we focus our attention on certain thoughts and tendencies we give them energy and power. If we focus on negative thoughts we give them power and they bring us down; if we focus on positive thoughts we give them power and they elevate our mood. Similarly, when we feed the habits associated with the threat and drive system, such as a habit of anger or a burning desire to get something we want, we give these power. This then strengthens the stressed out, perfection-seeking, anxious or angry versions of ourselves that we so often inhabit — and they condemn us to living out our days locked into stress and toxic emotional states that we see as being normal since so many other people are like this too.

But there is another way to live. This is to consciously focus on and feed the soothing-affiliation system. When we do this life flows and there is a sense of peace and contentment in our heart. We feel part of life and intimately connected to all those around us.

When we are in this mode of being, compassion becomes possible. When we are locked into the threat and drive system, compassion struggles. Now, when we talk about compassion we are not talking about a static quality but one that flows in different directions, and this brings us to the next topic.

Flow of Compassion

OTHER>SELF   SELF>SELF   SELF>OTHER

Image 3. Flow of Compassion. (Compassion Focused Therapy — Prof. Paul Gilbert.)

Paul Gilbert identified the 3-directional flow of compassion as being a key component of how we understand and train in compassion. The first is the flow of compassion from others to ourselves. The second is the flow of compassion from ourselves to ourselves. The third is the flow of compassion from ourselves to others. Our task is to create conditions for compassion to flow in each of these directions.

When his research unit carried out studies on this 3-directional flow they discovered that people found the flow of compassion from themselves to others to be the most natural and easy to do. This is also our general understanding of what compassion means: being compassionate to others. His research unit found that many people struggled with receiving love and compassion from others. They had blocks in this area. Their next discovery was even more important. They found that if people found it hard to receive compassion they also found it hard to give compassion to themselves. These two flows were found to be intricately linked. It is like we are driving a car with 3 cylinders but only one of them is working.

The conclusion that emerged from these research findings was an obvious one: just like our car will soon grind to a halt if we just run it on one cylinder, so too will our compassion run out of steam and we will find ourselves experiencing compassion fatigue and in some cases burnout. As we mentioned before, this is very common in the caring professions where people become very good at giving compassion to others, but are not so good at receiving it and are even worse at attending to their own emotional needs.

Consequently, we will start with the flow of compassion from other to self. We will start gently because many of us find this hard. Instead of focusing on receiving compassion from a person, we will focus on receiving compassion from a colour that is imbued with certain qualities because this is less threatening. We will also imagine being in a safe place and feeling welcomed by this place. Only once we have become proficient in these practices will we move onto receiving compassion from others by doing the *Compassionate Being* practice, which works with an idealised image of compassion. We will do this practice in Chapter 8.

We then return to the compassion practice that we are most familiar with: giving compassion to others. But now all three cylinders are firing in our compassion vehicle and the energy of compassion is now flowing in three directions. This is so important because now the practice of compassion is sustainable. This is basic common sense: if we give care and support to others, we also need to nourish ourselves otherwise we will not be able to care for others for very long.

Working with Resistance and Blocks

When we do the various practices around the flow of compassion we will notice that sometimes they go effortlessly and we feel open to the flow of compassionate thoughts, emotions and sensations. Through placing a consistent focus on these practices, our capacity for generating the flow of compassion grows and we experience the benefits. Once again, this is the practice of energy follows focus.

However, sometimes compassion doesn't flow effortlessly and we might feel resistance or blocks. When this happens we haven't failed; it is quite normal. We can see this as an opportunity to acquaint ourselves with our unique set of blocks and resistances to compassion. We don't need to get into a fight with ourselves. We can recognise that we all struggle at times with opening ourselves to the flow of love and compassion in our lives.

We can then draw on our mindfulness skills and become curious about our blocks or resistances and see what we can learn about them. This entails turning towards the experience of blockage or resistance and noticing the thoughts, emotions and sensations that are part and parcel of this experience. Holding them gently in our awareness with acceptance and kindness, we can learn to be with them directly and let go of the storyline of the past. This creates the conditions for insights to arise into these resistances and blocks. Gradually, we come to familiarise ourselves with these blocks and understand them. Over time, whilst they might still persist, they become less of an obstacle because we know them and learn to welcome them like an old friend.

Receiving Compassion

Many people experience blocks when it comes to receiving compassion from another. Since this is the focus of this chapter it might be worth exploring what kind of blocks might arise.

Firstly, we might feel that we are not worthy or good enough to be receiving compassion. Many of us feel this way in the modern West. When Tibetan Buddhist teachers first began teaching in the West they were astonished to discover how many of us don't like ourselves and see ourselves as being worthless and deficient. This block can be a very painful one as we begin to understand how hard we have been on ourselves throughout our lives and how much suffering this has caused within our own minds and within our relationships. Often, this is accompanied by overwhelming feelings of grief.

Secondly, we might not want to receive compassion from another because we perceive it as threatening. We might think that it puts us beneath the person who is offering the compassion and perceive that we are falling down in terms of social hierarchy. Moreover, we might feel that if we accept the compassion we will be beholden in some way to the person offering the compassion. This is a fundamental misunderstanding of compassion, which is without hierarchy. It is pity that involves hierarchy. True compassion comes from an understanding that we are all in this human life together and is without expectation of reciprocation of any kind.

Thirdly, we might have opened up our hearts to loved ones in the past only to be hurt by them. If this has happened to us repeatedly, we may have developed a coping mechanism of keeping our heart firmly shut down. While this coping mechanism may have served us in the past, it has the negative consequence of blocking authentic loving connections with ourselves and others. Now might be the time to have the courage gradually to open our hearts again to receiving love and care from others, and then to dare to be kind to ourselves.

Giving Compassion to Ourselves

As we begin to do this an inner confidence slowly begins to grow. As our teacher, Rob Nairn, used to say, 'If we accept and love ourselves unconditionally, what does it matter what others think of us?' With a growing feeling of self-love and self-acceptance, the world around us begins to feel like a safer and a more welcoming place.

Self-compassion is the foundation of compassion for others. Once we understand with clarity what causes us to suffer then we understand what causes others to suffer. As we see deeply into the messy human condition within ourselves, we begin to recognise and have compassion for other people we share our lives with. They are in the mud too. However, this is easier said than done because so many of us are cruelly critical of ourselves; many of us don't like or accept ourselves and feel that we are not worthy of love or compassion from ourselves. These can be some of the most painful blocks that we encounter in our compassion training. We will explore the inner self-critic, which is one of the biggest blocks to self-compassion, in Chapter 10, but there is quite a bit of work to do before we get there!

Extending Compassion to Others

In Chapter 11 we will explore the flow of compassion from ourselves to others. While we may find it relatively easy to wish those we love to be free from suffering, when we move on to cultivating compassion for those who we don't like, or who are our rivals, we arc likely to hit some resistance. We might be perplexed about the rationale for cultivating compassion to those who have hurt us in our lives. However, we will come to see that feelings of anger or resentment towards others always cause us to suffer, whereas the object of our negative feelings may be completely oblivious (or not care less) about what we think or feel about them. This situation is like eating poison and expecting the other person to get ill.

Our practice is to recognise the common thread of humanity running through all imperfect human beings in the world: that everyone is trying to be happy and avoid suffering but so often are going about it in the wrong way. There is a sadness and a poignancy about this that can open our heart to even the most hated rival or dreaded adversary.

It's not that we become a doormat or condone bad behaviour; instead we recognise our common ground with others and use this as the basis for being more empathic and kinder. From this empathic understanding we are able to communicate more skilfully with the difficult people in our lives — and if nothing else we can gain some equanimity. We begin to let go of blame and to forgive; and in so doing we gain great strength, wisdom and joy in the growing workability of even the most challenging of our relationships.

Imagination Based Practice

As we have already discussed, the human imagination is incredibly powerful and is linked with our physiology. If we sit down to a delicious meal we start to salivate! But if we think of a delicious meal, something similar happens. Similarly, when someone is cruel to us, our threat system is activated and so too the reactions of fight or flight. But if we are cruel to ourselves with self-critical thinking, something similar happens. Our threat system is activated, we become stressed and cortisol floods our system. If we think of how often the inner critic torments and bullies us then we can appreciate how much time we spend locked in the threat system.

On the other hand, if someone is kind to us and they speak to us in a friendly, warm way we feel held and supported. Something in us relaxes and we feel safe. Similarly, if we relate to ourselves in a friendly way and think kind thoughts, the inner response is the same. This is the basis of compassionate imagery. It is about learning to enlist our thinking and imagination in the compassionate project of being kind to ourselves and others. It is based on the principle that the brain does not know the difference between what is real and what is imagined. Therefore, thinking and imagining kind things has the same effect as doing kind things.

When people practise compassionate imagery, they often think that they have to conjure up picture-perfect images in order for the practices to be effective; and when they cannot do this they can get discouraged and give up imagery practice. But this is not how it works. We can imagine fleeting images that come and go just like we do when we daydream.

Also, for some of us our imagination produces images, while for many of us our imagination operates through felt sense or by simply knowing what is imagined. Instead of an image coming to mind feelings or thoughts come to mind. When engaging with the practices that follow it is important simply to follow the guidance and allow our own imagination to operate in its own way. We try not to think too much about what we are going to imagine. Instead, we trust that a deeper wisdom will guide our imagination and we become curious about whatever emerges.

We will use compassionate imagining for each of the three flows of compassion described above. In this chapter we will introduces two practices for the flow of compassion from other to self: safe place and compassionate colour.

Safe Place

Feeling safe and secure is a lifelong quest for human beings. When we are safe we function at our optimal best. We have a secure base from where we can relate with other people and co-create effectively with them. Feeling safe is also the foundation for compassion. It is a key element of the soothing-affiliation system that helps us to down-regulate the threat and drive systems.

In the context of compassion training we make a distinction between safeness and safety. What we mean by 'safeness' is somewhere we feel completely at ease, where we are free to explore and have a sense of expansiveness; it is not a place of escape or confinement. It is true that sometimes people like to imagine themselves under a duvet, or safely snuggled in bed, but the important thing here is that it should be a joyful place for us — one of freedom, not one of 'hiding away in bed'. The key thing with a safe place is feeling a sense of freedom.

This can be contrasted with a place of safety that is concerned with keeping bad things out. This is linked to the threat system. The problem with this type of place is that while there is a sense of relief, there is little joy and little freedom; it's really an image that is being created by the threat system to try to keep out threats. In some cases, however, people begin with creating a place of safety and then gradually work on becoming freer and more open, thereby creating the conditions for safeness.

We can approach the safe place in various ways. One is to actively create conditions in our lives in which we feel safe and secure. In the case of a formal sitting practice, this might entail setting up a place in your home that is devoted to your practice, performing symbolic things like lighting candles or incense, and making sure that you will not be interrupted or disturbed. When you enter your space, there is a sense of crossing a threshold into a soothing place, which holds a feeling of sacredness, and where nobody will intrude on you. When you sit down, there is the feeling that you are held and supported by this environment and you can then sink more readily into your practice.

Another approach is to imagine a place that feels safe and secure. Since we know now that the imagination is very powerful, even just imagining a place where we feel safe and secure can evoke feelings of being safe. In the first practice at the end of this chapter we will invite you to imagine a place that evokes feelings of safeness and belonging for you. It can be any place you like. It can be a place you once visited, somewhere very familiar like a favourite room in your house, or outdoors in nature. It can be an imaginary place, one you saw in a movie or read about in a book, or entirely your own creation. It can also be a combination of a real and imagined places. You might be on your own in this place or surrounded by other humans or animals. The key thing is to give your imagination free reign and let it spontaneously come up with a place that feels right for you.

An important part of this practice is to be closely in tune with our senses. We notice how the place looks, what sounds we can hear, what we can smell and what textures we can feel, and whether it feels warm or cold in our safe place. We then imagine that every part of this place welcomes us and takes joy in our being there. This is a place where we truly belong. The emotional atmosphere we try to create is one of playfulness and freedom.

Like any of the compassion practices, we can run into resistances and blocks, especially when we imagine that the place welcomes us and takes joy in us being there. If so, we can begin doing the safe place practice without imagining that the place welcomes us. Once we have built up a stronger sense of feeling safe, we can begin to explore our resistance to being welcomed.

The blocks to the safe place practice may be to do with feeling threatened as soon as we relax our guard and begin to allow ourselves to feel safe. Alternatively, they might be due to an underlying feeling of unworthiness. Once again, when we feel strong enough, we can begin to be curious about these blocks; we can create a welcoming space and allow the thoughts, emotions and sensations associated with these blocks to arise, without any agenda of fixing them. In this way we can create the conditions for insight to arise.

Compassionate Colour

Learning to feel safe is the foundation for all the compassion practices to follow. In the previous practice we began to open in small ways to receiving kindness and support from outside by imagining that the safe place welcomes us and takes joy in us being there. We then build on this receptivity in the next practice. Here we imagine receiving certain compassionate qualities in the form of a colour. This can be less threatening than receiving love and compassion from a person because many of us have been hurt by people in the past and we can instinctively block it.

Once again we work with our imagination. We bring to mind a colour that we associate with kindness and compassion. It can take the form of a soft mist, a warm radiance or an energetic presence. We give our imagination free reign and notice what spontaneously emerges.

We then imagine that the compassionate colour has certain specific qualities. We imagine that it is endowed with a quality of *stability and strength* that holds and supports us; it possesses *intelligence and wisdom* that knows what we have gone through and what we need right now; it responds to us with *warmth and kindness*; and it instils in us a sense of fearless *courage and commitment*. These are key compassionate qualities that we will explore in detail in later chapters. At this stage we imagine that the compassionate colour is charged with these qualities and we draw them into our being.

We do this by visualising the compassionate colour surrounding and enfolding our body. We imagine that we are soothed and supported by the compassionate colour just like we might bask in early morning sunshine. We bring to mind that the sole intention of the colour is to support us unconditionally.

We then imagine that the compassionate colour enters us through our heart centre or is absorbed through the pores in our skin. It fills us up and we imagine that every cell of our body is bathed in its qualities of compassion. We are filled to the brim with the qualities of strength, wisdom, kindness and courage.

When we do the practice we might notice that our heart opens to receiving the flow of compassion. If so, we simply stay present with the process and get used to the feeling of taking in these qualities. This builds a new habit of taking in what is good and wholesome from the outside. This is so important because it lays the foundation for self-compassion that research shows is closely linked with the ability to receive love and kindness from sources outside ourselves.

Some people might experience blocks in doing this practice. For example, one of the qualities might be more difficult to receive than others. Alternatively, we might resist the idea of the compassionate colour supporting us unconditionally. We might not feel worthy to receive compassion or we might find the experience of opening up to a flow of incoming kindness and support threatening.

When we experience resistance, it may be accompanied by emotions such as anger, anxiety or sadness, or a combination of different emotions. This does not mean that we have failed. We can reframe these experiences as an opportunity to learn about our unique set of blocks and resistances. This entails opening up to the thoughts, emotions and sensations — staying present and being curious — and perhaps saying 'yes' to whatever emerges within us. In this way the obstacles become part of the path.

Window of Tolerance

In this book we will offer many different practices to build our inner resources of compassion. To begin with choose those practices that help you to feel calm and safe. Once you have built up sufficient inner resources then try doing the practices that bring up blocks and resistances.

It is important is to stay within our window of tolerance. If we notice that an imagination practice is becoming overwhelming, we can stop doing it for the time being and come back to our intention. This means reaffirming our wish to cultivate compassion even if we cannot put it into practice right now. We can appreciate what a wonderful thing it is to want to develop compassion in our minds and in our lives. We can acknowledge that this is difficult, but we can keep going. In this world, where so many people lead selfish lives and cause harm to others, we can rejoice in setting our intention to become a compassionate and caring person. Even though a particular practice may be difficult to do right now, we can reaffirm our intention to come back to it later once we have built up more compassionate capacity.

Once we become familiar with these practices, by doing them on a daily basis they become a part of us. Then, when we face a challenge in our life, we can take a pause and bring to mind our compassionate colour. We can sense the energetic presence of the colour and feel its kindness, strength and wisdom enfolding and supporting us — and then we can act from this place. At those times when we feel insecure and unsafe, we can take a pause and bring to mind the sights and sounds of our safe place and feel its presence. This can then support us to respond more skilfully in challenging situations.

Practice Section

Formal Sitting Practice

Practice 12: Safe Place (20 minutes)
Begin by sitting in a relaxed and comfortable posture on a cushion or chair. Then pay attention to the rising and falling of your body as you breathe. To help settle your mind, try deepening your in-breath and lengthening your out-breath a little. See if you can regulate your breathing so that your in-breath and out-breath are of a similar length and rhythm. You might like to count to three or four on the in-breath and a similar count on the out-breath. When your mind begins to settle, let go of counting and let your breathing find its natural rhythm.

When you're ready, see if you can invite the image of a place into your mind — a place that could give you a feeling of safeness and calm. Let the place emerge of its own accord, allowing your imagination free reign. Imagine looking around you, what can you see? Notice any colours, appreciating their richness, the quality of the light, the time of day or night. Now focus on what you can feel. Notice the temperature, the feeling of the air around you. Maybe you are barefoot in your safe space, noticing the texture of the ground under your feet. Next, think about what you can hear. Are there any sounds? Are they intense or are they quite subtle? Now see if you can smell anything in your safe space.

Notice if there are any other people in your safe place, or if you are there alone. Sometimes we can feel safe in the presence of other people, other times not. See what happens in your case. Also, notice if there are any animals in your safe place, and whether they are pets or wild animals. Are there any sounds, like bird song, for example?

When you bring your safe place to mind, allow your body to relax. Becoming aware of your facial expression, allow your brow to become smooth. If your jaw is clenched invite it to relax. Perhaps you may invite a soft smile of pleasure at being there.

See if you can imagine that the place itself *takes joy in you being there.* Allow yourself to feel how your safe place has pleasure in you being there. If you are on a beach, the sea sand welcomes you and the waves welcome you. If you are in a forest the trees welcome you, the birds welcome you and the sky above welcomes you. If you are inside sitting by a fire in your home, the flames welcome you, and every part of your home welcomes you. Notice how you feel when you imagine that this place is happy with you being there. Even if the images are fleeting and come and go, see if you can sense an emotional connection with this place.

Know that this place is always available for you to return to. It is never more than a thought away. As soon as you bring it to mind, you can go back there again in your imagination and once again feel the sense of safeness, security and belonging.

Now, imagine the safe place dissolving and imagine that any feelings of safeness, security and belonging gather in a coloured sphere of energy in your heart centre, which you carry within you. Then spend a few moments resting at ease, appreciating having done the practice, and then get up and continue with your day, seeing if it is possible to maintain an inner feeling of being safe and secure.

Practice 13: Compassionate Colour (20 minutes)

Begin by sitting in a relaxed and comfortable posture on a cushion or chair. Then pay attention to the rising and falling of your body as you breathe. To help settle your mind, try deepening your in-breath a little and lengthening your out-breath. See if you can regulate your breathing so that your in-breath and out-breath are of a similar length and rhythm. You might like to count to three or four on the in-breath and a similar count on the out-breath. When your mind begins to settle, let go of counting and let your breathing find its natural rhythm.

Now imagine a colour that you associate with compassion, or a colour that conveys some sense of warmth and kindness. It might only be a fleeting sense of colour, but when you are ready, see if you can imagine your compassionate colour surrounding you. Imagine it enfolding you in a way that feels warm and soothing. Then, imagine the colour entering you through your heart area and slowly spreading through your body; or you might prefer to think of the colour like a mist or glow that just flows into your body.

As this happens, try to focus on your colour as having certain qualities: it has a quality of stability and strength that holds and supports you; it has a quality of wisdom that knows your struggles and what you need; it responds to you with kindness and warmth; and it instils in you a sense of courage that helps you to stay present with difficult feelings that come and go. Invite a facial expression of softness and kindness as you do this practice.

Now, as you imagine the colour flowing through you, focus on the feeling that the sole purpose of this colour is to help you, strengthen you and support you. If blocks and barriers arise (especially those linked to ideas that you don't deserve compassion) see if you can simply let them be present without agenda. If the blocks and barriers feel strong at times there is no need to give yourself a hard time — they are not your fault — and for now go back to the rhythm of your breathing or revisit your intention to be compassionate.

When you come to the end of your practice time, rest at ease for a few moments and appreciate the afterglow of the practice. Allow the colour to gather in a sphere of energy in your heart centre which you can carry with you as you get up and move into the next moments of your day.

Chapter Seven

Self-Compassion

In the last chapter we introduced the practices of safe place and compassionate colour. These are visualisation practices. Throughout this book we will be alternating between mindfulness-based practices and imagination-based practices. Some people connect with one and not the other, and for other people it changes over time. We suggest you experiment with both and see what works best for you.

In this chapter we will introduce a key mindfulness-based practice focused on self-compassion. This will create the conditions for the practice of the *Compassionate Self* in the next chapter. As we have kept saying throughout this book, compassion training proceeds in stages with one stage building upon another.

Self-Compassion

Chris Germer describes mindfulness as posing this question to our self, 'What do I notice?' whereas with self-compassion, the question we pose is, 'What do I need?' (Germer, 2009). This really goes to the heart of the distinction between the two. In the approach we take in this book, we start with mindfulness, build in acceptance and kindness, and then move on to self-compassion before we practise compassion for others. This is the natural order of progression.

However, it is not as linear as that. Many of these processes are happening at the same time; for example, we might go back and forth between self-compassion and compassion for others. It is an integrated and organic approach, but nonetheless mindfulness, acceptance and some basic feeling of kindness are the essential building blocks we need to have in place otherwise our practice of compassion is likely to falter.

Many people regard self-compassion as something a bit odd and self-indulgent, almost like we are pampering ourselves. But it is important to distinguish clearly between our wants and our needs. Self-indulgence is all about succumbing to our wants — and there are so many on offer in modern life — whilst self-compassion is about identifying and meeting our needs. This is not selfish at all. In fact, it is an important step towards maturity.

Many traditional Buddhist teachers are perplexed by self-compassion. The traditional Buddhist view is that we love ourselves too much and we need to go beyond self-fixation and focus more on others. In the Mahayana school of Buddhism it is taught that the sacred recipe for happiness is focussing on the welfare and happiness of others and not worrying about whether we are happy or not. Counter-intuitively, this is seen as the best way to find authentic and lasting happiness for ourselves.

But the problem in the modern West is that *we hate ourselves too much* rather than loving ourselves too much! When the Dalai Lama first convened a meeting of Western Buddhist teachers in the nineties, he was astounded by the prevalence amongst Western Buddhist meditators of self-attacking and self-hatred. He found it hard to believe. This was something unheard of in the Tibetan society he grew up in. It took him some time to appreciate how endemic this problem is for so many Westerners.

Yet this is the reality for so many people. The strange thing about self-hatred is that it results in very tight self-fixation. You might think that if we hated ourselves we would just not bother about our self, but in truth people afflicted by self-hatred are tortured by rumination, self-doubt, and self-involvement, all of which tie them into tighter and tighter knots until they become completely self-absorbed and out of touch with the needs and feelings of other people.

Self-compassion is the antidote to this painful self-absorption. We start by noticing what is going on in our mind and shift our focus from the repetitive inner stories to a neutral focal support, and in so doing we take the heat out of the thinking process. This is basic mindfulness. Then we learn to lean towards our difficult feelings — even the painful knot of rumination and self-loathing — so that we are not inflaming the situation by resisting it. As Carl Jung once (reputedly) aptly put, 'what we resist persists!' This is basic acceptance practice. We then learn to nurture kindness within ourselves by remembering when someone was kind to us, and when we were kind to someone else. We notice how kindness feels now in the body when we recall these memories. This is basic kindness. We covered all of this in Chapter 3.

Now we are ready for the practice of self-compassion. The basic elements are in place for us to begin to identify what we need and how we can best meet those needs.

Embodiment

When we begin to practise self-compassion a key starting point is embodiment. This is a theme running throughout the book. We touched on it in Chapter 4 and we will revisit it again now.

The body carries so much. It holds both physical pain and pleasure. We experience so many of the delights and joys of life through our bodies; but the body can also express a great deal of pain and suffering too. This might be physical injury or sickness, but it can also be emotional pain, sadness, and discomfort. When we meditate we come to see how there is a thin line between physical pain and emotional pain, and between physical sensations of pleasure and emotional states of joy and rapture. Quite simply, the body holds so much of our sensing, feeling, emotional lives.

Many people in the modern West are very disembodied. For many of us the reason for this is that we find it uncomfortable to be fully present within our bodies because our bodies can hurt a lot. Any genuine path of meditation and spiritual practice, however, requires that we consciously descend into our bodies and be willing to feel what the body holds.

This is a complex process. Many of us hold deep trauma and wounding in the body. And when we begin to practise mindfulness some of this becomes more conscious. What was always there, but frozen and unconscious, begins to unfreeze and enter conscious awareness. For many people this can be a rude awakening, but it is an important process to navigate. It might require the skilled assistance of a mentor or therapist, and it requires slow, patient work. But this is the work of true self-compassion and courage.

Some spiritual traditions speak of three levels of being: cognitive mind, physical body, and subtle emotional body. In Tibetan Buddhism a lot of focus is placed on purifying the subtle emotional body that runs between the other two. It is understood that there are subtle energy channels and chakras making up the emotional body and that emotional blockages can inhibit the free flow of energy within these channels and chakras. In modern parlance we speak more about the nervous system rather than the subtle emotional body. It is well understood that trauma can interfere with the subtle wiring of our nervous system and a therapeutic process is often needed to unblock this. Therefore, when we talk about 'body' in this context we are referring to both the physical body as well as the subtle emotional body that runs between the cognitive mind and physical body and links the two.

Many of the key themes of this book come together at this point. In Chapter 4 we said that compassion is a process of descent into the felt reality of our emotional being. Many of us are drawn to the idea of spiritual ascent — ascending to a higher level of consciousness — but the point we made is that the path of genuine compassion is a process of descent into the murky reaches of our emotional world that is so often held within our body and the personal history it carries.

Rob Nairn described this as the willingness to drop into our messy humanity and to accept ourselves 'warts and all'. For him, true compassion was to embrace this messiness and then to go forth into the world as a compassionate mess. We are willing to have our feet firmly on the ground and be in touch with the issues and difficulties that so many other people face. This has the capacity to awaken genuine compassion since we know first-hand what other people go through because we are in touch with this in ourselves.

Another image that we looked at in Chapter 4 was the Buddhist image of the lotus and the mud. Here again, the ancient texts warn against ascending prematurely because, like Icarus of old, we might fly too close to the sun and tumble back down to the Earth with a thump. The instruction once again is to descend to the bottom of the lake — a metaphor for our psyche — and to befriend the 'mud' of our experience because that is where the seed of compassion is to be found; it is beneath the mud of our shame and sorrow, our shadowy emotions and painful memories. Furthermore, the mud is the fertiliser that enables the seed of compassion to germinate and grow into a beautiful lotus flower that at some point in our life breaks the surface of the lake.

The point here is that the mud is to be found in our bodies — our emotional bodies — and the process of descending into the mud is the process of inhabiting our bodies fully. It is a process that begins with mindfulness training and finds its maturity with compassion training. Only once we fully drop into and make friends with the strange and unfamiliar feelings we find in our bodies can the process of compassion really start. Only then can the true spiritual emergence begin.

This journey is also described by the two aspects of compassion we described in Chapter 2. There needs to be a willingness to approach suffering in ourselves (first aspect) and then also a recognition that we need to build the inner resources and capacities to hold and respond to our suffering (second aspect). These two processes always go hand in hand. But, as we have mentioned a few times, we need to work on the second one first before we can approach the first one.

Before we approach the mud within ourselves we need to build our capacity to hold it and engage with it skilfully. This is so important. Contemporary writers and practitioners of mindfulness exhort us to stay within our window of tolerance and not to bite off more than we can chew.

Touch, Voice Tone and Smile

A practical way of getting in touch with what we feel in our emotional body is to notice how we feel in the physical body. Through our mindfulness practice we begin to notice how the body feels when the threat system is activated, such as the lifting of the shoulders, the tensing of the jaw, the curling of the fists or the pumping of the heart. We also begin to notice how the body feels when the drive system is activated, such as a feeling of restless agitation or a tightening in the throat. We each come to know how the activation of the threat and drive systems manifests in our own individual experience. Then in daily life we can become more in touch with those times when the threat and drive systems are activated.

Once an embodied understanding grows of how the overstimulation of the threat and drive systems cause suffering in our lives, a heartfelt motivation to relieve this suffering naturally arises. This is the second aspect of compassion mentioned above. We feel impelled to set a strong intention to stimulate the soothing-affiliation system whenever we notice the threat or drive system taking over our experience and driving us back into our heads.

Gesture and touch are powerful ways of activating this emotional system. When a friend is having a hard time we might gently place a hand on their shoulder and say reassuring words. For many of us this kind of gesture comes naturally and we don't even think about it. But when we are invited to do this for ourselves it can feel awkward and unnatural. Yet soothing touch is an important way of activating the soothing-affiliation system.

When we were young the physical touch of our parents or carers were important ways of helping us feel safe and held. Human beings depend on emotional co-regulation to help them regulate their own emotions. We need the empathic presence of other human beings to help us feel safe within ourselves. One of the underlying themes of this book, however, is that if we did not get this when we were young we can learn to do it now through a variety of methods, and one of these are physical gestures of self-soothing.

In the two practices we offer at the end of this chapter we will introduce gestures of self-soothing. The most common is placing one or both of our hands on our hearts. Alternatively, we can place a hand on our cheek, give ourselves a hug or hold our own hand. If we reflect on it, we might already have a self-soothing gesture, which we use when we feel challenged, such as rubbing the palm of one hand with the thumb of the other hand or placing our hands on our belly. We feel the warmth of the hands and cultivate a sense of unconditional support and commitment to ourselves by way of the soothing hand gesture. We can each experiment with different gestures of self-soothing so that we might find a gesture, which over time can help us create a felt sense of safeness within this body of ours.

We then learn to combine soothing touch with the settling breathing that we introduced in Chapter 3. This is another way of activating the soothing-affiliation system. We breathe more deeply than usual in a steady rhythm and equalise the in-breath and out-breath. This method of breathing relaxes the body physiologically, especially if we focus on releasing tension on the out-breath. If we get used to breathing in this way, our centre of gravity drops out of the thinking activity in the head into the sensory awareness of the body.

Through our gesture of self-soothing, rhythmical breathing and through maintaining body awareness, our body gradually becomes a safe container within which any strong emotions can play out. Instead of turning away from and suppressing unpleasant emotional feelings, we cultivate the stability and courage to allow these emotions to arise and display within our experience. When we do this without getting caught up in the stories about the emotions, the underlying psychological mechanisms giving rise to the emotions can also come into conscious awareness. This is the process of insight and it leads to personal growth and understanding.

Another ingredient that we will add to the mix is that of friendly self-talk. Many of us talk to ourselves in such a cruel and aggressive way. In our experience of working with people, what strikes us both is the power of the inner critic and how it rules the lives of so many of the people we work with. We will devote a chapter to this tricky inner character later in the book, but the important point at this stage is for us to lay the groundwork for learning to talk to ourselves differently. Rob Nairn often used to say that if somebody talked to us in the way that we so often talk to ourselves, we would very soon part company with this person and walk away; but when it comes to our own inner critic we tamely roll over and let it walk all over us. And what is more, there is no escape because this angry, condemning figure resides in our very own head!

In the practice that follows we will learn to talk to ourselves in a kind and friendly way, almost like we are learning to become our own best friend. But this is not as easy as it sounds and so it needs a lot of practice! Once again it is helpful to see that the negative self-talk originates from the threat system and is charged with emotions like anger and anxiety, whilst the positive self-talk originates from the soothing-affiliation system and is linked to feelings of safeness and contentment.

Linked to the friendly self-talk, is learning to bring a smile to ourselves just like we would smile at a friend or child that we love. Choden recalls looking at statues of the Buddha and noticing how the Buddha is often depicted with a half-smile, almost like he knew from a place of instinctive wisdom how important it is to bring some warmth and humour to how we engage with the unfolding experiences of this life.

In summary, the key elements we will be using when we practise self-compassion are the following: feeling grounded in the body, settling breathing, soothing touch, friendly self-talk and a smile that reaches the eyes. For those of you who might be thinking that this is starting to go in an overly touchy-feely direction, you will be relieved to know that there is solid science behind this approach!

Polyvagal Theory

A scientific perspective that informs the practice of self-compassion is that of Polyvagal Theory. It was developed by the neurobiologist, Dr Stephen Porges. It centres around the complex vagus nerve and its different branches. The dorsal vagal nerve network is associated with a threat response and is a very old part of the nervous system. It mediates our survival reactions of fight, flight and freeze. A more recent adaption is the ventral vagal nerve network that is connected to the soothing-affiliation system. It comes online when we feel safe. Porges (2011) once remarked that all human beings come into this world with a deep desire to feel safe in their bodies, in their lives and in their relationships. As we know from the last chapter, feeling safe brings out the best in us and we are able to connect, trust and co-create with others.

He identified a hierarchy of response with three levels. At our optimal best, the ventral vagal network mediates our relationships with ourselves and with others. But as soon as we begin to feel unsafe we drop down in the hierarchy and the dorsal vagal network comes online. This is the second level where we either fight or run away from the source of threat. The third level is that of freeze — when the danger is very intense we freeze on the spot and do not move. Many trauma reactions are connected to this level in the hierarchy.

Interestingly, the more recent adaption of the ventral vagal network arose from the freeze response of the dorsal vagal network through the secretion of the hormone oxytocin. When this hormone is released the freeze response 'unfreezes' as it were and we can relax, connect and be intimate with others. In this way the most ancient part of the threat system becomes the gateway to our more highly evolved response of connection, affiliation and co-creation.

The vagus nerve is part of the autonomic nervous system. It is not within our conscious control and yet it has a big impact on how we perceive ourselves and the world around us. Porges used the term 'neuroception' to describe how this perception occurs. It refers to a process whereby we are always unconsciously scanning our environment to detect sources of threat and possibilities for feeling safe. Neuroception then determines where we find ourselves in the hierarchy of response.

Even though it is involuntary, we do have some agency in that certain cues activate the ventral vagal network. Key ones are calm breathing, smiling and voice tone. This is plain common sense: if we walk into a room and someone smiles and talks to us in a friendly way, we feel safe, we relax and we feel that we can interact constructively with the person. On the contrary, if we walk into the same room and the person is emotionally unresponsive, they do not smile and they talk to us in a dispassionate, uninterested way, we might conclude that we are not welcome and quickly exit the room. We have dropped down the hierarchy of response to the second level, namely the flight response.

Interestingly, when Porges described smiling, he said that the cue for the ventral vagal network comes more from the eyes than from the mouth. It is a smile from the eyes. Once again this is common sense. We can all remember times in our lives when we forced a smile from our lips — perhaps for a photograph — but did not really mean it. Yet a smile from the eyes is hard to fake.

What is so important here is that *we can do this for ourselves*. If we work on the slow, rhythmical breathing, if we talk to ourselves in a friendly way and if we learn to smile at ourselves with kindness and warmth, then we can initiate the shift from the dorsal to the ventral vagal network and our inner environment can feel completely different. We can feel more proactive and more in tune with ourselves and with others. A whole different way of living becomes possible.

Yin and Yang

We are now approaching the point where we will weave the different elements of self-compassion into a practice. But there is one more thing to mention.

When it comes to embodying compassion, we learn to cultivate qualities such as kindness and warmth, strength and stability, courage and commitment, and wisdom and understanding. We have already done some visualisation practices in the last chapter that help us to express these qualities.

We can build on this by connecting to a sense of a strong back and a soft, open front. Kristin Neff, one of the world leaders in self-compassion research, refers to this as the Yin and Yang of self-compassion. The Yin is the tender, soft, allowing quality which is connected to the quality of kindness and warmth, and the Yang is the strong, protective quality that is connected to the qualities of stability and courage.

When we practise self-compassion we can rely on the strength and dignity of the spine — our strong back that supports and protects us. As we sit or stand tall we might feel that we embody qualities of strength and courage. It also helps to roll our shoulders back and down so as to open the chest. This embodies courage as well as an open, tender heart. With the foundation of a strong back, we can allow the front of our body to relax, trusting that it is supported by the spine. We can relax the face, allowing a slight smile on our lips, and we can relax the regions of the heart and belly. This posture of a strong back and soft front can support us in our self-compassion practice as well as when we move around in our daily lives.

Self-Compassion in Practice

Grounding in the body is a key element of mindfulness practice. It helps us become more embodied. We do it by gently scanning our body with our awareness and noticing any sensations that are present whilst also being aware of the weight of the body on the ground and how the ground holds our body unconditionally.

We now add self-compassion to the grounding stage by gently inclining towards those areas that call for our attention — not just noticing sensations and feeling them (mindfulness) but *responding* to what we are feeling (self-compassion). These are areas of discomfort or pain that can be either physical or emotional, or a combination of both. Sometimes, our bodies feel OK and there is no need to go looking for discomfort or pain if they are not there. In this case we can offer ourselves some kindness as way of building up our capacity to support ourselves during those times in the future when we do experience suffering.

Here we draw on the approach of Chris Germer and Kristin Neff and their wonderful practice of 'soften, soothe and allow' (Germer, 2009).

We begin by softening around any areas of discomfort or pain, or any 'tight edges' we feel within our bodies. If there are no specific areas of discomfort or pain we can simply soften throughout the whole body. Germer and Neff describe this stage as being like applying heat to sore muscles. Furthermore, we draw on the insights of the Polyvagal theory by using a friendly, warm voice tone as we say these words gently to ourselves: 'soften, soften, soften...' This engenders a feeling of being safe.

We then say the words 'soothe, soothe, soothe...' once again with a friendly voice tone. We also use the gesture of compassion that we explained in the section above. We can place one hand on our heart and the other hand on our abdomen, or on a part of our body where we feel pain or discomfort. But it is important that we do what feels instinctively right and do not just follow a formula because this is what we think we should do.

In this way we are bringing kindness and compassion directly to our felt experience. Many of our students have struggled with friendly self-talk and hand gestures at first, but the more they persisted with them the easier they became until finally they have become an indispensable part of their self-compassion routine.

As you can see we are interweaving the two processes of compassion all the time: we are opening more deeply to what we feel, whilst also consciously building our inner capacity to soothe and take care of ourselves. It is like we are strengthening the compassion muscle by training it.

The third part of the self-compassion practice is to say the words 'allow, allow, allow...', once again in a friendly tone of voice, really infusing the words with feeling. This expresses the attitude of acceptance. We are not softening and soothing ourselves so that the pain goes away, but just *because* we are feeling that way. We have no agenda that things change or that we feel better. We are willing to let things be as they are and change in their own time. It is like we sit in the middle of our internal guest house of the mind and leave all the doors wide open; we let the guests come and go as they choose and stay for as long as they like. Ironically, if we practise in this way difficult feelings and experiences move through us more quickly.

We then combine all three elements of the practice into a mantra of self-compassion and say these words gently to ourselves: 'soften, soothe, allow... soften, soothe allow... soften, soothe, allow...' and so forth.

When it feels right we let go of saying the self-compassion mantra and just rest in our experience as it is, without any expectation that we should feel any particular way. We then stay in this resting space for as long as we remain undistracted, but when we notice our attention getting lost in thinking, we work with a mindfulness support in the normal way.

We can also include self-compassion when we use breathing as a mindfulness support. If we notice any areas of tension, discomfort or pain, we can breathe into those areas of the body on the in-breath, opening as we breathe in and softening as we breathe out. If you like, you can place your hand on your heart, or use your own unique gesture, and even continue to say the self-compassion mantra — it is entirely up to you.

In this way, we incorporate self-compassion into the practice of mindfulness of breathing by directing it to those areas within us that feel tight, painful, tense or in need of care. We breathe in and open, breathe out and soften. We are not doing this to make things change or go away but to bring greater awareness to what we are feeling and to bring kindness and acceptance to what we are experiencing. Breathing in this way can be powerful as the breath is an effective channel for the flow of kindness and compassion.

When we come to the end of our practice session we can then share our practice with others. This is a way of affirming our compassionate intention and extending it to others. Therefore, we are not just focusing on taking care of ourselves, but we also make the wish that other living beings can better take care of themselves and so find happiness and fulfilment.

In the practice section at the end of this chapter, we will offer a mindfulness-based self-compassion practice that includes all the elements we have described above.

The Unholy Trinity

The practice of self-compassion is one way of dealing with a threat system that has turned in on itself. The threat system is designed to be fast-acting and it has a vital function in protecting us from the many dangers we encounter in life. When our ancestors roamed the wilds in search of food and heard a rustle in the bushes, the alarm bell of the amygdala sounded and they ran for their lives. Nine times out of ten it was not a tiger lurking in the bushes but something innocuous; but nonetheless this fast-acting response made sense because our survival was ensured in case it was in fact a tiger.

The problem for so many of us in modern life is not tigers jumping out of bushes but the tigers that dwell in our very own minds. These are tigers we can never escape from because we carry them inside us and we unwittingly feed them with our self-critical thoughts. The great psychiatrist, RD Laing, once famously said that the greatest fear of the modern human is the mind itself. We have subdued the outer world but we have not tamed our own minds. The tigers in the mind are a combination of many factors that are unique for everyone but the common ingredients are so often anger, fear and shame.

In a similar vein, Paul Gilbert has remarked many times that many of the stressors we face are internal — often in the way we speak to ourselves — and this problem is compounded by the fact that the emotional system that is equipped to help us calm down stress, namely the soothing-affiliation system, is itself compromised. Therefore, we find ourselves in a very difficult situation.

Chris Germer and Kristin Neff have made a significant contribution to this area too. Choden attended some of their first retreats on Holy Isle in Scotland when they taught their Mindful Self-Compassion programme. Choden was struck by Germer's term, 'the unholy trinity of absorption'. This refers to the three main elements of the threat system that have turned in on themselves.

He argues that the fight response has turned into self-criticism, the flight response has turned into self-isolation and the freeze response has turned into self-absorption (getting locked into spirals of rumination). This internalisation of threat is very likely to have its origins in modern child rearing. When our parents do not value us as children and put us down, we can internalise these parental voices and relentlessly criticise ourselves. And when we get sent to our rooms when we are angry and distressed (when in fact we need soothing and comfort) this can forge patterns of retreating into 'internal rooms of the mind' later in life. And when we are alone in our rooms we can fall prey to repetitive, self-critical thinking and become overly absorbed in it. Chris Germer referred to this 'unholy trinity' as a modern hell.

Image 4. Threat Reactions and Antidotes. (Neff, 2010: Mindful Self-Compassion (MSC) Training Program.)

As an antidote to these self-destructive patterns, Kristin Neff developed her self-compassion model with mindfulness being an antidote to self-absorption, kindness being an antidote to self-criticism and common humanity being an antidote to self-isolation. Common humanity is the realisation that we are not alone in what we go through because many others go through something similar too. The internal threat responses and their antidotes are set out in the diagram on page 131. These antidotes are another way of building up the capacity of the soothing-affiliation system.

You can explore these three antidotes by asking yourself the following questions (or you might choose to visit Kristin Neff's website www.self-compassion.org and click the option to test your level of self-compassion):

Mindfulness:
Do you tend to get carried away by the drama of a situation so that you make a bigger deal out of it than you need to? Or do you tend to keep things in perspective?

Common Humanity:
Do you tend to feel cut off from others when things go wrong, with irrational feelings that everyone else is having a better time of it than you? Or do you get in touch with the fact that all humans experience hardship in their lives?

Kindness:
Do you tend to criticise yourself or others, ignore the fact that you are suffering, or focus exclusively on fixing the problem? Or do you stop to give yourself care and comfort?

Self-Compassion Break

The daily life practice at the end of this chapter is the *Self-Compassion Break*. It addresses each of the elements of 'the unholy trinity' with the antidotes of mindfulness, common humanity, and kindness. Many of our students have found this practice to be very useful. It is short and easy to do and yet it goes to the heart of self-compassion.

As you go about your daily life, whenever you feel stressed, overwhelmed or anxious, try to pause what you are doing and simply acknowledge that you are experiencing a moment of suffering. This is the mindfulness element of noticing how you are feeling. This is simple yet powerful because in that moment we dis-identify from the stress energy that is propelling us forward on automatic pilot. It gives us the headspace to notice that many other people are going through a hard time too. This is the second element of common humanity that connects us to other human beings. This power of connection can open our heart and free us from the tight knot of self-absorption. The third element is to bring kindness to ourselves *just for that moment* — not for the rest of our lives or even the rest of the day — but just for a moment or two. Even if we struggle with being kind to ourselves we can manage a few moments of self-kindness. Here again we can use the gesture of hand on heart (or somewhere else on the body) and we can try to speak to ourselves in a friendly tone of voice. This practice is powerful in its simplicity and brevity. It is also the perfect daily life complement to the formal self-compassion practice described above.

Don't Go Looking for Suffering

In our practice of self-compassion it is important not to go looking for suffering. Rather, we can just wait until it emerges and then practise self-compassion. It can be counter-productive to go delving into past suffering such as childhood trauma. If we actively dwell on these past sufferings they can overwhelm us. Instead, we trust that our process of cultivating self-compassion will unfold in its own way and in its own time.

Once our compassionate capacity grows and we find that we can tolerate more pain and distress, past experiences which we had previously sat on and not been able to deal with, may arise naturally in our practice without us actively digging them up.

This is one of the key differences between meditation-based practice and psychotherapy approaches. In psychotherapy, conditions are put in place to actively explore past issues and traumas. In meditation approaches, we trust the process and trust that when we have enough capacity to hold our past struggles and issues, they will emerge in our practice of their own accord. Then we apply our mindfulness and self-compassion practice to be with what arises in an open and non-judgemental way. This creates the conditions for spontaneous insights to arise as part of the process of healing and transformation.

Heather likes to use the analogy of a scratch on the hand. If we leave it alone it will heal of its own accord; but if we are constantly scratching the wound it will get infected and it will not heal. In the same way, we do not provoke the trauma associated with the most difficult times in our lives, which is like scratching a wound. Instead, we practise patience and build our resources of compassion and trust so that when the time is right, challenging issues will come to the surface and we will then have the resources to hold them and facilitate healing.

Practice Section

Formal Sitting Practice

Practice 14: Self-Compassion (20 – 30 minutes)
Begin by sitting in a relaxed and comfortable posture on a cushion or a chair. Feel the weight of your body on your seat while sitting dignified, upright and alert. Then pay attention to the rising and falling of your body as you breathe. To help settle your mind, try deepening your in-breath a little and lengthening

your out-breath. See if you can regulate your breathing so that your in-breath and out-breath are of a similar length and rhythm. You might like to count to three or four on the in-breath and a similar count on the out-breath. If your mind is flighty and full of thoughts try placing one hand on your abdomen, feeling the movement of your body as you breathe. When your mind begins to settle a little let go of counting and allow your breathing to find its natural rhythm.

Now bring your attention more fully into your body. Become aware of the contact and pressure where your body rests on the seat or cushion beneath you; mind resting in body, body resting on ground beneath you. Now gently tune into the sensations in the body. Do this in a gentle and open way, allowing the sensations to present themselves to you. You may be aware of the temperature in the room; perhaps there is a slight pain in your right shoulder or a feeling of tension in one of your knees; or maybe there is a contraction in your stomach related to an emotion you are feeling.

Now let your attention be drawn to a place in your body where you may be holding a difficult emotion, pain or discomfort. *Soften* around this area of the body. The more you feel this area tighten and contract, the more you soften around it. It is like applying heat to sore muscles. You can say, 'soften... soften... soften...' quietly to yourself to enhance the process. Remember that you are not trying to make the sensations go away; you are just bringing kind awareness to them.

Now *soothe* yourself for struggling in this way. Put your hand over your heart and feel your body breathe. If you wish, you can also direct kindness to the part of your body that is under stress by placing your hand in that place. You can say kind words to yourself that arise spontaneously, or repeat, 'soothe... soothe... soothe'.

Finally, *allow* the discomfort to be there. Abandon the wish for the painful feelings to disappear. Let the discomfort come and go as it pleases, like a guest in your own home. You can repeat, 'allow... allow... allow'.

'Soften, soothe, and allow... soften, soothe, and allow...' You can use these three words like a mantra, reminding yourself to incline with tenderness toward your suffering. See if you can use a gentle voice tone, almost as if you are reassuring a frightened child; and if it works for you, relax your jaw and allow your lips to soften into a half-smile.

Now broaden your awareness and become aware of your experience as a whole, no longer just focusing on the difficult feelings. And now simply rest in the midst of whatever is present for you: thoughts, feelings, sensations and sounds; mind resting in the body, body resting on the ground beneath you, open to whatever you are noticing and feeling. When you notice that your mind begins to drift into thinking, then move onto the next stage which is using breathing as a focal support.

Rest your attention lightly on the natural rhythm of your breathing wherever you connect to it most easily in the body: this could be the breath coming and going through your nostrils, your abdomen rising and falling, the sensation of the breath leaving your body, or the feeling of your whole body breathing. It does not matter where you rest your attention, what is important is to have a light touch — not shutting out thoughts and emotions but allowing them to come and go. When you become aware that you have got lost in thinking, simply notice this and return your attention to the breath — no sense of succeeding or failing, just noticing and returning.

If you notice any painful feelings or sensations, then integrate self-compassion into the practice of mindfulness of breathing. As a way of soothing yourself you can place your hand on your heart, or over an area of your body where you feel the painful sensations or emotions. Then breathe into the area of your body where you are feeling distress or pain, opening with the in-breath and softening with the out-breath. After breathing in this way for a while, come back to your experience as a whole and allow your experience to be as it is without requiring that anything changes.

Once you come to the end of your designated practice session, spend a few moments resting without any focus and letting go of trying to meditate. As a way of concluding your practice session, you might want to do a simple sharing something like this: 'I intend to carry the practice of compassion into my daily life, with the motivation to connect to others who are like me and who struggle like me'. Then stretch your body and slowly get up. See if you can carry the awareness of your sitting session into the next moments of your day.

Informal Daily Life Practice

Practice 15: Self-Compassion Break

When you go about your daily life and notice that you are feeling wound up and stressed, find a safe place to pause for a few moments and then do this practice. Sit upright and feel the weight of your body on the ground beneath you. Bring attention to your breathing and try placing one hand on your abdomen and the other hand on your heart centre (or use whatever gestures work best for you). Then go through this process:

- Step 1: Acknowledge that 'this is a moment of difficulty'. This brings mindfulness to the fact that you are feeling stressed.
- Step 2: Say to yourself in a friendly way: 'difficulties are part of everybody's life'. In particular, what you are experiencing right now many other people are going through too. This allows you to feel connected to others.
- Step 3: Now say to yourself in a gentle way: 'may I respond to what I am going through with kindness, even just for

this moment'. If self-kindness does not come easy, you don't need to be too ambitious. You do not need to try to be kind to yourself for the rest of the day, but just for this moment of difficulty.

Now see if you can carry these feelings of mindfulness, common humanity and kindness into the next moments of your day. (Germer and Neff, 2019.)

Chapter Eight

Finding the Compassionate Friend Within

The main purpose of compassion training is to uncover the source of wisdom, strength, and courage within us. So many people look outwards for support and solace. There is a place for this — as we shall soon see — but the important journey is to turn inwards and reclaim our own wellspring of compassionate power. This is when things really change. Marianne Williamson (2017) sums it up in these words:

> 'Our deepest fear is not that we are inadequate.
> Our deepest fear in that we are powerful beyond measure.
> It is our Light, not our Darkness, that most frightens us.
> We ask ourselves, who am I to be brilliant, gorgeous, talented, fabulous?
> Actually, who are you not to be?'

It is like discovering an inner friend that walks step by step with us when we face the challenges of life. Many of us have a scathing inner critic that is always criticising our every move. We do not need to develop this part; it is always there and ever-vigilant, often in ways that are destructive. We will find ways of relating skilfully to this tricky inner character in Chapter 10.

But the inner compassionate friend — the one who can genuinely help us — is something that we need to gradually cultivate; and once cultivated it can be a source of immense emotional support and joy. It takes joy in our successes and it picks us up when we fall down. We describe it as the 'compassionate self'.

The Holder and the Held

Cultivating the compassionate self is based on the principle of 'the holder and the held'. This concept was articulated by the well-known American meditation teacher, Tara Brach. Each of us struggles with inner issues and demons and many of us experience emotional wounding and vulnerability. These are the parts of us that need to be held. But many of us suppress or deny these issues and often unconsciously require other people to take care of them for us. This is what happens in some intimate relationships and it can be the undoing of these relationships.

There is also a part of us that can do the holding, but we need to clearly recognise and cultivate this part. When we then identify within ourselves what needs to be held and take responsibility for supporting these parts of us, it is the beginning of genuine maturity. We start to grow up. This is the birth of the compassionate self.

This principle of the holder and the held also relates to our working definition of compassion: *sensitivity to the suffering of ourselves and others with a deep commitment to relieve this suffering and its causes.* The first part of this definition — *sensitivity to the suffering of ourselves and others* — relates to that which needs to be held in ourselves and is about moving towards suffering, not resisting or denying it. The second part of the definition — *with a deep commitment to relieve this suffering and its causes* — relates to building the capacity to hold and respond to our own suffering (and thereafter the suffering of others).

When we speak about cultivating the compassionate self, we are talking about cultivating the second aspect of compassion, the holder. But the two aspects of compassion are always acting together in that the holder is always responding to what needs to be held.

Different Approaches

In this approach to cultivating the compassionate self, we start with the sense of a 'compassionate other'. When we start training our hearts and minds in compassion it is sometimes easier to relate to qualities like loving kindness and compassion being outside ourselves because we can find it hard to acknowledge and own these qualities within ourselves. We need to go on a journey that takes us back to ourselves in the end.

Both the Buddhist and Evolutionary models approach compassion training in this way. They both start by relating to the qualities of compassion outside ourselves and then shift the focus to cultivating them within ourselves. There are, however, some significant differences between these two approaches when it comes to the compassionate other that are useful to point out, since the approach we take in this book is a synthesis of both these paradigms.

Evolutionary Approach

In Chapter 5 we described some of the key features of the Evolutionary model. We explored how compassion flows in different directions: other to self, self to other and self to self. In Chapter 6 we focused on the flow of compassion from other to self, and we continue with this focus here.

According to the Evolutionary model we come into the world hard-wired to receive love and compassion from others. We have inner templates in our bodies and brains for connecting with others and receiving their support and kindness, especially from primary care givers. This is part of our mammalian heritage. In the case of us humans, when we are young we depend on our primary care givers for long periods of nurturing and care before reaching adulthood — in contrast to some reptiles who lay eggs and once hatched the offspring need to fend for themselves.

This is a key principle in human psychology: co-regulation as the basis for self-regulation. The stability of emotional makeup and the nervous system depends on being securely attached to our primary caregivers, and this then becomes our inner blueprint for regulating our own emotions when we grow up.

For many of us humans, however, we did not receive the love and care we needed when we were growing up. This can result in emotional complications and difficulties that people can carry within themselves throughout their lives. But this is not fixed in stone. We can *imagine* receiving the love and care now that we did not get when we were young. We discussed the power of imagination in Chapter 6. The brain does not know the difference between what is real and what is imagined, and so what we imagine is very powerful. This is also made possible by the fact that the brain can rewire itself depending upon what we focus on and train in. This is the power of neuroplasticity. So we can visualise our ideal compassionate nurturer and imagine receiving the love and care that we never received when we were a child. This meets a deep need within us and literally begins to grow new neural pathways.

This is the rationale of the *Compassionate Being* practice which creates the conditions for the *Compassionate Self* practice. They are both based on the principle we mentioned that co-regulation is the basis for self-regulation. The *Compassionate Being* practice is a way of experiencing emotional co-regulation which then creates the conditions for self-regulation by way of the *Compassionate Self* practice. We offer *Compassionate Being* practice at the end of this chapter and the *Compassionate Self* practice at the end of the next chapter.

Buddhist Approach

This approach starts with the premise that we are fundamentally well and whole despite the many ups and downs in our lives. In Mahayana Buddhist texts, this is referred to as our intrinsic *Buddha Nature*. This does not mean our true nature is that of a fat, laughing Eastern figure sitting on a throne as is sometimes depicted in Buddhist statues in garden centres! It means that there is a big part of our being that remains intact and undamaged even though we may have gone through many disappointments, difficulties and struggles in our lives and feel like 'damaged goods'.

In Mindfulness Association trainings we often use the phrase 'nothing is wrong' as a way of reflecting back to our students their basic goodness even in the face of their insistence that they are flawed and scarred by life, carrying a large bag of woes on their backs!

The classic image used is that of the pauper in the Buddhist text referred to in Chapter One. Similarly, according to this view, each one of us has a wealth of inner qualities buried within us, but these are so often obscured by habitual tendencies of poverty and lack. These block us from seeing the abundance of life all around us and we make our home on the pile of manure which represents our over-identification with our personal issues and baggage.

Not seeing the basic goodness inside and the abundance outside is called 'ignorance' in Buddhism. To help us to see clearly, we need to go on a journey with a series of stages that take us back to our basic goodness — the lump of gold ore in the manure. The first stage is to relate to an entity outside of us, real or imagined, which is endowed with the qualities of basic goodness, love and compassion. Through praying to and interacting with this outer representation of wisdom and compassion, we imagine that these qualities are absorbed into us and we are filled to the brim with them. In fact, these qualities were there all along, but this process helps us acknowledge them and it helps them to come alive in our own experience. This is the meaning of grace and blessing in Buddhism.

We can see the same process at work in mundane settings. If, for example, we want to learn a skill or a trade we would work as an apprentice to someone who is very skilled and experienced. Part of the training will involve learning specific methods and for the teacher to correct us when we make a mistake. But there is another important aspect to the relationship: this is the intangible transmission of qualities and experience that no learning from books or proficiency in methods can impart. Something intangible is transmitted from teacher to student so that the latter finds the confidence to become a master-craftsman themself.

Both mundane and spiritual transmissions work in this way. As human beings we need to rely on another person, or a visualised image of another person, to transmit to us what we already possess deep inside. This is the role of the outer compassionate friend (or being) in the Buddhist context. Furthermore, just like the Evolutionary approach, Buddhism relies strongly on visualisation to facilitate the transmission of qualities from teacher to student.

Outer Compassionate Being

Some of our students have remarked that visualisation is not real; it is made up. But this is precisely the point. It is made up, but it works because the brain responds to visualisation just like it responds to the 'real thing'. If we see something sexy this stimulates us in ways we don't need to elaborate, and similarly, if we imagine something sexy it also has the same effect.

When we imagine an ideal compassionate being, it can take a variety of forms. The best thing to do is to imagine what feels right for you. Trust the spontaneous power of your own imagination. It can be human or human-like, inanimate or an image of light. It can be secular, religious, or something in nature. If it is inanimate, like a tree or a mountain or an image of light, imagine that that these are endowed with mind because we are primarily relating to the mind of the compassionate other. That is the key point. For those who are religiously inclined it might take the form of Christ or Buddha or Mohammed. We go with what resonates with us and touches our heart.

Something to be careful about is imagining people with whom we have close relationships like partners or spouses or parents. The reason is that we often have complex relationships with these people and when we imagine them we might get triggered in ways that are not useful for this practice. If we imagine a parent, for example, we might love and adore them, but when we bring them to mind, we might also get irritated by some of their quirks or habits, or we might recall times in our growing up when they did not give us what we needed. It is best to bring to mind idealised images because we are using them to invoke qualities and trigger particular brain systems.

Receiving Qualities

The next step is to imagine what qualities this being is endowed with. Bear in mind that the compassionate being can change from session to session but it is best to stick with one being for one session. It is best if we let our imagination be spontaneous and just see what comes up when we imagine its qualities. In this way we are connecting with a deep inner wisdom that will respond by providing the qualities we really need rather than the ones we think we might need.

If we feel that nobody ever listens to us, then our compassionate being listens closely and tunes into what lies unsaid behind our words. If we feel that we are misunderstood in life, then the compassionate being truly understands us. If we feel that nobody loves us, then the compassionate being truly loves and cares for us. If we feel that we do not deserve love and compassion, then our compassionate being deeply empathises with this and holds our sense of undeserving within a loving space.

With these qualities in mind, we give our imagination free rein and imagine how the compassionate being looks: its colour or shape and whether it is old or young. The reason for doing this is to make it feel personal and intimate so that it is not a distant or remote image. We notice its facial expression, the look in its eyes, its voice tone and how it speaks to us. These are very important for making us feel safe.

We then imagine the compassionate being coming towards us, we sense its pleasure in seeing us and bask in the feeling of its presence. If we like, we can imagine it coming to greet us in our safe place, which is a practice we did in Chapter 6.

When we are in the presence of our compassionate being we then imagine that it is endowed with certain specific qualities. The first one is that of strength and stability. We imagine that it is rock-steady and stable like a great mountain or a mighty tree. It is not overwhelmed by our distress and not put off by the strange thoughts that go through our head. We feel deeply held by it. The second quality is that of wisdom. We feel the warm gaze and presence of the compassionate being and sense how it understands our struggles and what we have gone through in life. The third quality is that of kindness and warmth. The strength and understanding of the compassionate being are not cool and impartial but warm and kind. When it speaks to us there is kindness in its voice and we feel love emanating from its eyes. We feel held and safe, supported, and loved. The fourth quality is that of commitment and steadfastness. The compassionate being is always there for us no matter what. Even though key people in our lives might have let us down in the past, we feel confident that this being will not let us down. We can relax and feel safe in its supportive presence.

As we spend time with the compassionate being we can imagine that it speaks to us, and we savour what it says; we can even imagine having a conversation with it. But the most important thing is simply to feel its compassionate presence.

We imagine that the qualities of the compassionate being are absorbed into us like a thirsty person drinking pure, clean water. We can enhance this process by imagining an energy radiating from the heart of the compassionate being transmitting these qualities directly into ourselves. The most important thing is to believe that the qualities of the compassionate being are now alive and present within us. We then spend some time savouring these qualities.

According to the Evolutionary approach, the compassionate being then fades away. But we know that we can call on it at any time through the power of our imagination. It is always available and it is only a thought away. According to the Buddhist approach, we imagine that the being dissolves into energy which is absorbed into us. We feel that it has become part of us.

Compassionate Observer

We are now at the stage of stepping into our own power and aligning with our own capacity for strength, wisdom and compassion. This brings us to the *Compassionate Self* practice. But before proceeding to this stage, it will be useful to revisit the concept of the Observer, which we touched on briefly in Chapter 3.

There are always two processes occurring simultaneously within us: a knower and that which is known. There is a part of us that observes and another part that is observed. People often makes comments like, 'I had a bad meditation and lots of difficult stuff came up'. So two things are always going on: stuff coming up (that is observed) and the one that notices stuff coming up (the observer).

A simple analogy for this process is sitting on a riverbank and watching the river flow by. The one sitting on the bank is the observer and what flows by are thoughts, feelings, mind states and emotions. Rob Nairn referred to the latter as the 'undercurrent'. These are our inner experiences of mind that flow beneath the polite face we so often present to the world.

When we do mindfulness training we learn to stay sitting on the riverbank and resist the pull of thoughts and feelings that drag us into the river. So when thoughts arise we notice them and return to a mindfulness support such as breathing or sound.

Once we have stabilised our attention in the present moment (once we have stabilised our seat on the riverbank) the next step is to train the observer. We realise that genuine change does not come from trying to change the content of the undercurrent, which is impossible because it is a manifestation of the past. We realise that change comes from learning to observe in a different way.

The first thing we come face to face with is the fact that our observer is quite dysfunctional; it is powerfully addicted to its conditioned likes and dislikes and to its deeply ingrained modes of reaction. When we like something we try to keep hold of it, and when we dislike something we try to push it away, or block and suppress it.

We also come to see that our sense of 'I' and 'me' is located in the observer. When we turn our gaze inwards we come face to face with an inner tyrant that insists on reality going its way and suffering in the process! Rob Nairn aptly described this inner tyrant as the egocentric preference system (EPS).

An important part of mind training is to face the EPS and acknowledge the suffering and havoc it so often causes in our lives and the lives of others. An equally important part of the training, which is relevant for our purposes here, is to begin to cultivate the wise and compassionate observer. This goes to the heart of compassion training.

The more we focus on this part of ourselves and learn to cultivate it, the more the momentum in our psyche shifts from the dysfunctional EPS mode to the wise and compassionate mode. A useful analogy in psychology is attachment theory. There is strong research evidence to show that early childhood rearing results in different attachments styles. If we grow up in a loving and supportive family, then it is likely that we will develop a secure attachment style that will make it easier to form stable and loving bonds when we grow up and form intimate relationships. Alternatively, if we grew up in an abusive, insecure, or unloving family then it is likely that we will form an avoidant, ambivalent or disorganised attachment style, which will make it so much harder to form stable and loving bonds when we mature into adults.

However, these attachments styles are not set in stone. Even if we grow up in a challenging family environment and developed an insecure attachment style, we can still learn to love and trust those close to us and gradually develop a healthy, loving attachment style alongside the one that was forged into us when we grew up. Yet it is well known that the original attachment style never entirely goes away. It is always there like a ghost in the machine. Nonetheless, through persistent emotional work we can shift the momentum of our psyche to the more healthy, stable and loving attachment style.

There is a direct link here with the compassionate observer. We can never entirely uproot the dysfunctional observer, or EPS, but we can shift the momentum of our inner lives from the one to the other. This has a big impact our relationships with others and with our lives in general.

It is useful to understand the cultivation of the compassionate self in this context. This can give us hope that big change is possible in our lives if we invest time and energy in cultivating our inner capacities for wisdom and compassion. The balance of power within ourselves can shift from the inner tyrant, the EPS, to a wise and compassionate friend that has our best interests at heart, and so too the best interests of other people and the environment we live in.

Inner Compassionate Self

This process starts by imagining the presence of the compassionate being outside us and receiving its qualities. It now finds its fruition in identifying with the compassionate self within us. In terms of the flow of compassion, we shift from receiving compassion from others to giving compassion to ourselves.

Just like we did in the compassionate being practice, we imagine the compassionate self in two stages. The first one is to give our intuitive wisdom free reign and imagine what being compassionate means for us. You could reflect on the question, 'What compassionate qualities would I like to cultivate?' and sit quietly for a while noticing what emerges. The second stage is to cultivate certain specific qualities. We began to get a taste and feel for these qualities when we did the compassionate being practice. Now we build on these qualities and elaborate them. There are four key qualities:

Stability and Strength: Often we see ourselves as weak and fallible when in fact we have a lot more strength than we give ourselves credit for. We can tolerate and hold much more than we think we can. One way of connecting to our innate capacity for stability and strength is by imagining our body to be like a mountain and our mind to be like the vast blue sky. Another image is that of our body being like a mighty tree with roots deep in the soil. Mindfulness lays the foundation for this quality and we started developing it in Chapter 3 with the *Body Like a Mountain* practice.

Wisdom and Understanding: Based on this quality of strength and stability, we reflect on how we just find ourselves in the flow of this life that has been shaped by so many factors beyond our control. So much of what arises in our experience is not of our choosing and not our fault. This draws on the insights of the Evolutionary model that we looked at in Chapter 5. We build the capacity for wisdom by stepping back and looking objectively at our experience through the lens of no blame. Mindfulness lays the foundation for this quality by developing our capacity of meta-cognition and refining our curiosity.

Warmth and Kindness: From this position of stability and wisdom we choose to meet our unfolding experience of body and mind with warmth and kindness. We open to what is present, allow things to be as they are and soften around the hard edges of our inner experience. We began to develop this quality with the *Self-Compassion* practice in Chapter 7.

Commitment: Based on the preceding qualities, we learn to stay present with what is difficult or painful rather than turning away from it and getting caught up in avoidance and distraction. There is a sense of commitment to our inner process, and to the wellbeing of others. Once again this is a quality that we started cultivating in Chapter 3 with the practice of mindful acceptance where we learnt to lean into difficulty rather than pushing it away. We always stay mindful, however, of remaining within our window of tolerance.

Method Acting

What is important is to find our own way of embodying these qualities so that they feel real and alive for us and are not just a set of abstract ideals. One way of doing this is by method acting. This is an approach used in Compassion Focussed Therapy. Here we imagine stepping into the role of the compassionate self and feeling it from the inside.

For example, if Brad Pitt was given the role of acting as the Dalai Lama he would most likely read up on his life, find out about his character traits and qualities, and then he might walk around imagining himself to be the Dalai Lama. In this way the compassionate qualities of the Dalai Lama would begin to feel tangible and alive for him. He might even go a step further and when he encountered difficulties in his life, he might imagine relating to those difficulties as if he really were the Dalai Lama. When it came to acting the part of the Dalai Lama in the film, he would have a direct personal experience of what being compassionate felt like, and this would come through in his acting. This is the approach of method acting — to get into the role by actually living the role yourself. This is one way of bringing the compassionate self to life.

In the case of Tibetan Buddhism, there is practice approach that is somewhat akin to method acting. It is the practice of imagining that our bodies are not solid but are rainbow-like and endowed with qualities of love and compassion. It is called deity meditation. One such deity practice is to imagine ourselves in the form of Chenrezig, the bodhisattva of compassion. We would do a formal sitting practice imagining ourselves to take the form of this deity and we would silently recite the mantra 'Om mani padme hung', which is a way of generating the energy of compassion within ourselves.

Once we finished doing the formal practice we would walk around and try to maintain the feeling of being the deity. We would try to see the world through the eyes of the deity and not see things with our mundane perception that is so often ruled by grasping and aversion. Instead we would learn to see the dynamic interconnectedness of all life that is constantly shifting and changing like the play of light in the sky. This is called sacred outlook in Tibetan Buddhism. We learn to shift into a wise and compassionate mode of being and maintain this mode of being as we go about our lives.

Whatever approach we take, it is by no means easy to stay centred in the wise and compassionate part of ourselves. This is because there are other powerful forces in the mind, like anger and desire and competitiveness, which are constantly trying to pull us into their force field. Consequently, in the next chapter we will draw on our circle of allies to support us when the going gets tough, and we will learn to place the compassionate self within its natural context, the mandala, and train to stay present at the centre of our personal mandala.

In the Practice Section, along with the *Compassionate Being* practice, we will offer the practice of the *Holder and the Held*. It builds on the *Self-Compassion* practice we did in the last chapter. It also lays the foundation for doing the practice of the *Compassionate Self* in the next chapter, which we will do with the support of the circle of allies and within the context of the mandala.

Practice Section

Formal Sitting Practice

Practice 16: Compassionate Being (20 – 30 minutes)
Begin by forming an intention to practise compassion for yourself and others, and then reaffirm your compassionate motivation: why you want to practise compassion.

Sit in a relaxed and comfortable posture on a cushion or chair. Then pay attention to the rising and falling of your body as you breathe. To help settle your mind, try deepening your in-breath a little and lengthening your out-breath. See if you can regulate your breathing so that your in-breath and out-breath are of a similar length and rhythm. You might like to count to three or four on the in-breath and a similar count on the out-breath. When your mind begins to settle, let go of counting and let your breathing find its natural rhythm.

Now soften around any uncomfortable or painful sensations in your body while allowing your experience to be as it is. It may help to place a hand on your heart as a gesture of self-soothing. Feel the warmth of the touch and the movement of the breath in your chest. If you like, you can form a half-smile, and adopt a gentle voice tone when you guide yourself. In this way consciously connect with a kind and compassionate attitude to yourself.

Now consider what qualities you would like your compassionate being to have: maybe complete acceptance of you no matter what; or maybe you would like your compassionate being to have a deep concern and affection for you; or a sense of kinship and belonging. For example, if you are a person who feels that they don't deserve compassion, then think about what kind of being you would need in order to feel deserving of love. If you are someone who believes that they don't feel understood, then imagine what kind of being you need to feel understood. So you are creating a compassionate being that is *ideal for you*.

With these thoughts in mind, focus on what your ideal compassionate being would look like. Would you want it to be old or young? Would it be male, female or without gender, or perhaps even non-human, such as an animal, the sea or light? When you think of your ideal compassionate being just notice what comes to mind. Over time different compassionate images or beings might come to mind. You don't have to stick to one version. Just see what happens and go with what you feel is helpful to you at any given time.

What would your compassionate being sound like? If they were to communicate with you, what would their voice tone be like? If your being is human-like what are their facial expressions? Notice how they might smile at you or show concern for you. Are there any colours that are associated with them? With these thoughts in mind, spend some time imagining your ideal compassionate being, that is perfect for you in every way; that fits your needs exactly.

Sometimes it can help to bring to mind your safe place and imagine that you meet your compassionate being there. Imagine that they approach you in your safe place and savour their pleasure in seeing you. Focus on the presence of your compassionate being and feeling safe in their presence.

Next imagine that your compassionate being has certain specific qualities. Focus first on the sense of *kindness and warmth* that you feel emanating from this being. You can imagine an energy of kindness streaming out from the heart of the compassionate being soothing you and enfolding you. Maybe the energy has a particular colour? Notice the feelings that arise in you as you imagine this.

Now focus on its *maturity, strength, and confidence*. It is not overwhelmed by your pain or distress; it is not put off by the strange thoughts that go through your mind. You feel held and supported in its presence. Spend a few moments imagining being with your ideal compassionate being as it manifests these qualities.

Next imagine that your compassionate being has great *wisdom* that comes from its life experience. What emanates from this wisdom is a deep desire to be helpful and supportive. It deeply understands and empathises with the struggles you go through in your life. It transmits to you the wisdom of no blame: none of this is your fault. You just find yourself in this life shaped by powerful forces beyond your control. Spend a few moments imagining being with your compassionate being and feeling this great wisdom enfolding you.

Now focus on your compassionate being having a very deep *commitment* to you. No matter what happens, your compassionate being is fully committed in supporting you to become more compassionate to yourself, to others and in coping with life. Spend a few moments imagining what it feels like when you sense your compassionate being is fully committed to caring about you and helping you on your life path.

Now simply bask in the presence of your compassionate being and imagine that these qualities are absorbed into you and become part of you.

You might then imagine that your compassionate being speaks to you and wishes you well. If you like, you can imagine it saying the following words to you:

- *May you be free of suffering (say your name in your mind).*
- *May you be happy (say your name in your mind).*
- *May you flourish (say your name in your mind).*
- *May you find peace and wellbeing (say your name in your mind).*

Focus on the warmth and feeling behind the words. You might also like to make up phrases that resonate with you.

As a way of ending the practice, you can either imagine that your compassionate being bids you farewell and fades away, or you can imagine that it dissolves into an energy which is drawn into your heart centre so that it is now fully part of you. Then rest loosely for a few moments, letting go of trying to meditate.

Always remember that this practice entails working with your own imagination. Through doing so you are opening the door to your own compassionate qualities and feelings and becoming familiar with the way compassion can help you. These qualities and feelings are accessible to you at any time because they are part of you.

Once you become familiar with this practice you can do it quite briefly. Sometimes all you need do is bring your compassionate being to mind, without necessarily going through all the stages. What is important is to connect to a felt sense of this being; this is often enough to give you a feeling of its presence and a sense of being helped and supported by it.

Practice 17: Holder and the Held (15 – 20 minutes)
Begin by forming an intention to practise compassion for yourself and others, and then reaffirm your compassionate motivation: why you want to practise compassion.

Sit in a relaxed and comfortable posture on a cushion or chair. Then pay attention to the rising and falling of your body as you breathe. To help settle your mind, have a go at deepening your in-breath a little and lengthening your out-breath. See if you can regulate your breathing so that your in-breath and out-breath are of a similar length and rhythm. You might like to count to three or four on the in-breath and a similar count on the out-breath. When your mind begins to settle, let go of counting and let your breathing find its natural rhythm.

Now gently scan your body and mind and notice if there is anything in your present moment experience that is calling for your attention. This might be an ache or pain in your body; a difficult mood or emotion; an energetic sense of feeling heavy or low; or it might be troubling thoughts and images in your mind. This is something in you that *needs to be held*. Simply acknowledging this is the important first step; so often we tune out of these aspects of our experience by suppressing them or by distracting ourselves with something else.

Now see if you can step into the part of you that can hold what needs to be held. It can help to imagine your body to be like a mountain or like a mighty tree with roots deep in the soil. This helps to connect to a sense of feeling stable and rooted. Next imagine your breath to be like the wind, or a gentle breeze caressing the mountain or blowing through the branches of the tree. Then imagine your mind to be like the clear blue sky that is vast and open. In your heart centre you sense the tender heart of compassion — a place of vulnerability and power. If you like, you can imagine this taking the form of a sphere of energy of a colour that you associate with kindness and compassion. This sphere has the warmth and clarity of early morning sunshine.

While rooted in the part of you that is the holder — body like a mountain, breath like the wind, mind like the clear blue sky with the sphere of compassion in the heart like sunshine — see if you can simply hold the part of you that needs to be held.

Holding it in a stable and reassuring way and looking at it with the eyes of wisdom; what you are experiencing arises from so many causes and conditions, not of your choosing and not your fault. Offer it kindness and warmth and let it be touched by the sunshine of kindness in your heart. Stay present with what needs to be held, not tuning out or rejecting your feelings (but staying in your window of tolerance).

See if you can find your own way of holding what needs to be held. Then rest loosely for a few moments and let go of trying to meditate.

Try to bring this practice into your daily life. This means being in touch with your changing inner landscape of feeling that needs to be cared for and held, and then stepping into the part of you that can do the holding. Notice what a big change this can make to your life.

Chapter Nine

The Mandala of Compassion

The principle of mandala is used by many spiritual traditions to depict an experience of wholeness and balance. The basic meaning of 'mandala' is centre and periphery. It can be drawn as a circle and it refers to an energy system with the centre point in the middle of the circle and the periphery lying on its circumference.

For the purposes of this chapter, we will draw on an understanding of mandala that has emerged within Tibetan Buddhism. Within this spiritual tradition there are many colourful paintings, or *tangkas*, that depict a meditation deity sitting in the middle of a square palace that is set within a circular mandala. These *tangkas* are adorned with richly textured colours that symbolise the powerful energies of the psyche that are going through a process of alchemy and transformation. The circumferences of some mandalas are depicted with fiery demons and wrathful energies that represent the conflict and drama that afflict so many of us as we navigate our way through everyday life.

In most cases the palace has four doorways that lead to the centre of the mandala. One interesting perspective is that the doorway to the centre represents one's dominant emotional affliction. For example, if anger is our main stumbling block in life, then the instruction is to put all our focus on taming anger, and once transformed anger becomes the doorway to the centre. Therefore, anger is both a major obstacle and a big opportunity. It can condemn us to endless rounds on the wheel of cyclic existence or it can become the vehicle for awakening.

The deity sits at the centre of the palace on a throne. It represents our innermost capacity for wisdom and compassion.

The panoply of deities in the Tibetan tradition symbolise the multiple manifestations of wisdom and compassion. In essence, however, the deity is our true identity once all our confusion and struggles have been peeled away. When we identify ourselves with the deity and hold the space at the centre of the mandala the world looks completely different. We see richness and abundance everywhere and we feel deeply connected to all of life.

Psychological Mandala

Image 5. Psychological Mandala.

This spiritual depiction of mandala has been adapted for our purpose and viewed in psychological terms. Choden spent some time working with Paul Gilbert and they developed a synthesis of the Tibetan Buddhist principle of mandala and the CFT notion of the compassionate self being the inner authority within the psyche that can hold and manage its conflicting parts such as the angry self, anxious self, sad self and so on. The diagram above is a depiction of the psychologised expression of the mandala principle.

From this perspective, the journey of the compassionate self is the journey to the centre of the mandala — to the centre point of one's own energy system. And whilst the centre is still and calm, the periphery is stormy and wild. The image used is that of a turning wheel. The centre is still but the perimeter is always moving and turning.

The periphery is where our emotional life is played out. It is where the powerful emotions of anger, desire, jealousy, and greed are to be found. These emotions drive the wheel. From a Buddhist perspective, this is called the wheel of life — the endless cycle of conditioned existence (called *samsara*) that keeps on turning and generating suffering until we become free of it. From an evolutionary perspective, the periphery contains the powerful drives and emotions that have emerged through the process of natural selection and which impel us towards survival and procreation. Most of the time we find ourselves on the periphery caught up in the drama of our conflicting parts. Just bring to mind how you feel during the course of an average day — how you move from feeling anxious to angry to sad, and how these parts of you are often in conflict with each other. Sadly, many of us spend our whole lives ensnared in confusion and turmoil with only fleeting moments of peace.

But there is another possibility, and this is to find the centre of our personal mandala — to make the inner journey to the still point of stability and peace where we are not tossed and turned by our conflicting emotions. This is the journey of the compassionate self. Our task is to find our way to the centre and to relate to our life experience from this perspective. The implications of this are huge: we begin to live our lives from a very different vantage point within ourselves and we begin to see our own experience and that of others in a very different way.

Qualities of Compassion

Each of the qualities of the compassionate self that we explored in the last chapter help root us in the centre of the mandala. We will explore these qualities some more now within the context of the mandala principle.

The quality of strength allows us to put down roots and feel anchored so that we are not pulled in different directions. What helps is to imagine our body to be like a mountain, or like a mighty tree, firmly held by the vast Earth beneath us.

This gives us the stability to stand back and realise that none of the stuff on the periphery defines who we are. None of it is personal. It is all the passing show. We begin to look at all the stuff that normally bothers and afflicts us with the eyes of wisdom. So many people feel the way we do. All that goes through our minds and hearts has gone through the minds and hearts of so many others stretching back in time. This enables us to relax a little; we now have some perspective. This is the quality of wisdom.

This quality creates the conditions for being kind to ourselves. We learn not to judge our experience because it is not personal. Non-judging lies at the heart of kindness. With this attitude, some space arises whereby we can start to bring friendliness and warmth towards all the thoughts, feelings, emotions and mind states that constantly arise within us. We start to be kind to the parts of us that show up on the periphery.

There is a Buddhist image of a patient grandmother who sits in the middle of a playground whilst all her many grandchildren play and squabble with each other. She simply holds the space and keeps an eye on them. It is only when they start fighting and exchanging blows that she intervenes to separate them. This is the quality of kindness that is infused with wisdom and strength.

What is also called for is the quality of commitment that is made up of courage and steadfastness. It is not so easy to stay present with all the conflicting parts of ourselves that rub up against each other on the periphery even if the previous qualities are in place. This quality comes from our mindfulness training in which we learn to incline towards and be accepting of difficult emotions and mind states. But we also need to be aware of the limits of our capacity. When things are too difficult it is important to shift our focus away from difficulty and pain even if this means that we stop meditating. It is important that we always operate within our window of tolerance and do not over-expose ourselves to suffering.

Finally, it is unrealistic that we will stay at the centre of the mandala all the time. We are likely to find that we are often pulled into the periphery and caught up in its dramas and strong currents of emotion. But we will know what the centre feels like because we will have touched this place in ourselves and we will have the skills to find our way back there. This is the most important thing.

Shift in Identity

At one level the process we are describing is basic mindfulness — we notice when we get lost in thoughts and mind dramas and we return our attention to a neutral focus in the present moment. Distraction causes us to fall back onto the periphery and the skill of mindfulness allows us to find the centre again.

The crossover to compassion happens when we connect to *qualities* in ourselves and actively cultivate these qualities. These are the qualities we have been describing above. Compassion entails changing our basic orientation to what we experience. It is like stepping into an identity from which we relate to things differently. This is not a tangible, solid identity in the way we normally perceive ourselves, but one that is both spacious and grounded, curious and allowing, wise and compassionate. This is what we mean by the compassionate self.

Mandala is the context that allows this shift in identity to happen. It provides a symbolic space in which the cultivation of certain qualities takes us to the centre of our inner world and places us in a different relationship to the forces within our personality that cause us strife and suffering.

As we have reiterated many times, however, the journey of compassion is not just about relating to suffering. Similarly, the mandala principle is not just a method for relating more skilfully to the parts of us that cause distress. It is also about learning to appreciate the wholesome, creative parts of ourselves and being grateful for the good things in our experience. This is something we touch on when we learn to draw our personal mandala.

The Eyes of Wisdom

The quality of wisdom progresses in stages. Initially we come to see that our thoughts and emotions are not who we are. They are more like guests coming and going through the guest house of our mind. Just like we do not experience sounds as being personal because they appear to happen 'outside' our minds, similarly we learn to see that thoughts and emotions are also not personal. This is a great relief. Most people spend their entire lives believing in their thoughts and mental dramas and thinking that these constitute who they are. This can bring great suffering, especially when the thoughts and feelings are negative. This level of wisdom is the fruition of mindfulness practice.

The deeper level of wisdom is to appreciate the value and richness of everything that shows up in our minds. This lies at the heart of the mandala principle. All our experience has great value, even the dark, shameful, lustful and frightened parts of ourselves. When we step into the shoes of the compassionate self and find the centre, we are then in a position to experience our life in a very different way.

We begin to look at our rage, sorrow, desire, feelings of inadequacy, and buried grief with the eyes of wisdom. If we look long enough then we can start to see the clarity and vitality in our anger and rage; we can glimpse the passion, zest for life and intelligent discrimination in our feelings of desire; and we can sense the enormous possibility for being proactive and effective in the energy of jealousy and competitiveness. This applies to each and every one of our so-called negative emotions. All of them have value; each one of them has something to offer us.

This is a profoundly positive perspective and it combines well with the practices of appreciation and joy which we come to later in the book. In Tibetan Buddhism this is called 'sacred outlook'. Put simply, we learn to see how the glass of our lives is half full rather than half empty.

External Mandalas

Mandala is not just an inner process of relating to the parts of ourselves. It is also about how we relate to life outside the bubble of our minds. We can relate to our work situation or family life as a mandala, in which we learn to find the centre and relate compassionately to the parts on the periphery. This is especially relevant in the case of families where different family members occupy different roles, often unconsciously. Our practice here entails becoming aware of the family dynamics and learning to find a mature and non-reactive perspective of the processes that are playing out. We learn to find the still point at the centre of all these processes and dynamics. We are then in a position to bring something constructive to the situation by offering understanding and kindness to what is going on.

But starting with ourselves is important. Just like we start with self-compassion and then learn to cultivate compassion for others, it makes sense to start with the inner work of the mandala and once we have some stability in this area we are in a better position to open up to the many rich and complex mandalas that make up our lives.

Circle of Allies

Once we have cultivated the compassionate self and touched the centre of our personal mandala, the next step is to build a support around it. In the beginning the mentality of compassion is vulnerable to being overtaken by stronger forces within the mind such as self-preservation and tribalism as well as by the parts on the periphery. Therefore, establishing sources of support is very important.

The circle of allies is just such a support. In African tribal traditions they speak of drawing on the power of the ancestors who are always there in the background to protect and guide the lives of the tribal members. For many African tribal people, relying on their ancestors as a source of support and wisdom is indispensable to a happy and fulfilling life.

In addition, Buddhist practice traditions have always seen lineage as an indispensable support to the cultivation of compassion and wisdom. 'Lineage' refers to the oral tradition of great spiritual teachers going back to the Buddha who have woken up to the truth of things and who have passed this living stream of wisdom from one generation to the next. It is sometimes called the 'whispered tradition', which implies that there is an energetic transmission of wisdom from one person to the next. It is not something written down in books or texts. When people practise they then draw on the support and living presence of the spiritual teachers of the past, and this is seen as being crucial to the process of awaking wisdom and compassion within oneself.

We are offering a secular adaption of this process in the circle of allies practice. For us, it is not necessarily about relying on ancestors or spiritual teachers of the past but bringing to mind people in our life who embody kindness, compassion, wisdom and maturity. These are people who inspire us and who embody the qualities that we want to develop in ourselves. They can be people we know, people who are alive or people who have died, as well as great icons of compassion such as Mother Theresa, Dalai Lama or Nelson Mandela. They can even be inanimate things in nature, such as trees or mountains, so long as they are imbued with the qualities of compassion. If we come from a particular religious tradition, we might choose spiritual beings or deities, such as Chenrezig, the Virgin Mary or Krishna. The most important thing is a felt sense of connection to these people or things and feeling held and supported by them. In a very basic sense, they are those who have our back.

There are different ways of doing the circle of allies practice. One way is to bring to mind the qualities that we have been exploring in the last two chapters: strength, wisdom, kindness and courage. We then choose another quality, such as joy, acceptance, forgiveness or whatever we feel we need in order to fully embody compassion.

When we do the practice we bring each quality to mind and imagine a being who embodies vast amounts of that quality. We then imagine this being sitting in front of us as we breathe that quality from them into our hearts and breathe it out to other people in our lives. As we do this, we imagine that our whole body and mind fills up with this quality until we feel that we embody limitless amounts of it. We can imagine that the quality is absorbed into the very cells of our body.

We follow the same process for each of the other qualities — imagining a being who fully embodies that quality and so on — until we build up a circle of beings, or compassionate allies around us. Then we imagine breathing in all the qualities together from all these allies and breathing them out to those who we share our lives with.

It is helpful not to think too hard about who the particular beings will be that will represent these different qualities. Instead, we can trust that a deeper wisdom will guide our imagination. When we do this we can often be surprised by who comes to mind, but this often leads to a more powerful and authentic experience in our practice.

Another simpler way of doing the circle of allies practice is to bring to mind people who embody qualities that we feel we need and imagine them sitting in a semi-circle behind us. Once again it is best to do this in a natural and spontaneous way and whenever people spring to mind we imagine them taking a seat behind us. It is best too if we imagine that we are aligned with our inner compassionate self. We then feel their presence as we do the practice and we imagine that their qualities are absorbed into us. We imagine that we are held and supported by their love, compassion and wisdom.

Drawing the Mandala

When we are doing compassion practice it can be useful to have a map of the journey we are undertaking. The mandala is such a map. It is important though to make it personal. It is not so useful to have an impersonal map of our inner world because this will not touch us deeply.

It can be helpful to draw the mandala and make it your very own. You can even give the parts on your periphery specific names and draw little images or figurines depicting them. You can do the same with the compassionate self at the centre. Give it a name and draw it in a way that resonates with your own felt sense of compassion. The more personal and specific you make it the better it will be. You can also revise your mandala from time to time and draw different versions of it depending on how your emotional world changes. Once you have finished drawing it, put it up somewhere close to where you meditate.

It can also be helpful to draw your circle of allies and depict them in a circle (or semi-circle) around the outside of the periphery of the mandala. Alternatively, you can imagine that they are in the sky above your compassionate self and draw them in a way that depicts this.

When Choden did a one-year retreat in 2016 he drew his personal mandala and gave each of the parts on his periphery evocative names like 'the frightened inner child', 'the raging tyrant', 'the sad and lonely one', 'the ambitious hero' and so forth. He put it up on the side of his shrine. He found it very helpful to have a picture that was personal and unique to his situation. When he was meditating and noticed that a strong emotion was taking hold of his mind, he would glance at the picture and say to himself, 'that is where I am right now, this part is trying to pull me into its orbit; all I need to do is to bring awareness to it and bring to mind the qualities of my compassionate self and I will find the centre again'. It gave him a feeling of headspace and it reminded him not to take the ups and downs of retreat and his inner dramas too personally.

Practice Section

Formal Sitting Practice

Practice 18: Circle of Allies (20 – 30 minutes)
Begin by forming an intention to practise compassion for yourself and others, and then reaffirm your compassionate motivation: why you want to practise compassion.

Sit in a relaxed and comfortable posture on a cushion or chair. Then pay attention to the rising and falling of your body as you breathe. To help settle your mind, try deepening your in-breath a little and lengthening your out-breath. See if you can regulate your breathing so that your in-breath and out-breath are of a similar length and rhythm. You might like to count to three or four on the in-breath and a similar count on the out-breath. When your mind begins to settle, let go of counting and let your breathing find its natural rhythm.

Now imagine your body to be like a mountain or like a mighty tree with roots deep in the soil, your breath like the wind, and your mind like the clear blue sky that is vast and open. In your heart centre try connecting to your tender heart of compassion — a place of vulnerability and power. To help do this, imagine that there is a sphere of golden energy (or another colour that you associate with kindness and compassion) in your heart centre that is imbued with the warmth and clarity of early morning sunshine.

Now bring to mind each of the qualities of compassion in turn. Start with the quality of stability and strength. Bring to mind a being who fully embodies this quality for you. It can be a living being, someone from the past or an image of light such as a deity. The important thing is that you feel a connection with this being or image and you sense this quality to be strongly present within them.

Imagine that this being takes a seat in a circle around you and breathe this quality into your heart. Imagine that your body and mind completely fills up with this quality and it is absorbed into every cell in your body. Think that you now embody limitless amounts of this quality and imagine breathing this quality to other people in your life so that it fills them up completely too.

Then go through the same process with the other qualities in turn: wisdom/understanding, kindness/warmth and commitment/courage. For each quality imagine a being or image who fully embodies this quality for you, breathe in this quality so that it feels you up completely and then breathe it out to other people you feel connected to in your life.

Now, choose another quality that you feel you need in order to fully embody compassion. It can be a quality such as joy, acceptance, forgiveness, or something else entirely.

Once you have completed this process imagine that you are now surrounded by a circle of allies who embody these different qualities of compassion. Spend a bit of time imagining them sitting around you and feel their supportive presence. Then imagine breathing in all the qualities together from all these allies and breathing them out to all those whom we share our lives with.

To conclude the practice, you can imagine one of two things: either your circle of allies dissolve into energy and this is absorbed into you so that their qualities are fully present within you; or you can imagine that your circle of allies bid you farewell and depart — remembering that you can call on them at any time that you need them.

Once more imagine your body to be like a mountain (or a mighty tree), your breath like the wind, your mind like the clear blue sky, and the sunshine of compassion in your heart. Then let go of trying to meditate and for a few moments rest loosely without any specific focus.

For daily life: once you are familiar with this practice, you can bring to mind an ally that embodies a quality you might need as you go about your life. For example, if you are struggling to cope with work pressure, you might imagine an ally who embodies the quality of strength and imagine breathing this quality into your heart and mind, and then breathing it out to others who might need that quality too.

Practice 19: Compassionate Self (30 minutes)
In this practice we cultivate the qualities of the compassionate self and this takes us to the centre of our personal mandala. If you like, you can first do the Compassionate Being practice from the last chapter (Practice 16) and imagine that the qualities of this being are absorbed into you, and then in this practice you embody those qualities yourself. Then focus the compassionate self on one part of your periphery. Choose a part that is active and calling for your attention, but in the beginning try not to work with the most difficult part. We need to build up our capacity in stages. You can also draw on your circle of allies to give you extra support when working with the parts. But this is your choice. It is best that you are guided by your own intuitive wisdom.

Begin by forming an intention to practise compassion for yourself and others, and then reaffirm your compassionate motivation: why you want to practise compassion.

Sit in a relaxed and comfortable posture on a cushion or chair. Then pay attention to the rising and falling of your body as you breathe. To help settle your mind, try deepening your in-breath a little and lengthening your out-breath. See if you can regulate your breathing so that your in-breath and out-breath are of a similar length and rhythm. You might like to count to three or four on the in-breath and a similar count on the out-breath. When your mind begins to settle, let go of counting and let your breathing find its natural rhythm.

Now consciously identify with your compassionate self that lies at the centre of your personal mandala. This is done in stages. Begin by imagining your body to be like a mountain supported by the vast earth below or like a mighty tree with roots deep in the soil. Notice how the vast Earth holds your body unconditionally. Connect to the sense of security and stability that comes from visualising in this way. You might discover that you can tolerate and hold more than you think you can. This is the strength quality of your compassionate self.

Build on this visualisation by imagining your breath to be like the wind, or like a gentle breeze caressing the mountain or the tree, and your mind vast and open like the clear blue sky. Body like a mountain, breath like the wind and mind like the clear blue sky...

Whilst staying connected to your compassionate self at the centre of the mandala, bring to mind something you are struggling with in yourself — a part of you on the periphery that has been activated — perhaps feelings of anger or anxiety or sadness, or a combination of these feelings.

See if you can bring this part to mind in one of two ways: either imagine this part as it plays out in your life, like watching a video of yourself as you go about your daily activities, being aware of how this part manifests in the way you think, feel, talk and move around; or you can simply connect to how this part feels inside you. The second approach is more subtle, so be sure to create a sense of perspective and objectivity with you identified as the compassionate self that is witnessing the part that struggles. Imagining your body like a mountain, your breath like the wind and your mind like the clear blue sky can help with this.

Now see if you can look objectively at this part of you that is struggling with the eyes of understanding. If you have drawn a personal mandala, it can be helpful to look at it while you are doing this practice as it brings things to life in a personal and evocative way. Notice how this part of you has arisen from the many complex forces that have shaped your life. See if you can connect with the wisdom of no blame. It is not your fault that you feel this way; it makes perfect sense given your life history, and many other people feel this way too. This is the wisdom quality.

Now see if you can bring some warmth and kindness to what you are feeling. You can use the self-compassion gesture of the hand on the heart and also the mantra 'soften, soothe and allow'. You can imagine the warmth of compassion being like a golden sphere in your heart centre — the sunshine of compassion in your heart. This is the quality of kindness.

See if you can stay connected to the part of you that is struggling, instead of avoiding it or getting lost in distraction. It is like you are communicating to this part of you that you are there for it and you are supporting it. This is the quality of commitment which takes some courage too. But remember to stay within your window of tolerance.

As you do this practice, be sure to remain connected to your compassionate self at the centre of the mandala. If you find that you get sucked into the drama of a particular part, or things feel too intense, then come back to mindfulness of breathing and re-establish the sense of body like a mountain, breath like the wind and mind like the clear blue sky.

You can also include your circle of allies in this practice. You can do this by bringing to mind people who embody qualities that you feel you need and imagine them sitting down in a semi-circle behind you. Try doing this spontaneously and whenever people spring to mind imagine them taking a seat behind you. Sense their supportive presence and imagine that their qualities are absorbed into you. It is like they have your back; they add their weight to your practice of the compassionate self.

The essence of this practice is simply to stay present with the part of you that struggles — just allowing the compassionate centre in you to be in relationship with the part that struggles. If other difficult parts or issues arise, then see if you can relate to them in a similar way too.

At the end of the practice, imagine that the part that struggles is drawn back into you and you continue to hold it with wisdom and compassion. Then rest for a while without any specific focus. Finally share the benefits of this practice with others who struggle like you do, making the wish that they find the wisdom and courage to relate skilfully to the wounded, painful parts of themselves.

Chapter Ten

Befriending the Self-Critic

For many of us the biggest obstacle to self-compassion is the critical voice in our head. It is something we can never escape from. It is always there ready to put us down. However hard we try nothing is ever good enough for the critic — we are always falling short. It condemns and criticises our every move. Many people live with this voice in their heads for their whole lives.

We are both struck by the immense suffering and damage inflicted by the critic. There is no escape from the inner critic because it is inside us, and moreover we just roll over and succumb to its tyranny and beatings.

The constant put-downs and negative comments of the critic trigger our threat system and keep us bound in a cycle of fear and shame. Many people live in a state of perpetual stress and hyper vigilance. Over time this can deplete our inner resources and result in poor physical and mental health. Furthermore, this is reinforced by a deeply held belief of lack of self-worth which can damage our relationships and limit our freedom to live life to the full.

From the point of view of the mandala, the critic is a part that lies on the periphery. As we discovered in the last chapter, we first need to dis-identify from the critic and find the centre of the mandala. We do this by consciously identifying with the inner compassionate self. From this perspective we are able to understand the critic and take care of the insecurities and fears that lie behind it. This is the focus of this chapter. We are learning to face the critic, understand what drives its condemning voice of shame and bring some compassion to it. All of the training and practise we have done so far lays the groundwork for this task.

Something that is important to clarify right at the outset is the difference between negative self-criticism and critical thinking. In the case of self-criticism there is a toxic attitude of condemnation and often ridicule that is expressed in cruel self-talk such as: 'Look how stupid you are, you always mess up, you are no good at anything!' This results in unclear thinking. Our mind is clouded by the negative attitude and the threat-based voice tone causes our minds and hearts to contract in fear like a cowering animal. Basically, very little good comes from this.

On the contrary critical thinking is often accompanied by an attitude of genuine inquiry and exploration, and it tends to come with either a neutral or friendly inner voice tone that does not fire up the threat system. This kind of thinking can be very proactive and lead to a great deal of clarity. By no means do we want to give up this faculty of critical thinking because it serves us well.

To be clear, not all of us have this inner critical voice. Some of us have been brought up in an environment relatively free of criticism and have an inner voice of compassionate self-care. Some of us have practised self-compassion such that the inner critical voice has either diminished in power or been transformed into one of compassionate encouragement and wise discernment.

For many of us the inner critical voice is not immediately apparent and operates within the mind in a disguised and subtle way, which we do not at first notice. As we begin to uncover our inner critic, it can undergo a process in which it stops being so blatant and begins to operate in the background of the mind in a way that can go undetected. For many of us transforming the self-critic is a life's work which takes many years of ongoing commitment to practise.

The Origins of Self-Criticism

Humans have evolved the capacity for self-awareness and metacognition that allows us to see our self in our minds eyes as a symbolic self-representation. While this opens up the possibility for thinking about ourselves in a positive way with self-acceptance, it also opens up the possibility for thinking badly about ourselves in a negative, self-judgemental way. How we end up thinking about ourselves depends greatly on the social context and culture we live in and the conditions of our early life and upbringing.

In an earlier chapter we described how our life is strongly conditioned by three distinct stories: the long story of how we evolved as gene-built biological organisms, the medium-term story of how social context and culture has shaped our perceptions and actions, and the short story of how our family life and upbringing have crafted our emotional makeup and personality.

According to the long story, we have evolved to live in tightly knit groups of mutual support and cooperation and in the distant past we would have died if we were thrown out of these groups. For this reason we are hard-wired to imagine how other people think about us and there is a strong survival imperative to think and behave in a way that will be approved of by others in our family or tribe. The inner critical voice often represents what we unconsciously think other people are thinking about us. In fact, most people aren't thinking about us at all! If we reflect on how much time we spend thinking about other people this becomes apparent. A better approach would be to think and act in accordance with our life values, rather than in accordance with how we think other people think we should be or act.

The medium-term story about the origins of self-criticism is the cultural context within which we find ourselves. In the modern West we live in a culture underpinned by Christian ideas of original sin, which encourages us to think that there is something fundamentally wrong with us. This is made worse by our individualistic capitalist culture, which blames the individual for their life circumstance within a system which celebrates success in terms of personal wealth and fame, which only a tiny minority can achieve, thus setting up the majority for failure. This is further exacerbated by our media and entertainment industry which thrive on shaming and humiliating those who come into the public eye and who do not conform to narrow social norms of success.

Living in this cultural context gives rise to a survival imperative to think there is something inherently wrong with us and to blame ourselves before anyone else does. This results in feelings of shame and humiliation as a way of keeping ourselves on the 'straight and narrow' and therefore protecting ourselves from being shamed or humiliated by others.

The short story of the origins of self-criticism is the family and life circumstances within which we grew up. Many of us were consistently shamed and humiliated as children as a way of ensuring that we conformed to the internal rules of our family and the norms of society. This was often done by well-meaning parents, carers and teachers who had bought into the prevailing social values of the time. We may have been brought up by carers who consistently withheld their approval so that as adults we are constantly seeking approval from others. We may have been trained not to show emotions such as anger or sadness because we were rejected by our carers at those times when we did.

It is common for us to blame ourselves for the experiences we had in our childhood. This has the advantage of leaving us feeling seemingly empowered in the sense that if we see ourselves as being to blame, we don't have to acknowledge the scary fact that we are vulnerable to the unskilful actions of immature adults around us.

Given these circumstances it is not surprising that we have developed a deeply ingrained habit of self-criticism as a coping mechanism to stay safe from the real or imagined criticism from others. If we chastise ourselves first, chastisement from those around us is less painful. If we blame ourselves first, blame from those around us is less painful. It is also not surprising that we are fearful of letting go of this self-protection mechanism.

The key point is that we did not choose our evolved human brains, nor the cultural context, family or life circumstance that we were born into. The long, medium term and short stories were imposed upon us. We just find ourselves in our unique life situation through no fault of our own. Therefore, the self-critic is not our fault but is the result of many causes and conditions beyond our control. However, once we recognise the suffering caused by the self-critic, we can choose to take responsibility and practise compassion in order to reduce this suffering.

It can feel overwhelming when we begin to acknowledge the damage caused by the self-critic to ourselves and our relationships and how this has greatly limited our freedom in life. We can feel eaten up by feelings of rage, shame and grief. It is easy to blame others, in particular those who brought us up and the leaders within our society. What we need to recognise is that this is no one's fault. It is the unavoidable messiness of the human condition, from the individual level to the societal level right back into the distant evolutionary past. We are all just doing the best we can in difficult circumstances. This applies to our parents and carers, however misguided they were. If we are honest with ourselves, would we have behaved any different from them if we had experienced the same life circumstances and conditioning? Probably not. No one is to blame.

The inner critic is painful to acknowledge, but it is far more painful if we let it run unchecked in our minds and rule our lives. Once we face it and engage with it compassionately, the shame and self-blame gradually diminishes. By doing so we can gain some insight into the workings of our own self-critic, make friends with it, and give it what it needs to be at peace. We can take responsibility for our life and learn not to buy into what our self-critic is telling us. Instead, we can set an intention to live in accordance with our life values, including compassion towards ourselves, towards those around us and towards the wider world. This leads to more skilful choices based on these values, rather than reactive decisions based on fear and shame. We provide an exercise at the end of this Chapter which explores our deeply held life values.

Experiencing the Self-Critic

For most people the self-critic is so ingrained and normalised within their mind stream that they barely notice that it is there. They can then unwittingly fall prey to its cruel whisperings and identify with the resulting feelings of unworthiness and shame without conscious awareness of the dynamics at play. The important first step is to face it honestly. This is the focus in this section.

To begin this process, it is helpful to understand what the self-critic is trying to do. You can explore this for yourself by using the following reflection:

Bring to mind a recent situation when the self-critic was strongly active in your mind. Then pose these three questions in a reflective way. This means dropping them into the mind and seeing what emerges without rushing for an answer.

What is the self-critic trying to do?
How is it trying to protect me?
Is this working as intended?

You might journal afterwards and write down whatever pops up. Try to pose these questions a few times a day and journal afterwards. This might reveal something about the function of your self-critic.

A core need for each of us is to love and be loved. When these needs are not met in childhood, a child can blame themselves rather than blame the parents or caregivers for the reasons we described above. This self-blaming in childhood is very often the genesis of the self-critic in adulthood. When we see these dynamics operating in our own experience we can get some distance from the cruel dynamic of self-criticism and begin to bring compassion to the frightened, wounded part of us that so often lies behind the cruel invective of the self-critic. We will explore this process in more detail now.

Choden recalls Paul Gilbert once leading a workshop on self-criticism and shame. During the workshop Paul said to the attendees: 'Imagine you attended an extraordinary workshop, not an ordinary one like this. The promise of this special workshop is that after three days you would no longer have a self-critic. It would be completely absent from your life for evermore. No doubt the workshop organisers would charge a hefty fee, but it would be worth it because your inner tormentor would be gone without trace'.

Then he paused and with a smile on his face said, 'What would your greatest fear be if you no longer had a self-critic?' He then led a group inquiry and wrote what people said on a flipchart. Interestingly, people voiced many fears if they lost their self-critic. These included: they would not be motivated to achieve anything; they would become lazy and self-indulgent; they would lack self-discipline; they would fall prey to bad habits; they would lose track of their life goals, and so on. In the end it was a long list and Paul was writing non-stop. The bottom line was that people recognised how this inner voice caused them a lot of distress, but nevertheless they were fearful of it disappearing for good.

Using the method of functional analysis, Paul then said, 'Okay let's test what you are saying by doing a practice in which we directly experience the self-critic and see clearly how it relates to us'. This practice is called *Experiencing the Self-Critic* (Practice 20) and it appears in the Practice Section at the end of the chapter.

In this practice, we begin by asking ourselves, 'How do I experience my self-critic?' Our critic may have well-worn scripts, such as 'Why am I such an idiot?', 'I am a total failure' and 'This always happens to me', or 'There must be something wrong with me'. It may embody an attitude or an emotion, such as anger or exasperation, or even hatred and distain. It may feel compelling and all-powerful and make us feel powerless, small, ashamed and humiliated.

We then create some distance between ourselves and the inner critical voice by imagining the critic as a character sitting in front of us. This is so important because it allows us to dis-identify with the critic. The problem with the voice of self-criticism is that we identify with it so tightly. We buy into it and then it disempowers us. Once we create some space between ourselves and it through visualisation, our wisdom can come into play. We can become curious about it, see it more objectively and be less under its power. The self-critic thrives on lack of awareness. As soon as we bring wise and kind awareness to it then it begins to lose its hold over us.

We are now familiar with using our imagination and we give it freedom to create a visual representation of our inner critic. It may take the form of a fairy-tale creature, such as a demon, a bogeyman or a witch. It may take an animal form, such as a wolf, a snake or a spider. It may be more ethereal, like a smoke or mist. It may take the form reminiscent of someone from our childhood, perhaps with the angry eyes or disdainful laugh of a parent or carer.

If we imagine our critic as a character, then we are able to interact with it, rather than feel that we are it. We are able to hear what it is saying. We are able to see and hear how it is expressing itself and the emotions or attitudes it embodies. We are able to recognise how it makes us feel, and what thoughts, emotions and sensations it evokes within us. We are able to give ourselves some self-compassion as we face our inner self-critic.

When we are able to view the self-critic with a bit of distance and perspective, this opens up a choice. We can continue to buy in to what the self-critic is saying or we can decide to be kind to the self-critic, but without buying in to its message.

Again, we apply the principle of energy follows focus. Each time we buy into the message of the self-critic, we feed energy into the habit of self-criticism and the power of the self-critic grows. If we do not buy into its messages, but instead offer ourselves compassion and relate to the self-critic with kindness, we feed energy into the habits of self-compassion and kindness and the power of the self-critic diminishes.

We then ask ourselves whether the self-critic has our best interests at heart. Often, the underlying motivation of the self-critic is to protect us but it is based on an outdated coping mechanism that helped us survive in difficult circumstances when we were a child but is no longer fit for purpose as an adult.

We then clearly see that even though it may have our best interests at heart, this is no longer working as intended. In fact, it has imprisoned us in a cage of fear. This has consequences now in preventing us from living fearlessly in the service of our deeply held values, possibly preventing us from loving unconditionally and forming healthy relationships. It is not that the self-critic is bad. It is a wounded part of us and as such our practice is to be kind and compassionate towards it.

Having guided people through the practice, Paul asked people to describe their self-critic. This fell into three categories: What form did your critic take? What emotions did it direct at you? How did this make you feel? He then wrote down what people shared on a flipchart. It was extraordinary what people described. For some the critic was a demon with large red eyes transmitting contempt and anger, for others it was a scolding parent wagging their finger with disgust and disapproval and for others it was a suffocating fog that drowned out any creativity and life force. People had no problem describing how their critic looked in vivid detail and they were very clear about the intense emotions it directed at them. In almost all cases it was destructive and had little interest in their happiness or wellbeing. And, when the question was posed, 'How did this make you feel?' people unanimously reported that they felt awful being at the receiving end of the incessant abuse and attacks of the critic.

Paul then stepped away from the flipchart with great aplomb like a barrister about to make a decisive point in a legal case! He pointed to the previous flipchart sheet posted on the wall in which the greatest fears of losing the critic were listed. He then pointed out the glaring mismatch between these legitimate concerns and the actual behaviour of the critic. It was clear to all present that their self-critic could not address these concerns at all. In fact, it would undermine them. It felt like a huge penny dropped! Even if the original intention of the critic was to protect us from hurt in the past, it was very clear that this is no longer working as intended now.

The question then arises: how do we meet the legitimate concerns we identified at the start of the process, and furthermore, how do we also take care of the self-critic and the fear and wounding lying behind it? What part of us is best equipped to do this job?

The answer to this question is clear from the last chapter. It is the compassionate self that is best equipped to take on this role. In the preceding chapters we have gradually been building our capacity to step into this part of our being.

We can reframe this question as follows: what school would we choose to send our beloved child to? Would we send them to a school where the teachers scold and beat them every time they make a mistake and highlight their every fault, where there is a heavy atmosphere of fear such that our child is terrified of making mistakes and does whatever they can to appease the teachers? Or would we send our child to a school that nurtures their strengths and abilities whilst also acknowledging their weaknesses and supporting them to develop skills so that their weaknesses can become strengths? Any sane parent would send their child to the latter school.

The key point is that we are shifting from the threat system, which is like the school that criticises and induces fear, to the soothing-affiliation system where the compassionate self takes charge, which is like the school that supports and nourishes our beloved child.

Compassion for the Self-Critic

Once we are more familiar with our self-critic we can begin to offer it some compassion and understanding. However, we need to acknowledge that working with the self-critic can bring up strong emotions and at times this may feel overwhelming. We may find ourselves crying. There is no problem with this, so long as we stay within our window of tolerance. Often, the experience of crying, and even deep sobbing, can be a cathartic release of previously suppressed emotions.

Choden recalls Paul Gilbert once saying that when we cry the soothing system comes alive. This is a relational system and so if it does not get the nurturing it needs in childhood, it shuts down. It is like it becomes frozen and turns to ice. When we engage in therapy or do compassion-based practices like we are offering in this book, the ice can begin to thaw until finally the water begins to flow again. This can take the form of deep sobbing and crying. When this happens, it is helpful to see this as a positive development even though it might feel bad at the time. It is also important to reach out for support because connection with supportive friends and mentors assists the process of release by allowing ourselves to feel safe and held.

However, if we do feel overwhelmed, a skilful approach is to step back from this work, with an intention to approach it again when we feel sufficiently safe and resourced. We can rejoice in our intention to offer compassion to the self-critic, even if it is proving difficult to do in practice. We can engage in mindfulness or compassion practices that nourish us and help us to feel safe and aware. For some of us this might be a body scan, compassionate imagery or a mindful walk in nature. We can focus on cultivating more joy in our minds, by focussing on a daily life practice of gratitude and appreciation. This counterbalances the suffering that might come up when working with the self-critic. Whenever our capacity for compassion becomes depleted, resourcing ourselves with the practice of joy can replenish us.

Once we feel ready to offer compassion to the self-critic, we begin by consciously identifying with our inner compassionate self. We do so by feeling into its qualities as we learnt to do in Chapter 8. The more we step into this part of ourselves the easier it becomes. Once again we bring to mind the self-critic, imagining it in front of us and noticing how this feels. We try to get a real sense of its presence, how it looks and the emotions in its eyes.

We then interact with the critic and ask it some questions. We ask the self-critic what is driving it and what it is scared of. We don't think about these questions, but allow our imagined self-critic, in whatever form it takes, to tell us in its own words and in its own way what is driving it and what it is scared of. By using our imagination in this way we are able to get in touch with a deep healing wisdom within ourselves. We then try to remain open and curious about what the inner critic has to tell us. We stay in touch with our experience, noticing any thoughts, emotions and any physical sensations that may arise. This process is set out in Practice 21 below.

Becoming aware of what is driving the critic is a crucial part of the healing process. Sometimes the critic can tell us what is driving it, other times it does not know and we need to find a way of skilfully looking behind the cruel invective of the critic to detect what is there. Many people have remarked that there is a vulnerable, fearful part of themselves lying behind the harsh words of the critic. This is like a wounded dog who barks aggressively and jumps up to bite us but is in great pain and needs tender loving care. The skill here is to appease the aggressive posturing of the critic so we can take care of the wounds that need healing. When we do this the intensity can go out of the recurring inner voice of self-criticism because the real issue has been seen and approached. The once aggressive dog can start wagging its tail and curl up next to us on the sofa!

As our compassionate self we then say to the critic, 'It's not your fault'. In making this statement we recognise that the self-critic arose due to a myriad of causes and conditions that weren't chosen by the critic, or by us, but were due to the many complex forces that shaped our lives. Then, from this perspective of understanding the bigger picture, we offer the critic some compassion by saying phrases such as, 'May you find peace' and 'May what is driving you find peace'. There may be other phrases of well-wishing that come to mind, depending on your personal inner critic and what it has expressed, such as 'May you feel safe' or 'May you experience kindness'. It is important to remember that when we say these phrases we are not trying to get rid of anything and we are not trying to get rid of the self-critic. Instead, we are welcoming and caring for the self-critic as a wounded part of ourselves.

As we offer the self-critic some compassion we notice what happens. Sometimes the critic will change — possibly in a minor way, such as a relaxation in the body or a change of facial expression. In other cases the self-critic may transform into a completely different character. Again, our practice is to give our imagination free reign and for the practice to unfold in its own way. We trust that we don't need to figure anything out and that any understanding or change will happen in its own way and in its own time. As always, we stay in touch with our present moment experience of thoughts, emotions and sensations.

If we do this practice regularly and cultivate an attitude of welcoming the self-critic, hearing what it has to say, and offering it some compassion, we gradually become more familiar with how it feels when the self-critic arises within our experience, and we gain some skills in relating to it skilfully. Then, in daily life, when something goes wrong and the critic starts speaking to us in a cruel and condemning way, we are more likely to recognise what is happening and apply the skills we have learnt.

When we do this, the condemning inner voice of self-criticism gradually diminishes. We do not change into some directionless blob that breaks all the rules and creates havoc. Instead, we are freed up to live more courageously, guided by our life values rather than being driven by fear.

Compassionate Self-Management

The process of working with the critic leads us from destructive self-criticism to compassionate self-management. Right at the outset we identified how people think that they need the harsh words of the critic to keep themselves in line and to prevent them from causing harm to others. But when we explored what actually takes place we saw how the critic is not the one best suited for this job. It might have been suited to the job of protecting us when we were children, but no longer now when we are mature adults.

When we follow the route of destructive self-criticism we get locked into the threat system. This is a fear-based approach like the example quoted above of the school where your kid gets beaten every time they make a mistake. The voice of self-criticism arouses stress hormones within our bodies that cause us to inwardly contract and become very self-absorbed. This can lead to intense feelings of unworthiness and shame. Simply put, we feel awful! Clearly this does not help anyone, least of all someone we might have hurt or wronged. The perverse logic of self-criticism is that through relentlessly beating ourselves up we become far less sensitive to the needs of others.

The other approach is to operate from the soothing system. We learn to step back from the inner voice of criticism and take care of ourselves. This allows us to connect to our life values and to act from these instead of from fear and shame. This is a compassion-based approach. We are now in a position to notice and respect the needs of others. We move from shame to remorse. Instead of beating ourselves up for doing something wrong to someone else, we cultivate genuine concern for them and act in a way that alleviates any hurt or pain. We move from being self-absorbed to being focused on others. Furthermore, our faculty of critical thinking has an important role to play in evaluating our behaviour, but it is not enslaved to the condemning voices that emanate from the threat system. Instead, it emanates from our soothing system and is firmly tied to our life values.

Practice Section

Formal Sitting Practice

Practice 20: Experiencing the Self-Critic (20 – 30 minutes)
Begin by forming an intention to practise compassion for yourself and others, and then reaffirm your compassionate motivation: why you want to practise compassion.

Sit in a relaxed and comfortable posture on a cushion or chair. Then pay attention to the rising and falling of your body as you breathe. To help settle your mind, try deepening your in-breath a little and lengthening your out-breath. See if you can regulate your breathing so that your in-breath and out-breath are of a similar length and rhythm. You might like to count to three or four on the in-breath and a similar count on the out-breath. When your mind begins to settle, let go of counting and let your breathing find its natural rhythm. Take some time to connect with and ground in the body.

Now bring to mind a memory of a recent time when you felt the presence of your self-critic or think of something that you often criticise yourself about.

When you start to hear the inner stream of words that the critic usually chastises you with, see if you can imagine these words coming from a visual image of your self-critic in front of you. Notice any details about its appearance: its eyes, facial expression, colour etc. Then also notice what kind of emotions it is directing towards you. Let it express itself in the way it habitually does.

Now bring your attention back to yourself and feel what the self-critic brings up in you: the one it criticises. You may wish to place your hands on your heart and stay connected with the body as you do this. Ask yourself this question: does the self-critic have my best interests at heart? And if so, does this actually work as intended?

Now let the image of the critic fade in your mind and come back to simply resting; mind resting in body, body resting on ground. Notice any residual feelings after doing this practice, in particular how you feel in your body.

Reflection afterwards:

- *What form did your critic take?*
- *What emotions did it direct at you?*
- *How did this make you feel?*
- *Does the critic have your best interests at heart?*
- *If the answer is yes, then does this work as intended?*

Practice 21: Compassion for the Self-Critic (20 – 30 minutes)
Begin by forming an intention to practise compassion for yourself and others, and then reaffirm your compassionate motivation: why you want to practise compassion.

Sit in a relaxed and comfortable posture on a cushion or chair. Then pay attention to the rising and falling of your body as you breathe. To help settle your mind, try deepening your in-breath a little and lengthening your out-breath. See if you can regulate your breathing so that your in-breath and out-breath are of a similar length and rhythm. You might like to count to three or four on the in-breath and a similar count on the out-breath. When your mind begins to settle, let go of counting and let your breathing find its natural rhythm. Take some time to connect with and ground in the body. Now consciously identify with your compassionate self that lies at the centre of your personal mandala. This is done in stages. Begin by imagining your body to be like a mountain supported by the vast earth below or like mighty tree with roots deep in the soil. Notice how the vast Earth holds your body unconditionally. Connect to the sense of security and stability that comes from visualising in this way. You might discover that you can tolerate and hold more than you think you can. This is the strength quality of your compassionate self.

Build on this visualisation by imagining your breath to be like the wind, or like a gentle breeze caressing the mountain or the tree, and your mind vast and open like the clear blue sky. Body like a mountain, breath like the wind and mind like the clear blue sky…

Now once again bring to mind the self-critic and imagine that it is present in front of you. Get a real sense of its presence, how it looks and the emotions in its eyes.

Now see if you can look behind the harsh words of the critic to what drives it. It might even be helpful to pose these as questions to the critic: 'What is driving you? What are you scared of?'

Spend some time just sitting and reflecting, posing these questions and not expecting any quick answer. Stay in touch with sensations in the body.

Now, as the compassionate part, what do you want to say to the self-critic?

Reflecting on how the self-critic came into being trying to protect you, how does it feel to say to the self-critic: 'It's not your fault'?

Now send the self-critic a message of well-wishing: 'May you find peace, may that which is driving you find peace'. How does this feel?

Does the self-critic change when you pay it compassionate attention? Do you understand a little more about the self-critic's underlying motivation?

Reflection afterwards:

- *What is driving the self-critic?*
- *What is it scared of?*
- *How does it respond when you say, 'It's not your fault'?*
- *How does it respond when you make the wish that what is driving it finds peace?*
- *Explore these questions in a small group if you are doing this practice in a group context; or if you are doing it on your own, spend some time writing a response to these questions in your reflective journal.*

Practice 22: Reflection on Life Values

Human happiness is dependent on living a life with meaning, in accordance with our deeply held values, but rarely do we take the time to reflect on what our true values are. We may notice that we behave differently when we are at work, at home, or with our parents, adopting different sets of values so as to fit in. In order to live authentically, we need to be clear about what our own life values are. Deep down what values would we like our life to stand for? This exercise can help us to clarify this.

Values are a direction of travel as opposed to a goal. For example, if you value honesty, then it is an ongoing journey to be honest with others and with ourselves. It is not something you can finish and then tick off your to do list. It is like travelling in the direction of East. You never get to East, but just keep going around the world. Begin this practice by placing the body in posture, with a pen and paper or your journal to hand. Continue by forming an intention to allow your imagination free reign and to reflect honestly on your life values, and then reaffirm your compassionate motivation: why you want to practise compassion.

Sit in a relaxed and comfortable posture on a cushion or chair. Then pay attention to the rising and falling of your body as you breathe. To help settle your mind, try deepening your in-breath a little and lengthening your out-breath. See if you can regulate your breathing so that your in-breath and out-breath are of a similar length and rhythm. You might like to count to three or four on the in-breath and a similar count on the out-breath. When your mind begins to settle, let go of counting and let your breathing find its natural rhythm. Take some time to connect with and ground in the body.

Imagine that you are at an event celebrating your life achievements. Anyone you want can be there, alive or dead, real or imagined. Allow your imagination free reign.

Now imagine a first person gets up to give a speech about you. Someone who you deeply admire and respect. Imagine that they say all the things you would most like to hear about what your life stands for and the values you most want your life to stand for. This might be in relation to your relationships, your work or education, spirituality, recreation, your community, the environment or health and wellbeing. Let go of any feelings of self-consciousness and see if it is possible to really hear what they are saying.

Then a second person gets up, possibly from a different realm of your life and gives a speech about you. In their speech they describe the qualities you most want to embody in your life.

Now imagine that a third person, possibly a mentor or someone who's life has inspired you, gets up to give a speech about you. In their speech they articulate your heart's deepest desires for how you want to live in and interact with your world and those with whom you share it with.

Now allow the imagined event to fade and spend some time grounding in the body and connecting with the breath. Then drop these questions in to the mind, like dropping pebbles into a pond and watching the ripples. There is no need to answer the questions, to make anything in particular happen or to figure anything out. Simply allow any responses to the questions to arise in their own time and their own way. You can jot the answers down. The questions are:

- *What do the speeches say about my deeply held values?*
- *What do they say about what I want my life to stand for?*
- *What do they say about the values and qualities I most want to embody?*
- *What do they say about how I want to live in and interact with the world?*

Then rest for a few moments to end the practice.

You can make a list of your key values to carry around with you in your purse or wallet or you can write them in your phone. Set an intention to live in accordance with your values. Then refer to your list of values regularly, as you move through your life. You may struggle at times, but see if you can offer yourself compassion and encouragement, and just keep going in the direction of your values.

Informal Daily Life Practice

Revisit Practice 5 in Chapter 2 and practise gratitude and appreciation.

Chapter Eleven

Widening the Circle of Compassion

This is the stage in our journey where we shift our focus to compassion for others. A point we have made many times in this book is that compassion flows in three directions but most people see it as a one-directional flow (self to others) with the result that they can experience compassion fatigue and even burnout. Hence our strong focus so far on being open to receiving love and compassion from others and giving compassion to oneself. This brings balance and engenders resilience.

It might be worth briefly recapping our compassion journey thus far. To begin with we cultivated mindful awareness, with acceptance, as a way of getting in touch with our experience in an honest and open way. Mindful acceptance provides us with a safe foundation to return to if our compassion practice becomes too challenging. Through practices such as RAIN (Chapter 3), we cultivate our ability to recognise and allow what is happening within ourselves, giving it ample room to express itself, whilst also gradually stepping back from what is arising in order to get some headspace and perspective. This is the first aspect of our compassion training, cultivating a sensitivity to our suffering.

We then build up our inner resources to hold and respond to what arises within ourselves, using compassionate imagery practices, gratitude and appreciation and the self-compassion practice of soften, soothe and allow. In this way we gradually develop a felt sense of inner safeness and strength. This is accompanied by warmth and non-judgement towards our fallibilities and a sense of appreciation and gratitude for our strengths, which give rise to a deep commitment to ourselves, as we are, no matter what.

At this point in the journey we are likely to be clearer about what triggers us and causes us to suffer through being with our difficulty and confusion with openness and honesty. Simultaneously, we are likely to be clearer about how to relieve that suffering, without resisting or wanting things to be different, but through a courageous commitment to our own flourishing. From this position of insight and understanding into what causes us to suffer and how to relieve that suffering, we are in a much stronger position to see with clarity what causes those around us to suffer and how to relieve their suffering.

This point is worth repeating because it is the reason why we practise self-compassion first. It is only when we see what causes us to suffer and how to relieve that suffering, that we can do this in a genuine way for others.

When we then move on to practise compassion for others, we can sometimes encounter resistance and blocks and sometimes these can feel overwhelming. When this happens, we follow an approach we have applied throughout this book: we fall back to the previous level of practice. In this case we fall back on self-compassion. We recognise that this journey is difficult and requires us to face some dark places within ourselves and so we tend to our own suffering through the practices of self-compassion that we are already familiar with. We then take some time to build more capacity with the intention to come back and face that which is currently overwhelming once we feel safe enough to.

Sometimes even the practice of self-compassion can feel overwhelming and when this happens we rejoice in our intention to be compassionate and then fall back to the practice of mindfulness. When the going gets tough, we support ourselves with the mindfulness practices that nourish us. It won't always be tough and so when the situation lightens we can go back to practising self-compassion and then compassion for others.

The problem with compassion for others is that we are hard-wired to offer love, kindness and support to our family and tribe. This can flow naturally and easily, but what is not so easy is to extend these feelings to all those many beings who are not part of our family or tribe. Therefore, some practise is required to overcome our evolutionary conditioning and widen our circle of concern to all living beings.

This is why we will be applying the Buddhist model of the Four Immeasurable Qualities of loving kindness, compassion, joy and equanimity. This model is designed for expanding our circle of concern from those who are close, to those who are strangers, then to adversaries and finally to all living beings. We have adapted the theory and practice for a secular audience and approach the cultivation of these qualities in an experiential way.

In this chapter we will focus on loving kindness and equanimity. In the next chapter we will focus on compassion (tonglen practice) and sympathetic joy.

Four Immeasurable Qualities

The Four Immeasurable Qualities are also known in the Pali language as the Four Brahmaviharas. Their literal translation is the *Four Divine Abodes*. Pali was the language in which the teachings of the Buddha were originally written down.

They are:

- *Maitri* (Sanskrit) or *Metta* (Pali), is generally translated as loving kindness but a more accurate description is gentle friendship and active good will towards all living beings. This quality is accompanied by the wish, 'May all beings be happy and create the causes for happiness'.
- *Karuna* (Sanskrit and Pali), is generally translated as compassion and arises when our loving kindness meets suffering. This quality is accompanied by the wish, 'May

all beings be free from suffering and from creating the causes of suffering'.

- *Mudita* (Sanskrit and Pali) is generally translated as sympathetic or empathetic joy and is best described as rejoicing in the good qualities and good fortune of ourselves and others. This quality is accompanied by the wish, 'May all beings experience deep joy, untainted by suffering'.
- *Upeksa* (Sanskrit) or *Upekkha* (Pali), is generally translated as equanimity and is best described as an attitude of impartiality and even-mindedness in relation to what life throws at us. This quality is accompanied by the wish, 'May all beings dwell in equanimity, free from attachment, aversion and ignorance'.

These four qualities provide balance to our compassion practice in that we are not exclusively focused on suffering, but we are also attentive to flourishing. As we move about our lives we do so with an attitude of gentle friendship and curious engagement. Where this gentle friendship meets suffering, compassion naturally arises. Where it meets positive experiences or good fortune, joy naturally arises. Furthermore, these three qualities of loving-kindness, compassion and joy are underpinned by the quality of equanimity. This means that we are willing to expand the reach of our hearts and minds in an impartial way to embrace all living beings. We do so gradually and learn to extend the practices of kindness, compassion and joy beyond our narrow preferences of like and dislike. In this way we go against our evolutionary programming of just focusing our love and concern on our immediate family and tribe and train to open our hearts to strangers and adversaries too.

The view in Buddhism is that these limitless qualities are already present within us as latent potentials. Each of us is endowed with the capacity to be limitlessly kind, compassionate and joyful. Furthermore, each of us has the capacity to extend the reach of our hearts to include all living beings. However, these qualities are obscured by ignorance. This is the belief in a solid, permanent sense of self, which separates us from other people and life at large. This belief is mistaken because life is intricately interconnected, and any sense of solidity and separation is pure illusion. Yet, if we adhere to this belief we become increasingly egocentric, putting our own needs and wants before those of others. In the short term this might appear to serve us, but in the long term it drives a wedge between who we think we are and the truth of who we truly are and how life is — and the only outcome is suffering.

Through wishing that all beings be happy and create the causes of happiness, we re-align ourselves to the truth of how life is — dynamic, changing and interconnected — and gradually free ourselves from the trap of egocentricity. Ironically, the more our egocentricity weakens, the happier we become. The Dalai Lama is one of the happiest people in our world and lives by his motto, 'Be kind to everyone, and if you can't be kind at least do not harm'. He goes on to say that if we focus on the happiness of others, we might benefit other people but we will definitely benefit ourselves. One of the great discoveries in life is that the root cause of our happiness is not egocentric concern but concern for the wellbeing of others. This perspective lies at the heart of the Four Immeasurable Qualities.

Practising the Four Immeasurable Qualities

We bring these qualities to life by following the practice approach used by the famous Tibetan Buddhist nun, Pema Chodron (2009). She devised a four-stage approach: contact, encourage, expand and notice the effects.

We first make *contact* with each of the qualities by starting where it is easy and uncomplicated and using our imagination to bring to mind a person (or an animal) for whom this quality is easy to generate. Taking the example of loving kindness, we begin with a person towards whom our heart opens unconditionally. We start with someone with whom we have an uncomplicated relationship, perhaps a grandchild, grandparent, niece or nephew or a favourite aunt or uncle. Sometimes our relationships with closer family members can be complicated and less unconditional. Alternatively, we can choose to start with a pet, or a squirrel we see in the park, or the robin in our garden. For some people it is easier to start with themselves, but for most of us it is easier to start with others.

We then *encourage* the flow of loving-kindness by saying phrases that amplify the feelings and make them stronger. We either say them softly to ourselves or silently in our heads. It is important that these phrases feel genuine and meaningful and are appropriate to the person we are bringing to mind. Also, it is important to imbue them with feeling and not just to use stock phrases that are commonly used if we do not have a feeling for them. In the next section we explore different options for loving kindness phrases. The main point here is that we are building on the loving kindness we already have and making it stronger.

The next step is to *expand* these qualities by widening the reach of our hearts beyond those for whom it is easy to generate the feelings of loving-kindness, compassion and joy. This is where the quality of equanimity is important because it underlies each of the other qualities and helps us to go beyond our habitual likes and dislikes and expand these qualities in an impartial way to all living beings everywhere.

In the case of loving kindness, we begin this process by directing loving kindness towards other classes of beings and notice what happens. We explore how it feels to direct loving kindness towards so-called 'neutral' people — those who are strangers and whom we neither like nor dislike. They are people we might encounter on a daily basis, like those working at a coffee shop we frequent or people working at the supermarket checkout. We then explore how it is to direct loving kindness towards a so-called 'difficult person', someone we find challenging. With difficult people it is important to tread carefully and start with those who are mildly annoying and gradually work up to our nemesis who might have hurt us badly. Then we extend gradually to all beings with whom we share our planet: humans, animals, including birds, fish and insects. We can even include beings on other planets, if we believe there may be some out there!

The last stage in the process is to *notice the effects*. As Pema Chodron loved to say, 'If your heart opens to all beings, including adversaries and enemies, this is excellent; if instead you feel shut down and blocked this is excellent too!' (Chodron, 2009). Whatever occurs is part of our own unique learning. Learning about our blocks and resistances is very important because we are learning about how we shut down. We become curious and explore how these manifest for each of us. Do we feel avoidant, numb, dissociated, or do we have a fervent resistance to opening our hearts? Where we experience blocks or resistance or challenging emotions we bring mindful awareness, allowing the natural display of these experiences within our embodied presence, without agenda. In this way we create the conditions for insights to arise, of their own accord, about the blocks we experience and so create the conditions for the blocks to transform themselves.

When we practise the Four Immeasurable Qualities in this way sometimes the feelings do not flow. People sometimes remark that the phrases feel empty; they mouth the words to themselves but they do not feel anything. Like any new activity it can take time to get the feel for it, and we often need time to warm up to the practices. If the lack of feeling persists, however, we can instead focus on our intention to be kind, compassionate and joyful. Intention is powerful. It creates the conditions for the qualities to arise in their own time and in their own way.

It is important to distinguish intention from expectation. An intention sets a direction of travel that is open-ended, whilst an expectation is fixed on a desired outcome. We set our intention to cultivate and live by these qualities, but we don't make it into a goal or expectation to beat ourselves up with if we fail to achieve it. Instead, we recognise that it can be challenging to cultivate these qualities. The human condition is messy and not one of perfection. We recognise that we will fail over and over again, but setting our intention is creating the conditions for future success, so long as we keep going. So we set our intention over and over again.

We can see our practice of cultivating the Four Immeasurable Qualities as a playful dance. We move to the edge of what feels okay, delight in any opening up of the compassionate heart and bring mindful awareness and self-care to any closing down of the heart. In so doing, we step forwards and backwards between mindfulness, self-compassion and compassion for others, in a never-ending process of opening our hearts.

The Tibetan Buddhist teacher, Chogyam Trungpa, spoke poignantly about each of us having a soft spot within us — a vulnerable heart, which is tender to the touch, just like a bruise. Living a life of compassion requires this tender heart of ours to open up to the pain and suffering in the world and be touched; yet this can be painful, just like pressing on a bruise. For many of us this soft spot has been sorely wounded by our life experiences and so we have built up rigid defences to protect it from further wounding. But this also shuts us off from living in a full and loving way. It is also understandable that we may feel reluctant to drop these defences too quickly, which is why we need to go carefully with these practices. If we persist, however, they will open the heart and expose our soft spot. At first this may feel like a shaky vulnerability, but this is actually a good sign. It often arises together with a sense of unconditional cheerfulness. The two go hand in hand.

Widening the Circle of Loving Kindness

Whereas compassion focuses on the relief of suffering, loving kindness focuses on the promotion of happiness. The Buddhist aspiration prayer that goes together with this quality is: 'May all beings have happiness and create the causes of happiness'.

Loving kindness is a wish for the physical wellbeing and psychological happiness of ourselves and others. We navigate life with warm engagement to all the circumstances we find ourselves in and gentle friendship to all the people or animals we interact with. It can be felt as a steady, unconditional sense of kindly connection that touches all experience and all beings, without exception.

Each of the Four Immeasurable Qualities has a 'near enemy', which is something that might easily be mistaken for it. The quality of loving kindness is unconditional and is to be contrasted with the near enemy of conditional love that requires something in return. Loving kindness is also different from passionate desire, which is closely linked to neediness and attachment, and is tied up with meeting our own needs and wants. This can have a contracted, grasping feel to it in contrast with loving kindness that is open, without expectations or assumptions, and asks for nothing in return.

The so called 'far enemy' of loving kindness is anger and hatred. This is its polar opposite. Therefore, if someone struggles with anger — anything from mild irritation to passive aggression to resentment or rage — loving kindness is a good practice to do. It operates as an antidote to anger. We cover this in more detail in our book, which we co-wrote with Rob Nairn, called *From Mindfulness to Insight*.

The contemporary practice of loving kindness, popularised by teachers like Sharon Salzberg, goes with the following types of wishes:

- *May I and others be happy.*
- *May I and others be well.*

- *May I and others be safe.*
- *May I and others live with ease.*

When you practise cultivating loving kindness, you can use these phrases or choose phrases that are meaningful for you. It is important that the phrases feel genuine and heartfelt because we are trying to make contact with feelings of loving kindness we already feel and then build on them.

We start the practice with a dear friend, who may be an animal or human friend, and with whom we have an uncomplicated relationship. It is a person or animal that naturally causes our heart to open when we bring them to mind. We imagine that they are sitting next to us or in front of us. This might involve visualising them or just feeling their presence, depending on how our imaginations work. It can be helpful to imagine them in the context we know them in, for example our home or workplace. We might imagine making a gesture of welcome towards them, such as a smile or a pat on the shoulder. We notice any thoughts, emotions or physical sensations that arise when we bring our dear friend to mind, remembering there is no right or wrong way for us to experience the practice.

Then we begin by saying kind wishes for our dear friend and become curious about what happens. If we experience a flow of kindness — an opening of our heart towards our dear friend — we pay attention to it. Applying the principle of 'energy follows focus', if we give attention to these feelings they grow. Alternatively, if we experience any feelings of shutting down, numbness or resistance we pay attention to these feelings with mindful awareness and acceptance. We become curious about what is happening, without getting caught up in any stories and without trying to make anything happen or figure anything out. We simply remain open and curious and see what happens.

Then we include ourselves in the practice. We first remind ourselves that just as our dear friend wishes to be happy, so do we, and we then extend our loving kindness to both ourselves and our dear friend, by saying phrases like these, 'May we be happy, may we be well, may we be safe, may we live with ease'. Again, we notice what happens: any opening or closing down. Then we move onto the next stage which is to focus only on ourselves by saying phrases like these, 'May I be happy, may I be well, may I be safe, may I live with ease', again noticing what happens.

Next we expand on the feelings of loving kindness we have generated. We start doing this by focusing on a neutral person. This might be someone we regularly come into contact with, but whom we do not know or have any strong feelings of like or dislike towards. It might be someone we see on a daily basis, perhaps in the local shop, bus stop or nearby park. We bring them to mind and notice how this feels. We make a gesture of welcome towards them and remind ourselves that just as we and our dear friend wish to be happy, so does this person. Then we say the phrases for them, 'May you be happy, may you be well, may you be safe, may you live with ease'. Again, we notice any flows of kindness, any blocks or resistance, remembering that there is no right or wrong way to feel.

Then we move onto a so-called 'difficult person', who is someone we find challenging or annoying. It might be someone who pushes our buttons. As stated above, we start with people that we find mildly irritating and over time move onto more challenging people, such as those who have hurt us. We bring this person to mind and once again notice how it feels to make a gesture of welcome to this person. Again, we remind ourselves that just as our dear friend, our self and the neutral person wish to be happy, so does this person. Then we experiment by saying the loving kindness phrases to this person and notice what happens. We pay attention to any thoughts, emotions or sensations in the body.

If we don't experience feelings of kindness when we do the practice, we can remind ourselves of our intention to be kind, which is very powerful. Over time the intention will gradually give birth to the feelings. Sometimes people do not notice much happening in the practice itself, but nevertheless experience changes in their daily lives. We might notice ourselves becoming kinder and responding differently to situations. We can recognise that this is the fruition of our loving kindness practice, even if it often feels like we are getting nowhere in the practice itself. The heartfelt intention to be kind and sticking with the practice will surely result in transformation over time.

Another way of doing this practice is simply to allow people to pop up spontaneously and then greet them with the loving kindness phrases. In this case we don't have to intentionally bring people to mind, and go through the categories of dear friend, neutral and difficult person. Instead, we rely on a deeper wisdom. It can be interesting and sometimes surprising to see who pops up!

To end the practice we widen our circle of loving kindness to include more and more human beings and animals. We might do this geographically, starting with our local area and widening out to our country, then our continent, until eventually we extend loving kindness to all living beings on the planet and throughout the whole universe. To begin with we include as many beings as we feel comfortable with and gradually expand this over time. As always, we stay in touch with the body and notice how the practice feels.

If the practice becomes challenging or overwhelming, we can take a moment to rejoice in our intention to generate loving kindness to these many living beings, and then drop back to self-compassion or mindfulness practice. In so doing we build up our resources until we feel ready to extend kindness to others again.

Cultivating Equanimity towards All Beings

In the context of the Four Immeasurable Qualities, equanimity is an impartial state of mind that is not dry and impersonal but is charged with feeling. It is warm and inclusive and we care for all living beings equally. Pema Chodron defined equanimity as fully abiding in our own experience without believing in the opinions and judgments that arise; and when opinions and judgments do arise, we practise equanimity in relation to them too (Chodron, 2009).

It's 'near enemy' is indifference, apathy or cool detachment, which is very different from equanimity's quality of warmly embracing the world and those with whom we share it.

The opposite, or so called 'far enemy' of equanimity is prejudice, resentment and taking sides in a conflict or dispute. The underlying state of mind here is egocentric preference in which we are ruled by our habitual likes and dislikes. This might take the form of grasping at what we like, aversion for what we dislike or indifference to what does not interest us. The practice of equanimity that we describe below is the antidote to this divisive mentality.

When it comes to practising equanimity there are two aspects to focus on. The first relates to steadiness and balance. A useful image is that of the ballast of a ship that keeps the vessel steady in stormy seas. Similarly, when it comes to our meditation practice and how we navigate our daily lives, the quality of equanimity helps us to remain grounded and stable in the face of intrusive thoughts and everyday ups and downs. This aspect of equanimity is cultivated through mindfulness practice which is a pre-condition for the compassion practices we are describing in this book. Therefore, we will not focus on it here.

The second aspect of equanimity is cultivating a big perspective. A useful image is climbing to the top of a mountain and looking down at a city far below. We are less caught up in all the hustle and bustle of city life, whilst also seeing much more than if we were standing in a noisy street. The way we get this big perspective is by not being a slave to our habitual preferences of like, dislike and indifference. This allows our hearts and minds to open up to a bigger experience of living that is our natural birth right. We have already started to get a feeling for this bigger space of awareness in the loving kindness section above.

A very helpful way of practising the second aspect of equanimity is by doing the practice *Aspiring, Dissolving and Equalising* developed by the Buddhist teacher, Aura Glaser. This practice can be found in the practice section below. Before doing the practice it will be helpful to explain each of the stages.

The *Aspiring* stage is the same as the loving kindness practice described in the previous section. We make contact with feelings of loving kindness we already possess and build on them by using phrases. We then expand them to other people we know and like, to strangers and finally to people we find difficult and aversive. In so doing we are consciously stretching our capacity for offering loving kindness. Many of us may not to find it too difficult to generate loving kindness to strangers since we have neutral feelings to these people. But when it comes to people we do not like, those who push our buttons and annoy us, it may not be so straightforward. This is the main focus of the aspiring, dissolving and equalising practice.

The main point with this stage is not to pretend or manufacture feelings of loving kindness when we do not genuinely feel them. There is always a danger with these practices of creating a false positive — of wishing people well when in fact beneath the surface we are seething with resentment and anger. It is much better to acknowledge what we are actually feeling and work with these feelings. So, when we do this stage of the practice we simply become curious about what happens when we cultivate kind feelings to adversaries or enemies. If genuine feelings of kindness flow that is good, and if we feel blocked and resistant and nothing flows, that is good too. We might start mouthing phrases of kindness and instead feel blocked, numb or angry. Instead of feeling disappointed that our loving kindness practice has run aground we simply acknowledge that this is what is going on for us now. We do our best to maintain our intention to be loving and kind, whilst owning what we are actually feeling now. In this way our practice is genuine and realistic.

In the *Dissolving* stage, we then shift perspective and try to view the object of our enmity, love or indifference through the eyes of other people. It is called 'dissolving' because we are trying to dissolve our fixed projections on other people. In the case of people for whom we find it difficult to extend feelings of kindness, we try to see the same person through the eyes of other people. Whereas the very sight of this person might fill us with anger and resentment, there are other people who dearly love this person. We might find them impossible to deal with in the work situation, but in their home situation they might be loving and kind and bring joy to all those around them. Also the vast majority of people are likely to see them in neutral terms because they do not know them and so they do not arouse strong feelings of like or dislike.

What does this tell us? It shows very clearly that our feelings of dislike relate to our own *perception* of this person. It is to do with us and our particular relationship with them. It is not as if 'enemy' or 'difficult person' is a label they carry around on their forehead. This is very empowering because now we can do something about it. Since our difficulty with them is something to do with us and our own perceptions, the situation is workable. If they were intrinsically bad and difficult there would be very little we could do.

Here we are not condoning the unskilful or damaging behaviour of the difficult person, but recognising our messy common humanity. Much unskilful behaviour arises out of a person's suffering and is likely to cause them more suffering. It is not as if we become a doormat, instead we balance compassion for ourselves with compassion for the difficult person. Often the fruition of our compassion practice is an increased ability to set boundaries, based on increased clarity and compassion for all involved.

We can also apply the dissolving principle to those who are near and dear and to strangers for whom we have neutral feelings. In the case of someone we love and feel close to, we first connect to our own feelings of love and closeness when we bring this person to mind. Then we step into the shoes of someone who doesn't know them and imagine what that would be like. Next we step into the shoes of someone who doesn't like them and imagine what that would be like. Through doing this we can see very clearly that 'being a loved one' is not intrinsic to this person as there are others who don't know them or don't like them. This helps to dissolve our solid projections of like and dislike.

We can do the same for a stranger. There are so many people we encounter who do not arouse any strong feelings at all. They can be like nameless, unfeeling entities passing us by. It can then be helpful to put ourselves in the shoes of a partner or family member who dearly loves this person. This can help bring this person to life as a breathing, feeling person who longs for happiness and fulfilment just like we do. Finally, we can put ourselves into the shoes of someone who dislikes this person and see how it affects our perception. Although to us this person appears bland and neutral, some will love them and others will dislike them, and so they are not neutral to everyone. Once again this helps to loosen up our fixed perceptions of people.

The third stage of the process is *Equalising*. Here we broaden our perspective and reflect that just like us, all living beings want to be happy and free from pain and suffering. Just like us, they want to be safe and healthy. Just like us, they make mistakes and mess up. Just like us, they sometimes act from confusion and cause harm to themselves and others. Just like us, they yearn to be loved and accepted.

These many living beings who want what we do include those who are near and dear to us; those who are strangers and for whom we have neutral feelings; those who cause us difficulty and might be seen as adversaries or enemies; and those countless living beings who we have never met. The bottom line is that there is more that connects us than which separates us. This even applies to our most hated adversary. When it comes to the most important things in life, we are all the same. We then let the humanity of these many different beings touch our hearts.

We are all subject to powerful drives and emotions that are hard-wired into us by the long process of evolution. Each of us is subject to a lifetime of conditioning that has shaped us in powerful ways beyond our control. At a deep level we are all just doing our best, often in difficult circumstances. We recognise that we are all subject to the messiness of the human condition, trying to be happy and not to suffer, but often going about it in an unskilful and counterproductive way.

The important point here is that we are focusing on the person and not their actions. We are not condoning the negative actions of others. These need to be addressed in the appropriate way. We are not trying to bypass or suppress our negative feelings and reactions that might all have justifiable causes. We are also not trying to get rid of our preferences of like and dislike. This is a very realistic approach of bringing all these things to light and being honest about how we are. We acknowledge our limitations and preferences but then chose to see through them all to a deeper truth — that of our common humanity with others.

To reiterate, this is expressed by the simple truth, 'Just as I wish to be happy and to be free from suffering, so do you, so do we all'. It can be very heart opening and liberating to walk through a crowd of people, some we know and many we do not know, and say this phrase to ourselves, while letting the poignant humanity of other people touch our heart. We can apply this to animals and insects too and notice how it feels.

Finally, we contemplate all beings and conclude with the aspiration of the Four Immeasurable Qualities:

- *May all living beings be happy and create the causes of happiness;*
- *May they all be free of suffering and the causes of suffering;*
- *May they all experience great joy and wellbeing untainted by suffering;*
- *May they abide in equanimity free from preference.*

Again, if at any point the practice feels too challenging we can step back to self-compassion, to rejoicing in our compassionate motivation and to our mindfulness practice.

Practice Section

Formal Sitting Practice

Practice 23: Widening Circle of Loving Kindness (20 – 30 minutes)

Begin by forming an intention to practise kindness for yourself and others, and then reaffirm your compassionate motivation: why you want to practise compassion.

Sit in a relaxed and comfortable posture on a cushion or chair. Then pay attention to the rising and falling of your body as you breathe. To help settle your mind, deepen your in-breath a little and lengthen your out-breath. See if you can regulate your breathing so that your in-breath and out-breath are of a similar length and rhythm. You might like to count to three or four on the in-breath and a similar count on the out-breath. When your mind begins to settle, let go of counting and let your breathing find its natural rhythm.

Now soften around how you feel in the body, allowing your experience to be as it is. It may help to place your hand on your heart as a gesture of self-soothing. Feel the warmth of the touch and the movement of the breath through your chest. If you like, you can form a half-smile, and adopt a gentle voice tone in how you guide yourself. In this way consciously connect with a kind and compassionate attitude to yourself.

Now bring to mind someone you care about — it could be a child, friend, partner, parent or an animal. Focus your loving feelings on them. Name them in your mind and say two or three loving-kindness phrases as you breathe out. You can choose some phrases from this list or make up your own:

- *May you be well and healthy.*
- *May you be free of suffering.*
- *May you be happy.*
- *May you flourish in your life.*
- *May you find peace.*
- *May you be free of danger.*
- *May you live your life with ease.*

What is most important is the flow of feeling, not the actual words or phrases. If you find that the feelings do not flow so easily, then stay with your intention to be kind and compassionate.

Now gradually expand the circle of loving-kindness to include other people and animals. You can do this in a spontaneous way, letting people flow through your awareness and greeting them with one of more the above phrases, or phrases of your own. Notice how it feels to consciously direct feelings of loving-kindness to whomever moves through your awareness.

It can be helpful to think of your loving-kindness spreading out in a circle, with yourself at the centre, and each time you say the phrases for a new person or group of people, you can think of your circle of loving-kindness growing bigger. Then you practise loving-kindness for everyone within the circle, including yourself. You can move back and forth between yourself and the others, as this can help to emphasise that we are all the same; we all want to be happy and to be free from suffering.

To enhance this practice, as you breathe out you can imagine that you transmit a warm golden glow from your heart that touches the person you are relating to, bringing them peace and wellbeing. Notice the sensations around your heart and the feelings in your body as you do this. Become aware of any feelings of pleasure and joy that arise, when you imagine that they become happy and free of suffering.

Before finishing the practice, imagine that your circle of loving-kindness expands outwards in a limitless way, including all living beings everywhere. At this point allow the practice to dissolve, and then simply rest, noticing how you feel in the body and staying in touch with the felt sense of the practice.

Alternative: If you want to do the practice in a more structured way, then you can follow the same approach as above, but extend the loving-kindness phrases progressively to the following groups of people:

- *a person or animal for whom loving-kindness flows naturally and easily;*
- *yourself as you are;*
- *a neutral person, someone whom you neither like nor dislike;*
- *a difficult person — someone with whom you have experienced difficulty or conflict;*
- *a group made up of the people or animals from the categories above, including one for whom you feel kindness, yourself, a neutral person and a difficult person;*
- *pairs of opposites, such as young and old, rich and poor, those in good health and those in poor health;*
- *finally, all beings everywhere, without exception or distinction.*

Daily Life Loving Kindness

In daily life we can set an intention to promote the physical and psychological wellbeing of ourselves and of those around us.

We can do this each morning, perhaps using the words of the Dalai Lama, 'May I be kind to everyone I meet today (including myself) and if I cannot be kind may I at least do no harm'. We might remind ourselves of this intention during the day, for example, by setting an alarm to go off on our phone.

We can also set an intention to take any opportunity that presents itself to do random acts of kindness. We might let someone into a traffic queue or hold a door open for someone. We might send a friend a joyful text or make someone a cup of tea. Do these things with the intention to be kind and pay attention to how it feels. Then at the end of the day, reflect back on what happened. You might like to journal about these daily life acts of kindness, noticing how it feels as you do so.

Practice 24: Aspiring, Dissolving and Equalising (20 – 30 minutes)
Begin by forming an intention to practise equanimity, and then reaffirm your compassionate motivation: why you want to practise compassion.

Sit in a relaxed and comfortable posture on a cushion or chair. Then pay attention to the rising and falling of your body as you breathe. To help settle your mind, deepen your in-breath a little and lengthen your out-breath. See if you can regulate your breathing so that your in-breath and out-breath are of a similar length and rhythm. You might like to count to three or four on the in-breath and a similar count on the out-breath. When your mind begins to settle, let go of counting and let your breathing find its natural rhythm.

Now soften around how you feel in the body, allowing your experience to be as it is. It may help to place your hand on your heart as a gesture of self-soothing. Feel the warmth of the touch and the movement of the breath through your chest. If you like, you can form a half-smile, and adopt a gentle voice tone in how you guide yourself. In this way consciously connect with a kind and compassionate attitude to yourself.

Someone Who Is Close

Now bring to mind someone you hold dear and imagine that they are sitting in front of you or going about their daily business. This can be a visual image or a felt sense of them being present. They might be a parent, child, partner or an animal for whom you feel a natural flow of love and care.

[*Aspiring*] Now direct the following heartfelt wishes to this person by saying these phrases silently on your out-breath (or make up your own phrases):

- *May you be well and happy (say their name).*
- *May you be free of pain and suffering (say their name).*
- *May you experience joy and wellbeing (say their name).*

Connect to the flow of loving-kindness to your loved one and pay attention to the feelings that arise in you when you focus on your wish for them to be happy and free of suffering. If the feelings do not flow so easily then remain connected to your intention to be kind and supportive.

[*Dissolving*] Now shift perspective and reflect for a moment that while it may be perfectly natural for you to feel love and care for this person, to someone else — at work for example — your loved one may be seen as hostile and aggressive and may even be the object of loathing. And then for most people, your loved one elicits neither attachment nor aversion. Therefore, see how your feelings arise out of your particular relationship; they are not intrinsic to that person.

[*Equalising*] Now reflect that just like you and your loved one, the people who do not like them and the people who are indifferent to them, all want to be happy and free of suffering. In this respect all are equal. Then let the image of your loved one fade and spend a few moments tuning into the feelings that may have arisen in you, noticing how this feels in your body.

Someone Who Is Neutral

Now think of someone that you neither like nor dislike but have some form of contact with on a daily basis. It might be a bus driver, the person who serves you coffee as you walk to work, a classmate or someone you see on the train every morning. Bring an actual person to mind.

[*Aspiring*] Now imagine this person faced with suffering in some way, perhaps dealing with conflict at work, struggling with addiction or depression, or feeling lonely and unloved. Then allow your heart to feel tenderness and concern for this person, and say the following phrases silently on your out-breath (or make up your own phrases):

- *May you be well and happy.*
- *May you be free of pain and suffering.*
- *May you experience joy and wellbeing.*

Notice how you feel when you say these phrases. Perhaps there is a natural flow of care and concern, or perhaps you feel indifferent or even irritated by the exercise. If you notice yourself feeling shut down, irritated or resistant, simply be curious about this and notice where you feel this in your body. Is there tightness in your face, jaw or shoulders, or tension and contraction in some other part of your body? Try to be gentle and honest, not suppressing the emotions you are feeling.

[*Dissolving*] Now shift perspective and think that this person, to whom you may feel indifferent, loves and cares for some people. There are people who look forward to seeing them when they come home from work; there are things in their life that they cherish. In this way, reflect that your indifference or neutrality is about you and the way you see things; it is not intrinsic to them.

[*Equalising*] And now reflect that just like you this person wants to be happy; and just like you this person wants to be free of suffering and pain. Just like you they want to be loved, safe and healthy; and just like you they do not want to be despised, lonely or depressed. Let the poignancy of this person touch you. Then let the image of this person fade and spend a few moments tuning into the feelings that may have arisen in you, noticing how this feels in your body.

Someone Who Is Difficult

Now think of someone you dislike, or who may have done you some harm, someone who is an adversary or competitor, or someone you know but have little time or regard for. Bring a particular person to mind and imagine that they are present in front of you.

Imagine this person faced with suffering in some way, perhaps dealing with conflict at home or at work, struggling with addiction or depression, or feeling lonely and unloved. Perhaps you can see that one of the reasons they are difficult is because they are suffering in some way.

[*Aspiring*] Now direct heartfelt wishes to this person by saying the following phrases silently on your out-breath (or make up your own phrases):

- *May you be well and happy (say their name).*
- *May you be free of pain and suffering (say their name).*
- *May you experience joy and wellbeing (say their name).*

Notice how you feel when you make this aspiration. Is there a natural flow of tenderness and care towards this person, or does your heart feel contracted and resentful, not really wanting them to be happy and free of suffering? Simply notice how you are feeling — there is no right or wrong way to feel. We are not trying to force out a feeling of compassion or pretend to be compassionate. Be curious and tune into how you are feeling in your body — is there tightness in your face, jaw or shoulders, or tension and contraction in some other part of your body? Maybe you feel the very opposite of compassion, and that is completely okay. Just affirm your intention that one day you may open your heart more fully than today.

[*Dissolving*] Now shift your perspective and reflect that other people might see your adversary in a very different light. They might be adored by some, even though you cannot stand the sight of them. They might be a loving parent at home and very tender with animals. In this way, reflect that your feelings and reactions may have a lot to do with you and your relationship with this person. In this sense 'enemy' or 'difficult person' is not intrinsic to the person, like a label they walk around with that is fixed to their forehead. This does not mean to say that you must condone their negative actions.

[*Equalising*] And now, once again, reflect that just like you this person wants to be happy; and just like you this person wants to be free of suffering and pain. Just like you this person wants to be loved, safe and healthy; and just like you they do not want to be despised, lonely or depressed. Let the humanity of this person touch you. In essence they are just like you. We are not condoning their actions, nor suppressing them; we are simply seeing through them and connecting with the bigger picture — that there is more that connects us than separates us. Despite our many differences, we are fundamentally the same when it comes to wanting to find happiness and avoid suffering.

Then let the image of this person fade and spend a few moments tuning into the feelings that may have arisen in you, noticing in how this feels in your body.

Opening Out to All Others

Now contemplate people you know, going through them person by person. Begin with friends, and then move on to people you have less connection with, like those who serve you coffee as you walk to work or sell you the morning newspaper. Then gradually open this up to include adversaries and those you find difficult. Imagine that just like you these people want happiness and don't want to suffer; just like you they don't want to feel stress and anxiety; just like you they want to feel safe and ease; just like you they want to be loved and accepted. The more personal you make the reflection, the more powerfully it will move you. Now gradually expand your awareness to take in other people who live or work near you, those in your neighbourhood and town, those who live in the same country and continent, and finally all living beings everywhere. And now, imagining all beings everywhere, you can conclude with the aspiration of the Four Limitless Contemplations:

- *May all living beings be happy and create the causes of happiness.*
- *May they all be free of suffering and the causes of suffering.*
- *May they all experience great joy and wellbeing untainted by suffering.*
- *May they abide in equanimity free from limiting attachment and aversion.*

Then let go of the practice and spend a few moments tuning into the feelings that may have arisen in you, noticing how this feels in your body.

Daily Life Equanimity

In daily life, as you walk down a street or as you sit in a café watching people walk by, try to notice your emotional reactions of like, dislike and indifference. Notice your automatic assumptions and prejudices about these different people you don't even know. Try doing this with honesty and kindness without judging yourself, because other people are like this too.

Then experiment with saying these phrases silently to yourself as people pass you by: 'Just like me this person wants to be happy and avoid suffering; just like me they want to feel safe and ease; just like me they want to be loved and accepted.' Make up your own phrases. See if you can connect with the common humanity that we all share with all others.

Chapter Twelve

Taking and Sending

The main focus of this chapter is the practice of tonglen, a powerful and transformative compassion practice. However, before we do this practice we will explore the third Immeasurable Quality of sympathetic joy. This balances the focus on suffering that is part of any compassion practice with a focus on joy and appreciation. It also helps us build our inner resources for containing and responding to suffering.

Sympathetic Joy

Sympathetic joy is a wish for the good qualities and good fortune of ourselves and others to grow so that we can all flourish and be happy in our lives. It stems from a realisation that we cannot be genuinely happy if those around us are suffering and that we are bound to be happier if those around us are flourishing and happy too. This is simple common sense. If we are only focused on our own good qualities and taking delight in our own good fortune, then our joy will inevitably be limited. If, however, we take joy in the many good qualities and good fortune of each and everyone around us, then our potential for joy is unlimited.

It can be tricky to rejoice in the good fortune of adversaries and those we do not like or find difficult. But even when it comes to people like these, it is simple common sense that if their good qualities and good fortune were to grow and they were to flourish and be happy in their lives, they would surely be less difficult to be around.

In essence, sympathetic joy is based on a simple principle. If we are jealous and resentful of the good fortune and happiness of others, this negative attitude affects our *own mind*. It is toxic and corrosive and undermines our wellbeing. But the person we are jealous of is unaffected by our jealousy and resentment. They remain happy while we become miserable. However, if we practise sympathetic joy we share in their happiness and good fortune and both of us are happy. Therefore, it is a win-win approach to life.

The 'near enemy' of joy is over-excitement, hedonism or grasping at pleasant experiences in a compulsive and addictive way. This stems from an egocentric approach to life in which we seek out the highs and good times for ourselves, in contrast to sympathetic joy which is selfless and other-focused, as indeed are all the Immeasurable Qualities. Furthermore, cultivating this quality results in a quiet upwelling of joy and contentment in contrast to the excitement and buzz of its near enemy.

The 'far enemy' or opposite of joy is competitiveness or jealousy. These emotions often stem from poverty mentality, which is an inner experience of lack or deficit. It is a 'glass half empty' approach to life, in which we only see the downside of things and focus on the negative qualities and bad things that happen to ourselves and others. This results in a desperation to fill that sense of lack and to compete for scarce resources with others who seem to have more than we do. It is also a breeding ground for envy and covetousness as we feel resentful and jealous of those who have what we want and lack.

The opposite of poverty mentality is an attitude of abundance in which we feel grateful for all the good things in our lives and the lives of others. This is a 'glass half full' approach to life that naturally gives birth to the quality of sympathetic joy. In Chapter Two we offered some practices for cultivating gratitude and appreciation that we have suggested people go back to again and again as a way of cultivating the 'glass half full' approach to life.

Furthermore, in the book which we co-wrote with Rob Nairn, *From Mindfulness to Insight*, we look in more detail at how to transform the emotional affliction of jealousy and cultivate the antidote of sympathetic joy.

The contemporary practice of sympathetic rejoicing, goes with the following types of wishes:

- *May the good qualities of myself and others grow.*
- *May I and others experience good fortune.*
- *May I and others flourish in our lives.*

In traditional Buddhist texts, sympathetic joy is associated with the following wish:

- *May all beings experience deep joy untainted by any suffering.*

The rejoicing practice we offer at the end of this chapter follows the practice approach we described in the last chapter. This involves contacting feelings of joy we currently experience, encouraging its growth by using aspirational phrases, expanding it to include different classes of people, and noticing the effects of this practice which might either be the increase of sympathetic joy or encountering blocks and shutting down.

Just like we did in the *Widening the Circle of Loving Kindness* practice, we start with a dear friend and say phrases of rejoicing for them. We then move onto a neutral person and then include ourselves in the circle of rejoicing too. The crunch comes when we choose a rival or someone we are jealous of as the person we rejoice in. This is when we might start shutting down and saying, 'No, not them!' Rob Nairn recounts a story of teaching this practice in South Africa and encouraging people to rejoice in the happiness of adversaries and enemies. One person retorted, 'Well I might consider wishing my enemy to be happy, but *not too happy!*'

We end the practice by symbolically extending our circle of sympathetic joy to include all living beings. Throughout the practice we stay in touch with our thoughts, emotions and sensations, staying open and curious to any feelings of shut down and blocks to the flow of sympathetic joy. As we know well by now, these are just as much part of the practice as the open-hearted flow of joy and appreciation.

In the practice section we also offer a practice for appreciating and rejoicing in small groups. This is a lovely practice and very popular on the retreats we run. As part of this practice people are invited to walk outside and notice things in the surroundings they take delight in. When people return to the practice space they are invited to sit in small groups and gently name the things they took delight in, along with other things in their lives that they take joy in too. The other people in the group sit and listen and simply rejoice in the delights of others. This is a very good practice for integrating one's own gratitude and appreciation with that of rejoicing in the delights of others.

Compassion

It goes without saying that we have been exploring compassion throughout this book. Within the context of the Four Immeasurable Qualities our focus is now on the flow of compassion from self to others. Just as we did with the other Immeasurable Qualities, we start where it is easy to generate compassion and gradually expand it more and more until it becomes limitless.

The 'near enemy' of compassion is pity. This is close to compassion because it involves feeling sorrow for the misfortune of others. But it differs from compassion in that there is a subtle hierarchy where we place ourselves above the person who is suffering. The image that comes to mind is someone on the high horse of good fortune looking down on those who are lowly and miserable. This engenders a subtle ego inflation of putting others down. Likewise, if we experience self-pity, this includes a sense of putting ourselves down.

What pity lacks is the perspective of equanimity where we appreciate how we are all in this life together. We all suffer in our differing ways and we all yearn for happiness and wellbeing. When we practise compassion we put ourselves in the shoes of another person to know what it feels like to suffer the way that they do. We are on the same level as them, not above them. Equality is a crucial component of compassion. We recognise that if we were subject to the same causes and conditions as other people, we would suffer in exactly the same way as they do.

The 'far enemy' of compassion is cruelty. This can range from gross forms such as cruelty to animals to more subtle forms such as trampling on the needs of loved ones through fixating on our own egocentric desires. The practice of compassion is an antidote to egocentric desire. This is something that we explore in more detail in the book, *From Mindfulness to Insight*.

Tonglen

The main practice we focus on under the compassion section of the Four Immeasurable Qualities is tonglen. It is a practice that features strongly in Tibetan Buddhism and is part of the Seven Points of Mind Training (or Lojong) dating back to the eleventh century when the Indian monk, Atisha, first introduced these teachings in Tibet. Lojong is comprised of a set of slogans that each impart a pith instruction. At the heart of this approach is welcoming adversity instead of pushing it away and making obstacles part of one's path. This has been a theme throughout this book. Lojong and tonglen have been popularised in the West by teachers such as Chogyam Trungpa and Pema Chodron.

'Tong' means sending and 'len' means taking. The key instruction of this practice is to give away all our happiness and good fortune and take on the suffering and misfortune of others. This goes directly against our usual egocentric tendency of keeping hold of good feelings and pushing away negative feelings. Many people instinctively resist tonglen when they hear this and one of our students remarked that 'life is already difficult and stressful and the last thing I want to do is take on the suffering of others!' But if we can get over our initial reaction and persist with the practice it can bring an unexpected freedom and release. For many of our students tonglen has proved to be a powerfully transformative compassion practice.

It can serve us in the most challenging times of our lives, such as severe illness or bereavement. It gives us a way to help ourselves and those around us at times when nothing practical can be done to improve a situation and when we feel lost and disempowered. For example, when we sit next to a close friend who is dying, tonglen is a practice we can turn to. We can silently sit beside them and breathe in their suffering on the in-breath, transform this in our heart, and offer them peace and wellbeing on the out-breath. With tonglen any form of adversity is workable and this can instil in us a sense of confidence and hope.

Initially the process of tonglen seems counterproductive but if we reflect more deeply it turns out to be simple common sense. We will offer a series of reflections to demonstrate this.

Our first reflection is 'What is it like to try to keep pain and suffering out?'

When we pose this reflection in workshops the overwhelming response we get is that it is exhausting to try to keep pain away and moreover resistance only compounds the pain we feel. We explored this in Chapter Two when we looked at the metaphor of the two arrows. What we resist persists and if we resist the unavoidable pain of life, which makes up 10% of the problem, we end up adding an additional 90% which then turns the pain into suffering. Instead, if we allow ourselves to feel this pain, the 90% falls away. This is what tonglen helps us do.

Our second reflection is 'What is it like to hold onto happiness?'

The response we get to this reflection is that it is not possible to hold onto happiness and grasping at it is exhausting because it is like trying to take hold of a rainbow. Moreover, the action of grasping distorts the happiness we feel. In the words of William Blake, 'He who binds to himself a joy does the winged life destroy; but he who kisses the joy as it flies lives in eternity's sun rise'.

Our third reflection is 'What is it like to let the suffering in?'

Initially people balk at the prospect but when they reflect more deeply they feel a sense of relief because they realise that it is not as challenging as expected. Letting suffering in does not make it worse. It is the only thing that makes sense as it gives the suffering the space to change and transform.

Our fourth reflection is 'What is it like to give happiness, joy and wisdom, the positive qualities away?'

The response we always receive is that this is a heart opening experience and it allows our positive qualities to grow, rather than to diminish. It leads to genuine happiness and wellbeing.

For Pema Chodron the root of suffering is closing down our hearts and minds and the root of happiness is opening them up. In her book *Start Where You Are* (2003) Pema Chodron speaks of the mind and heart being like our own special room where all the doors are closed and the windows barred. We work very hard to keep the conditions inside our room within our tight parameters of like and dislike as this keeps us within our comfort zone. When someone we don't like tries to enter the room, we can get very defensive and reactive. Also when life circumstances don't go the way we like, we add more layers of armour to protect our room and while this might help keep out the thing we don't like, it also constricts our hearts and minds more and more. We feel more closed in and defensive. This ego contraction is the root of suffering and this is also the main focus of the tonglen practice.

It takes courage and practise to open our hearts. As we mentioned before, Chogyam Trungpa, in his book *Training the*

Mind (2005), talks poignantly about a soft spot in the heart, which is tender and sore like a bruise or an open wound. This is what we are protecting in our boarded up room. Through the practice of tonglen, we begin to open the windows a tiny crack. This lets the air in, but it also exposes our tender and vulnerable heart to the inevitable vicissitudes and discomfort of life. The key message of the tonglen practice is that if we stay in our window of tolerance and gradually open our heart to the pain of life, this will not harm us or cause us more pain; instead it will enliven us and reconnect us to the wonder and joy of life. But it is important that we proceed slowly and stay within our window of tolerance.

Compassionate Breathing

For this reason a good way to begin the process is to do a practice called Compassionate Breathing. This is an adaption of tonglen devised by Chris Germer and Kristin Neff as part of their Mindful Self-Compassion training programme.

The key difference from tonglen is that compassionate breathing entails breathing in happiness on the in-breath and breathing out happiness on the out-breath too, whereas tonglen involves breathing in suffering on the in-breath and breathing out happiness on the out-breath. So it is much easier to do. What is useful with this practice is that we get used to the breathing process and we start with positive feelings before moving on to transform negative feelings.

Many people find this practice very helpful. It works by enlisting the power of intention and imagination. When we breathe in we imagine drawing in positive energies of healing, vitality and wellbeing from the environment around us and imagine that these energies completely fill us up and permeate every cell of our body.

Intention is powerful. Just think about walking in nature and all the beauty and vitality and wholesome energies all around us. A lot of the time we are not open to receiving these life affirming energies because we inadvertently block them through dwelling on our worries and issues. This is the negativity bias of the brain that we described in previous chapters. Through intending to connect to the positive we open a window in our hearts and minds to invite it in.

To begin with we breathe in positive energy and then simply relax and let go as we breathe out. We do this for a while until we feel we have built up some inner capacity, a bit like filling our inner gas tank. Once we feel sufficiently resourced we then imagine breathing out positivity and wellbeing to those people who are in our immediate vicinity. On the in-breath we breathe positive energy in and on the out-breath we breathe it out to those around us. In this way we alternate between self-compassion and compassion for others.

This practice is very helpful in everyday stressful situations. If, for example, we find ourselves in a deadlocked meeting at work, instead of tearing our hair out we can do this practice, offering kindness to ourself on the inbreath and offering spaciousness and ease to the other people in the meeting on the outbreath. Given that all of life is intimately interconnected, so too is our meeting and even this subtle shift in focus and attitude can bring about a significant easing up of the tensions and stresses of the people in the meeting. Similarly, we can use the compassionate breathing practice in many other situations in our daily lives too.

Practising Tonglen

We are now ready to start doing the tonglen practice itself. It is useful to reflect that this practice trains us in the two aspects of compassion that we described in Chapter Two. These two aspects make up our working definition of compassion, which is 'sensitivity to the suffering of self and others with a deep commitment to relieve suffering and its causes'. When we take in suffering we are turning towards it and becoming sensitive to it, which is the first part of the definition, and when we send out compassion, we are offering relief from suffering which is the second part of the definition.

There are some key components to the practice of tonglen. These are: the compassionate self, the sphere of compassion in the heart and the breathing process.

We always do the tonglen practice from the perspective of our compassionate self. If we try to do the practice as our ordinary selves it can feel like there is too much to take on. This is often a complaint made by people who are new to the practice. By now we should be familiar with identifying with our inner compassionate self by cultivating the qualities of kindness, strength, courage and wisdom. This has been an ongoing theme in our practice since Chapter Eight.

Another familiar theme from previous chapters is imagining a sphere of light or energy in our heart centre. This sphere is the agent of transformation. It is a place of vulnerability and power through which we are able to transform all the negative energies and suffering into the energy of compassion. Many mystical traditions see this as being located in the heart centre — not the physical heart but the centre of the chest. When we practise tonglen we breathe suffering into this place.

The underlying principle here is that all energy is fundamentally pure, it is just that it gets distorted in different ways and these show up as emotional afflictions and suffering. In both the tantric tradition of Buddhism and the Alchemist tradition of the West there is an understanding that we can purify negative emotions and redeem their inherent purity, which then becomes a source of healing and vitality instead of being a source of suffering. This is the essence of the tonglen practice and it is the function of the sphere in the heart centre. For those who find it that it does not work for them to imagine a sphere in the heart, another approach is simply to feel a compassionate presence in the heart centre and imagine this to be the focus of transformation.

The third key component in the tonglen process is breathing. When we take in suffering we imagine doing so as we breathe in, and when we send out compassion we imagine doing so as we breathe out. The reason why the breath is used as a vehicle for the practice is because it is a natural process happening all the time. But it is important not to be too literal about breathing in suffering. We do not literally breathe suffering into our lungs and chest. This is where it can start to feel too much. In some Buddhist versions of tonglen people are instructed to breathe in the suffering of all beings in the form of smoke which they breathe into their hearts. If we take this too literally we might start coughing and spluttering and give up the practice! Instead, as we breathe in we can imagine drawing suffering towards our heart centre, where all of it gets transformed by the sphere in the heart and as we breathe out compassion flows out from the sphere. It does not need to be breathed into our lungs and chest. The breathing is useful because it lends a rhythm and flow to the practice.

One way of getting a feeling for the tonglen practice is to imagine sitting by a campfire late one night under the stars in a chilly clearing in a forest. The fire is starting to die down and as the cold begins to bite we blow onto the embers. We also add twigs and leaves and kindling wood as fuel to get the fire going again. As we blow on the embers they consume the fuel and glow more brightly whilst emitting heat as we huddle up close. The more fuel we add and the more we blow on the glowing embers the brighter they get and the more heat they generate.

This is a helpful analogy for the tonglen practice. We can imagine the sphere of energy in the heart centre as the ember of the fire and as we breathe into it, it glows more brightly and draws in as fuel any negativity, toxic energy or stress that we might be feeling. The more fuel there is, the brighter it glows and the more 'heat' it generates in the form of vitality, compassion and positive energy. In the practice section below we will offer a way of priming the process of tonglen by using the embers of a campfire image.

Tonglen Movement

A useful next step is to do a movement practice that expresses the process of tonglen through physical movement. Many of our students really get tonglen when they do this practice. They find that the gestures of tonglen movement give them an embodied feeling of taking in suffering and sending out compassion.

Also, tonglen is generally taught by starting with the taking in of non-specific suffering, like an atmosphere or negative vibe. Many of us are sensitive to atmospheres and can immediately sense a gloomy atmosphere in a place or amongst a group of people. In this instance, we use the non-specific form of tonglen as part of the movement practice.

We describe how to do tonglen movement in the practice section below. Since many people connect very well with tonglen movement and find it preferable to sitting tonglen, it is also permissible to do the movement practice whilst relating to suffering in a specific way by focusing on another person, or oneself, as described below.

Tonglen for Another

We use tonglen to take in suffering in a specific way by first focusing on another person and then ourself. We do it in this order because it is generally easier to focus on another person as it requires more skill in imagining the practice in relation to ourselves. We then extend the practice to include all beings everywhere.

Just as we did with the loving kindness and rejoicing practices, we start with someone (or an animal) we feel close to and for whom feelings of compassion flow easily and naturally.

We bring this person or animal to mind using our imagination. One option is to visualise the person in the context we know them in (at home, at work or somewhere else). Another option is to get a feeling of the presence of this person and sensing how they suffer. A third option is just to know the person or animal is there and how much they suffer. We can use any of these options or a combination of all three. It all depends on how our imagination works. The important thing is to bring this person to mind and let their pain and suffering touch us. It needs to feel alive and genuine.

We then breathe a little deeper and make the in-breath and out-breath a similar length and rhythm. As we do so, we get in touch with our compassionate heart and begin to breathe in the suffering of the person in front of us into the sphere in our heart centre. This causes the sphere to glow, like blowing on the embers of a fire. All the suffering is transformed by the sphere in our heart, like the twigs and leaves that are consumed by the glowing embers of the fire. None of the suffering gets stuck; it is all transformed into the energy of compassion. Then we breathe out this energy of compassion to the person or animal in front of us. It becomes exactly what they need to relieve their suffering and bring them joy and wellbeing. We can imagine the process of tonglen on every breath or every third or fourth breath. It is important not to feel overtaxed by the practice and to do it in way that feels manageable and relaxed.

As we breathe in, we imagine breathing in the texture and atmosphere of suffering, however that might manifest for us. The suffering may be visualised as a colour or mist. Alternatively, it may be imagined as a feeling, or it may be expressed in words. We might breathe in a grey mist of suffering. We might breathe in feelings of sadness, anger, fear or claustrophobia depending on the type of suffering the person we are focusing on is experiencing. We might breathe in and say words to ourselves representing the texture of suffering, such as 'heavy, hot, tight, suffering' or representing the feelings of suffering, such as 'sadness, fear, isolation'. We might use a combination of imagery, feelings and words. We allow our imagination to manifest in its own way and in its own time.

As we breath out, we imagine breathing out compassionate relief in whichever way spontaneously comes to mind to relieve the suffering of the person concerned. It might be love or ease or spaciousness or something practical that meets their needs. The compassionate relief that we breathe out may be a colour or a mist radiating out from our compassionate heart. Alternatively, we might transmit feelings from our compassionate heart, such as joy, kindness, courage or openness, depending on what is most needed to relieve their suffering. We might breathe out and say words to ourselves representing the texture of the relief, such as 'bright, soothing, open relief' or representing the qualities of compassion, such as 'calm, kind, courageous compassion'. Again, we allow our imagination to express itself in its own way and in its own time.

If we experience a reaction or block to taking on the suffering of another person we can shift the focus of the practice to the block we are experiencing. Whilst being curious and accepting of this block, we can imagine breathing it into the sphere in our heart where it is completely transformed, and then breathing out to this part of ourself exactly what it needs. If we find that difficult, we can simply rejoice in our wish to transform the suffering of ourselves and others and step back to doing a mindfulness or self-compassion practice from before. We can then set an intention to come back to the tonglen practice when we feel adequately resourced.

For some people the tonglen practice can feel a bit contrived in the beginning; but try to keep going because there is a magic and beauty to this practice that comes through practising it. Sometimes we can feel numb, drowsy or distracted, in which case just explore how numbness, drowsiness or distraction feels with acceptance and curiosity. Always remember that there is no right or wrong way for this practice to unfold and that whatever happens provides us with an opportunity to become familiar with our habits of mind.

Once we have become familiar with doing tonglen for someone who is close to us, we can follow the usual approach from the Four Immeasurable Qualities of focusing on other people who are near and dear, then extend it to people we feel neutral towards, and finally extend it to those we find difficult and triggering. The reason for extending outwards in this way is to loosen up our preference system of like and dislike because this is what keeps us contracted and locked in suffering. This is the equanimity aspect of the Four Immeasurable Qualities that underpins each of the other ones.

This does not need to be done in a formulaic way, but it can be done quite intuitively and spontaneously. We might start the practice with someone who is a dear friend that we know is suffering. Maybe the dear friend is experiencing anxiety, in which case we bring to mind others who are also experiencing anxiety and do the tonglen practice for them all. This is the classic Buddhist approach to doing tonglen — we focus on one person and then imagine that the suffering of all beings who suffer in a similar way is breathed into our heart too. What is important here is to understand that all of this suffering will not overwhelm us, all of it is fuel for the process of transformation in our compassionate heart, and all of it is transformed and offered to these many beings that they may find relief from suffering. But this step depends on our confidence in the practice and how resourced we feel. If it is too much to begin with, then it is best to leave this step out and just practise tonglen for the original person we brought to mind.

As the practice progresses, gradually the suffering we are breathing in lessens and becomes exactly the same as the compassionate relief that we are breathing out until finally we are breathing in the qualities of love and compassion and breathing them out. Then we allow the tonglen practice to dissolve and rest in open awareness.

Tonglen for Self

This variation of tonglen can form part of tonglen for another when we feel stuck and blocked doing that practice. If this happens, we then make our experience of feeling stuck the focus of our practice. We described this above. It can also be done as a standalone practice. The same key elements we described in the sections above apply to tonglen for self: compassionate self, sphere in the heart and using the breath as a medium for the practice.

Many people find this practice very helpful in relating to parts of themselves they are struggling with. For example, if we feel very anxious tonglen is a useful way of engaging the energy of anxiety and it gives us a method for working with it in a very direct and immediate way. We breathe the anxiety into the sphere in the heart and imagine it being transformed into a proactive energy that serves us and does not hinder us.

A helpful way of approaching self-tonglen is using the mandala model that we described in Chapter Nine. We begin by imagining that we identify with our compassionate self. This takes us to the centre of our personal mandala. Once there we become attuned to what is active and needing attention on the periphery. There might be anger or frustration present, or maybe anxiety or perhaps feelings of sadness. Tonglen gives us a way of positively engaging with what is moving through the mind at the level of the periphery. Each time a difficult emotion arises we welcome it and breathe it into the sphere in the heart, feeling it transform and imagining that the wisdom and vitality within the emotion is released. We then send this back to the part of us that is struggling. This can instil a feeling of confidence within us. Everything feels workable. Even negative and heavy and stuck emotions can be welcomed, drawn in and transformed. The more we do it, the more we trust in the transforming potential of compassion through the practice of tonglen.

Tonglen on the Spot

Tonglen on the spot is a daily life application of tonglen. This term was coined by Pema Chodron and refers to the fact that tonglen is best applied in life when we encounter difficulty, stress or suffering. It is important to practise tonglen in the formal way as described above because this refines the skill and gives us a feeling for the practice. But just like most other compassion practices the important thing is to bring it directly into our lives. Here we apply it intuitively and spontaneously whenever we encounter situations of stress, difficulty or suffering.

For example, we might be walking down a city street heading towards a meeting when we encounter a person who is homeless sitting on the side of the road. In situations like these it is very easy to turn away from the palpable suffering of this person. We might even reach into our pocket and throw them a coin or two, less out of generosity and more out of a wish not to really see them. In situations like these, tonglen is a practice we can turn to as a way of working directly with our feelings of avoidance and aversion. Instead of speeding away after we have made our token offering we take in the reality of this person's life as they sit on the sidewalk. We let their pain touch us and then use the tonglen method of breathing their suffering into our hearts, imagining it transform, and then breathing out a compassionate energy towards this person that takes the form of whatever they most need in that moment. In this way we are turning towards whatever suffering we encounter in our lives by breathing it in and we practise relieving that suffering each time we breathe out.

The net effect of this practice is that we allow ourselves to feel connected to this person. The more we do this as we go about our lives the more enlivened and connected we feel. We sense that we are part of something bigger than our immediate preoccupations and daily issues. We are part of life and life is part of us. This is the gift of tonglen.

Another aspect of this practice is that whenever we experience something joyful and pleasing in our day, we offer these good qualities to others as we breathe out. In this way we are not grasping onto the pleasant and uplifting moments of our day, but we are willing to let them go and to give them to others. Ironically, we do not lose anything. Our happiness and wellbeing increases.

Practice Section

Formal Sitting Practice

Practice 25: Rejoicing (20 – 30 minutes)
Begin by forming the intention to practise compassion for yourself and others, and then reaffirm your compassionate motivation. In particular, bring to mind the verse in the Four Limitless Contemplations:

May all beings experience joy and wellbeing.

Next follow the mindfulness stages of settling, grounding and resting. Take a few slightly deeper breaths, focusing in particular on the out-breath; in so doing, bring your awareness more fully into the body, feeling the contact and pressure of your body resting on the ground. Mind resting in the body, like the body rests on the ground.

Now soften around how you feel in the body, allowing your experience to be as it is. It may help to place your hand on your heart as a gesture of self-soothing. Feel the warmth of the touch and the movement of the breath through your chest. If you like, you can form a half-smile, and adopt a gentle voice tone in how you guide yourself. In this way consciously engender a kind and compassionate attitude to yourself.

Begin the practice with someone you care about and for whom it is easy to rejoice. Think of their happiness, pleasure or good fortune. Engender the mind that feels no jealousy or competitiveness. Make the aspiration that their good qualities expand and grow. You can use simple phrases like: 'May your good qualities grow and grow; may you flourish in your life'. Cultivate this aspiration until it feels genuine.

Now expand your circle of rejoicing to include other loved ones, family and friends. Reflect on their qualities, opportunities, prosperity or good fortune — rejoice in each of these things and make the wish that they increase.

Once you have become accustomed to the practice, extend it to strangers and people you feel indifferent towards. Bring to mind actual people you have contact with on a daily basis.

Now expand your circle of rejoicing to people you dislike and find challenging. Focus in particular on people you are jealous of. Actively cultivate the wish that their good fortune increases and they become happy. For example, if you are jealous of someone's popularity, then make the wish that they become even more popular and derive great happiness and joy from this quality.

If you encounter resistances or blocks and the feeling of rejoicing does not flow, then tune into how you feel in your body and notice any areas of tension and stress. Work with the self-compassion approach of breathing into any areas of tension, softening around them and allowing them to be present. Then reaffirm your intention in this way: 'At this moment I can't open my heart to this person, but I maintain the wish that one day I'll be able to open my heart more fully than today'.

Now expand your circle of rejoicing to all living beings everywhere, making the wish that all their good qualities grow and that they flourish. You can conclude with the verse from the Four Limitless Contemplations: *May all beings experience joy and wellbeing*. Then rest without any particular focus.

Practice 26: Compassionate Breathing (15 minutes)

Begin by forming an intention to practise compassion for yourself and others, and then reaffirm your compassionate motivation: why you want to practise compassion.

Sit in a relaxed and comfortable posture on a cushion or chair. Then pay attention to the rising and falling of your body as you breathe. To help settle your mind, try deepening your in-breath a little and lengthening your out-breath. See if you can regulate your breathing so that your in-breath and out-breath are of a similar length and rhythm. You might like to count to three or four on the in-breath and a similar count on the out-breath. When your mind begins to settle, let go of counting and let your breathing find its natural rhythm.

As you breathe in imagine that you are breathing in a healing energy of compassion from the environment around you. It is endowed with the qualities of kindness, vitality and wellbeing. Through intending to connect with the healing energies around you, you open to the possibility of receiving them. You can imagine that this healing energy takes the form of a colour that you associate with kindness and compassion.

As you breathe in this healing energy of compassion it completely fills up your body and mind and permeates every cell in your body. In particular imagine it going to those parts of you that need healing and care. As you breathe out simply relax and let go.

Do this until you feel sufficiently filled up and resourced with the healing energy of compassion. Then, as you breathe out imagine breathing out this healing energy of compassion to all those who are in your immediate vicinity. Think that it gives them exactly what they need: if they are stressed, it brings them calm; if they are sad, it uplifts them; if they are lonely, it brings support; if they are in pain, it brings relief from pain.

As you breathe in, kindness and compassion flows in. As you breathe out, kindness and compassion flows out. Once you have set up the process, trust that it happens by itself without any effort on your part. In this way you are integrating the process of self-compassion and compassion for others using the breath as a medium.

Once you come to the end of your designated practice session, spend a few moments resting without any focus and let go of trying to meditate. As a way of concluding your practice session, you might want to do a simple sharing something like this: 'I intend to carry the practice of compassion into my daily life, with the motivation to connect to others who are like me and who struggle like me'. Then stretch your body and slowly get up. See if you can carry the awareness of your practice session into the next moments of your day.

Practice 27: Tonglen Movement (5 – 10 minutes)
Begin tonglen movement by standing in an upright posture with your feet a hip-width apart and then place one foot slightly in front of the other. Tune into your breathing and breathe a little deeper than usual, making the in and out breaths a similar length and rhythm. As you breathe in, shift your weight onto the back foot and lean slightly back. Then as you breathe out, shift your weight onto the front foot and lean slightly forward. You can change feet from time to time.

Then add the arms. Start with the hands on the heart, getting in touch with your innate capacity for limitless compassion symbolised by the sphere in your heart centre. As you breathe out, move your hands forward and out to the sides in a gesture of giving or sending. As you breathe in, move your hands back to your heart in a gesture of gathering or taking in.

Next, when you draw your hands towards your heart centre on the in-breath, imagine you are drawing in any negative atmosphere or energy from the environment around you, which is completely transformed by the sphere of compassion in your heart centre. Even if there is no discernible negative atmosphere in the place where you are doing the practice, you can still imagine breathing in any feelings of suffering that might be present in the locality where you are. Then, as you extend your arms out on the out-breath, imagine breathing out compassionate relief from suffering wherever this is most needed.

Now integrate all the elements of the practice as you move. As you breathe in take in any suffering with a gesture of gathering. As you breathe out send out compassionate relief with a gesture of giving. You can also do the tonglen movement in a specific way by focusing on someone else or yourself, in which case follow the practice instructions below and integrate them into your movement practice.

After doing the movement for 5 – 10 minutes come back to standing with your hands on your heart centre and then move your hands back down to your sides and conclude the practice.

Practice 28: Tonglen for Another (20 – 30 minutes)
Begin by forming the intention to practise compassion for yourself and others, and then reaffirm your compassionate motivation: why you want to practise compassion.

Sit in a relaxed and comfortable posture on a cushion or chair. Then pay attention to the rising and falling of your body as you breathe. To help settle your mind, deepen your in-breath a little and lengthen your out-breath. See if you can regulate your breathing so that your in-breath and out-breath are of a similar length and rhythm. You might like to count to three or four on the in-breath and a similar count on the out-breath.

When your mind begins to settle, let go of counting and let your breathing find its natural rhythm.

Now consciously identify with your compassionate self: body like a mountain, breath like the wind and mind like the clear blue sky, with a sphere of compassion in your heart centre that radiates warmth like sunshine.

Now imagine that sitting in front of you is someone in your life whom you know to be suffering. Open yourself to this person's suffering and let yourself feel connected with them, being aware of all their difficulties. Feel within you a strong compassionate intention to release this person from their suffering and its causes.

Breathe in the other person's suffering, in whatever form it takes, and visualise it coming into your heart-center where the sphere of compassion burns it up like fuel, strengthening your capacity for compassion and wisdom. As you breathe out, consider that you are sending to the other person, in whatever form it takes, all your healing love, warmth, energy, confidence and joy.

You can imagine the sphere of compassion in your heart centre like the embers of fire. When you breathe into the sphere it glows just as when you breathe onto the embers of a fire. Similarly, just as the glowing embers of a fire consume twigs and leaves as fuel and emit heat, so too does the sphere in the heart consume the suffering you breathe in and emit the warmth of compassion as you breathe out.

Allow your imagination to imagine the energy of suffering that is breathed in, in its own way, for example as texture, colour or felt sense, as is described above. You can focus on the flow of feeling: being open and connected to this person's pain, drawing it towards you on the in-breath and letting it touch your heart, and then offering this person feelings of spaciousness, loving-kindness and care as you breathe out. Similarly, you can allow your imagination to imagine the energy of compassion that is breathed out, in its own way, as is described above.

Also, if you find yourself feeling blocked or going numb, then shift your attention to these feelings in yourself and make them the focus of the practice, breathing in these feelings on the in-breath and breathing out spaciousness and freedom from being blocked on the out-breath.

Continue this 'giving and receiving' with each breath (or every second or third breath) for as long as you wish. At the end of the practice, consider that your compassion has completely dissolved all the person's suffering and its causes, filling them with wellbeing, peace, happiness and love.

As your tonglen practice becomes stronger, you can gradually imagine others who are suffering in front of you — colleagues, patients, relatives or even strangers — and practise taking in and transforming their suffering, offering them all your happiness, clarity, understanding, forgiveness and love. Feel a firm conviction that all their suffering and negativity is relieved. Allow yourself to feel a sense of joy that you have been able to successfully free others from their pain and suffering.

As you conclude each session of tonglen, dedicate its positive energy and healing power to those you have visualised and all other living beings too.

Practice 29: Tonglen for Self (20 – 30 minutes)

Begin by forming the intention to practise compassion for yourself and others, and then reaffirm your compassionate motivation: why you want to practise compassion.

Sit in a relaxed and comfortable posture on a cushion or chair. Then pay attention to the rising and falling of your body as you breathe. To help settle your mind, you might like to deepen your in-breath a little and lengthen your out-breath. See if you can regulate your breathing so that your in-breath and out-breath are of a similar length and rhythm. You might like to count to three or four on the in-breath and a similar count on the out-breath. When your mind begins to settle, let go of counting and let your breathing find its natural rhythm.

Now consciously identify with your compassionate self: body like a mountain, breath like the wind and mind like the clear blue sky, with a sphere of compassion in your heart centre that emits warmth like sunshine. Imagine that this takes you to the centre of your personal mandala.

As you become aware of the parts that lie on your periphery, notice if there is a part that is active and calling for your attention. While remaining identified with the compassionate self, bring awareness to this part of you that is struggling — perhaps feeling lonely, fearful, misunderstood, angry, or troubled by physical illness or grief. As you look towards this part of you and become aware of the suffering you've been carrying, pay attention to the detail of your experience. Let its pain and struggle touch you and hold it with a warm and compassionate concern. If you notice any resistance to opening to yourself in this way, just become aware of this resistance and hold it gently in your awareness.

Now consider and allow this suffering as an energy and with each in-breath imagine that you breathe it into your heart centre, where the sphere of compassion burns it up like fuel, strengthening your capacity for compassion and wisdom. As you exhale, imagine that you freely give out understanding, joy, unconditional love and peace, in the form of an energy of compassion, to the suffering part of you. Allow your imagination to imagine the energy of suffering and energy of compassion in its own way, maybe with particular textures, colours, feelings or words.

Focus on the flow of feeling: being open and connected to the pain of this part of you, drawing it towards your compassionate self on the in-breath and letting it touch your heart, and then offering this part of you spaciousness, loving-kindness and care as you breathe out.

There is no need to imagine too ardently — just set up the process and trust that the breathing does the work. What is important is the intention of drawing suffering towards you and breathing out release from suffering on the out-breath, and then trusting that the process happens by itself.

As you continue the practice, imagine that this part of you is gradually relieved of suffering and filled with wellbeing and joy. Each time you conclude, consider that the practice has been completely effective: this part of you is released from all pain and distress and is now happy and at peace. Then rest loosely without any specific focus.

Finally, dedicate any positive energy and healing power to all other living beings who suffer like you do.

Informal Daily Life Practice

Practice 30: Appreciating and Rejoicing *(in small groups)*

Begin by walking outside in nature and notice the things you take delight in. These might be small things like the smell of a spring blossom, the cool wind on your face or the smile of a child. Pay attention to these positive experiences, spend some time appreciating them and absorb their goodness and vitality. Then come back inside and sit in small groups of four to six people and prepare for the practice by settling and grounding in the usual way. Tune into the moment and the people who are sharing this moment with you. Then bring to mind the things that bring you joy and pleasure, both from walking outside and from your life in general. These might be significant events or small fleeting moments. Begin to softly name these things as they come to your mind, allowing the feelings of joy and pleasure to expand and inhabit your body, mind and emotions. This can be done in a spontaneous way, with different people in the small group softly naming moments of joy, and then pausing as a way of savouring this experience.

As you resume the naming of your delights, while keeping the connection with your own sense of joy, begin to tune into the joy of others, by allowing ourselves to resonate with the things that they are naming and rejoicing in their happiness.

Can you resonate with their happiness, even when you don't share their enthusiasm for a particular pleasure? What does this feel like and what effect does it have on your own feeling of joy?

After doing this practice for about 15 minutes, fall back into silence and simply rest with the feelings brought up by the practice. Then share in the small group what it was like to do this practice together.

Practice 31: Tonglen on the Spot

You can practice tonglen in everyday life situations. This is often when it is most effective. For example, if you're walking down a street and you notice someone in pain or distress, on-the-spot tonglen means that you do not just close down and rush away. Let the humanity of this person touch you, breathe in their distress with the wish that they be free of suffering, and then send them warm wishes and feelings of happiness on the out-breath.

If you find that the other person's pain brings up fear or resistance in you, then do tonglen for these feelings and reactions in yourself. The idea behind this practice is to work through your own blocks and resistances, so that you can relate to changing life situations in a fresh and open way.

Here is another example of tonglen on the spot. If you have missed a train and feel irritated and upset, on the in-breath imagine drawing into your own irritation all the frustration of others who are angry and irritated about late transport. Imagine it is transformed in your heart centre and then breathe out relief for the frustration of others on the out-breath. This has the effect of expanding outwards and counteracting the tendency to contract inwards around our own irritation and distress.

Alternatively, if you experience some feelings of happiness and joy, instead of grasping onto these feelings and keeping them for yourself, use the tonglen method and offer these feelings to others as you breathe out, in this way sharing these feelings with those around you.

Chapter Thirteen

Compassion in Action

As long as space endures,
and as long as sentient beings exist,
until then, may I too remain
to dispel the sufferings of the world.
Shantideva

By Kristine Mackenzie-Janson and Fay Adams

At this point, let's circle back to motivation and take another look at its importance. We have been generating our compassionate motivation at the beginning of each practice and we may now have a sense of its power, like a force that propels our practice in the right direction. A truly compassionate motivation can be summarised thus — to nurture ourselves and our potential and turn our attention towards benefitting others as best we can. However, we may have come to realise that, in reality, our motivations are complex, inconsistent and mixed. That said, by committing over and over to a compassionate motivation, we are gradually opening more fully to our ever-present compassionate heart, giving it the possibility to express itself in our thoughts, feelings and actions.

In this chapter we will look at how the compassionate heart can be a powerful force not only for our sitting practice, but also for our way of being in the world, enabling us to act with courage and compassion either quietly and modestly in our own backyard or with big vision and grand strokes in the world at large.

Basic Goodness

There is an age-old debate about whether, as humans, we are basically decent, or basically depraved and selfish. This question has preoccupied philosophers, anthropologists and scientists of all kinds for centuries (Bregman, 2021), not to mention spiritual practitioners.

Over the course of modern history the view that we are violent and greedy by nature has been favoured, but just recently an array of academics from psychologists to biologists have been arguing that this grim view of humanity needs radical revision (Gabbatiss, 2017). Most agree that although we are indeed wired for violence and greed, we are also wired for caring, joy and cooperation. What shows up for us depends on culture and life circumstances.

We are deeply conditioned to notice and cultivate our self-interest and not to acknowledge the potential for caring that lies at the core of our being. Perhaps the Christian idea of original sin has something to answer for here. Moreover, we are subject to the continuous onslaught of bad news coming to us through the media making us over-focused on all the troubles of the world. Yet if we pause to look, the potential for selfless caring has been there all along. It's just that we tend to screen it out.

Evolutionary biologist, Dacher Keltner, says we should re-imagine human evolution as the survival of the kindest, rather than the fittest! It is only in the last few decades that science has begun to explore the presence of positive emotions and drives, and now Keltner and others are persuading us that we should confidently trust that humans are essentially good (Keltner, 2010).

How does it feel to pause and let this touch your own experience of life? If you *felt* deep within you that your basic nature is good and that your care for others and the world is a powerful force that dwells within your heart all the time, how would that change things for you? And if you *felt* that you could trust this capacity in others, would your experience of the world shift? Of course, the opposite is also true. This is not to deny the harsh reality of human ill-will, greed and destructiveness that has wreaked havoc on our planet. The shift is to realise that basic goodness is *also* a truth, and one that we can live by. It all comes down to what we choose to believe in and give our energy to.

David Adams, a neurophysiologist and psychologist, researched how people's beliefs about human nature influenced their likelihood of taking action for peace. Adams and others conducted studies on student attitudes, and they observed a negative correlation between the belief that violence was innate and peace activism. 'If you think that war is inevitable, why oppose it?' he said (Brach, 2020).

In the practice section below, we offer a practice for valuing basic goodness that has always been present but which we have mostly taken for granted. Far from being a distant dream, it is woven through every aspect of our lives. It is a basic connection to feeling. We are feeling beings and so we are very vulnerable to life's beauty as well as to its suffering. Buddhist nun, Pema Chodron, writes of basic goodness in the following way:

(It) is available in moments of caring for things when we clean our glasses or brush our hair. It's available in moments of appreciation when we notice the blue sky or pause and listen to the rain. It is available in moments of gratitude when we recall a kindness or recognise another person's courage. It is available in music and dance, in art, and in poetry. Whenever we let go of holding onto ourselves and look at the world around us, whenever we connect with sorrow, whenever we connect with joy, whenever we drop our resentment and complaint, in those moments [basic goodness] is there. (2000)

In his book *Born to be Good*, Dacher Keltner describes the prevalence of positive emotions at the heart of human nature across all cultures (2009). These include our propensity to appreciate and smile, emotions like awe and amusement, how readily we respond to kind touch and the many modest moments of goodness we encounter day to day.

The Spiral of the Work That Reconnects

Having opened the door to basic goodness in ourselves, we will now explore how we can bring our compassion into action in a wider context, in the community and society we are part of, and in the environment and world we live in.

First, let's revisit our working definition of compassion: *Sensitivity to suffering of self and others, with a strong commitment to relieve this suffering and its causes.* If we want to grow our compassion and actively contribute to creating the world we'd like to live in, it will require us to expand the reach of our hearts and turn towards what is difficult. Yet that's not straightforward in a world that faces so many challenges: from the climate crisis to social injustice; to the loss of ecosystems and species; and to poverty, racism and inequality — all of which can feel overwhelming. Of course, none of us can solve these big issues on our own, and luckily we don't have to. As Joanna Macy, whose work we will explore more in this chapter, says: 'You don't need to do everything. Do what calls your heart; effective action comes from love. It is unstoppable, and it is enough' (Macy and Johnstone, 2012).

Therefore, each of us can do what we can and practise compassion in action in those areas that are closest to our hearts. In the words of Frederick Beuchner, we're called to 'the place where your deep gladness and the world's deep hunger meet'. Finding this place requires a willingness, an openness and (re) connecting with both our love and concern for the world and what's happening around us.

Buddhist scholar and environmental activist, Joanna Macy, has developed a pathway which many people have found to be extremely helpful called *The Work That Reconnects* (https://workthatreconnects.org/). It's often depicted in a spiral shape, which can be a useful container for holding big topics in a way that turns debilitating worry into powerful compassionate action. It is an 'outer practice' that is a seamless extension from our practice of mindfulness and compassion on the cushion.

Gratitude

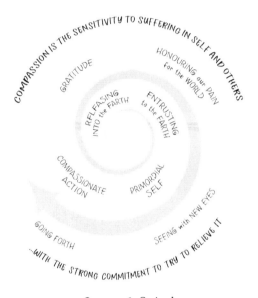

Image 6. Spiral

The spiral starts by resourcing ourselves through connecting with gratitude for what's good and wholesome in this life. Not only does gratitude and appreciation give rise to good feelings, but it opens us up to what we love and therefore what we want to care for and protect. For example, if we connect with the joy of the first hint of spring in the air, this opens us to the interdependence between the cleanness of the air and our own good health. In fact, when we look deeply, we can see a profound relationship with all life around us, and this awareness of interconnectedness together with gratitude is a powerful motivation to move beyond our comfort zone and grow our sensitivity to the suffering in ourselves and in the world around us. We may even come to honour our pain for the world we are part of and see it as the other side of the coin of our love for the world.

Honouring Our Pain for the World

This can range from sensing the struggles of those who are near and dear to opening up to the reality of other human beings who live in a different part of the world and who look different to us or have different values and beliefs, but who struggle in similar ways to those we love and hold dear. Despite apparent differences, everyone longs to be happy and healthy, safe and free from discrimination and oppression, with equal opportunities for flourishing in their life. Honouring our pain for the world might also include connecting to the suffering of animals or other living species which are facing threats to their ecosystem or even extinction. And then there's the pain that comes with connecting with places that are threatened, whether it's a local woodland that is due to be cleared for some new road or railway, or an entire ecosystem whose existence is endangered by the climate crisis, pollution or 'development'.

It may seem that allowing ourselves to feel this pain is needlessly upsetting since, after all, what good are my tears to big wildfires on the other side of the world, to melting icecaps or to systemic oppression of minority groups? But, through numbing our pain, our love can't flow freely, and our growing compassion may have a reach and effect that we can't yet fathom.

Seeing with New/Ancient Eyes

With this increased sensitivity to the suffering in ourselves and others, we may again need resourcing to see what the *strong commitment to try to relieve it* might look like. Connecting with empowering and inspiring perspectives can help here. There are many such perspectives within which we can redefine our sense of identity and community. Some of these may feel new to us in Western industrialised and individualised societies, but perhaps they were more familiar to our ancestors and indigenous cultures alive today — hence the term 'seeing with new/ancient eyes'.

In his book *The Myth Gap* (2017), Alex Evans argues that what the world needs most is 'a larger us and a longer now'. We looked at how to practise widening our circles of compassion in Chapter 11 of this book, and this sense of 'us' doesn't have to stop at human beings but could include animals and plant life too — 'all sentient beings' as it's often phrased in Buddhist texts. We can draw strength from our ancestors who survived in very challenging circumstances to pass on the precious gift of life to us now. Connecting with the generations to come can be a powerful motivation to live in such a way that we leave them with the best chances for flourishing.

Power is often seen as something there is only a limited amount of — 'if you have it then I don't'. This could be called 'power over'. Yet, there is another kind of power that is not based on hierarchy in this way, which we might call 'power with'. It is the kind of power that comes through collaboration, and the question that goes with it is: 'what am I part of?' It is the drop in the ocean, which seems tiny and insignificant, but together with many other drops forms a powerful wave. When reflecting on what enabled good and important things to come about, you may find that it was your patience, tenacity, kindness, deep listening, or acceptance that made it so — qualities that we might not normally think of as ingredients of power, but gathered together, they can bring about powerful changes. Also, it's clear that no one person will be able to save the world all by themselves, but as the saying goes, 'though I am only one person, I can be one person who makes a difference'.

Going Forth

The last phase of the spiral is about how we might like to respond. It's important here not to fall back into hopelessness and say: 'I'm just little me, what difference can I make?' The book called *Active Hope* (2012) that Joanna Macy wrote with Chris Johnstone about the spiral we have just described here, was a very important one for Kristine, one of the Mindfulness Association tutors. After her son was born at a time when she was feeling overwhelmed by worries about the climate crisis, the book opened up new ways of relating to hope and to what is actually possible. The authors of *Active Hope* do not see hope as a form of passive optimism in which we cross our fingers and hope for the best. Instead, they see it as something we can practise; it is a verb, something we can *do* on a daily basis. In each moment it's possible for things to stay the same, deteriorate or get better. The question is what each of us can do to make the outcome we hope for become more likely, rather than less likely. This is always possible, no matter how bleak the situation. Practising hope in this way gives us agency to contribute meaningfully, even if what we do feels woefully inadequate compared to the size of the problem. After all, we never know what our actions are part of and where they may lead, as Rosa Parks discovered with her refusal to give up her seat on the bus for a white person. She never would have guessed that it would play such an important role in the American civil rights movement. Similarly, Greta Thunberg never would have guessed the big impact her decision to go on strike from school each Friday afternoon would have on the world environmental movement.

This movement from gratitude to honouring the pain for the world, then finding new perspectives and being inspired to act, is one that we can move through again and again in small and big ways, as we practise engaging meaningfully with the world around us and bringing our compassion into action.

Deep Grounding

As we wind our way around the spiral of this compassion in action practice, we can resource ourselves through the connection we have with the earth. As part of the grounding stage in each mindfulness and compassion practice we take refuge in the ever-present support of Mother Earth, and we can consciously nurture this connection to further support us on our path as compassionate warriors.

Connecting with the earth is not a conscious thinking-mind experience. We're venturing below the analytical, conceptualising, busy tendencies of usual daytime mind. Instead, this kind of connecting is like our dreams — it seems to happen in the darkness and in the depths. We're dropping down into a world that is phenomenally vast and rich and incredibly nourishing and safe. When we drop down through the body into the earth, we find a place of visionary imagination, sensual experiencing and instinct and we also may begin to discover a deep union with ourselves, other beings and all of life. The possibility of dropping down into this place can reunite us with the ground of our being — our fundamental presence as part of all existence, which has always been there beneath the ups and downs of our daily life.

There is a Native American saying which goes like this: 'The earth does not belong to us, we belong to the earth'. We can extend this understanding to our own body which, born of the earth, also does not belong to us. What if we don't have dominion over our body and instead belong to its sentience, just like it belongs to the earth? As Guy Claxton says 'We do not have bodies, we are bodies' (Claxton, 2015). The modern discipline of neurobiology confirms the understanding that our biology *is* our consciousness. Really admitting this truth requires us to radically rethink and re-feel ourselves and our place in the world.

The 'Engaged Mindfulness' course from the Mindfulness Association explores the four stages of the spiral through practices inspired by the *Work That Reconnects* together with deep grounding mindfulness and compassion meditations. In the context of this book, we offer a practice connected with the spiral, which you can find in the practice section below. We begin this practice by connecting with the earth's presence, and from there we can reflect out loud with another person or write down on a piece of paper what moving through the spiral might look like for us in any given moment.

Warrior of Compassion

Having explored the awakening heart as an inner experience, we then turned our attention to its embodiment in the world. We have honestly explored our ability to engage with what we see happening in the world, both in the environment and in terms of social justice. We have begun the hard work of moving through the world as a warrior of compassion.

Recall the story of Chenrezig, the deity of limitless compassion, from earlier in the book. You may remember how he made a vow to act for the benefit of all beings and not to rest until he had freed them all from suffering. Within Mahayana Buddhist tradition this vow is called the *Bodhisattva Vow*. A *Bodhisattva* is a warrior of compassion, who powerfully strides out into the world to make compassion manifest. This sounds like a very grandiose undertaking, fit for deities, but perhaps not for us. However, in the Buddhist tradition, 'thinking big' is an important part of encouraging our minds to exceed their limitations, which are often caught in a perspective that is unrealistically short-sighted.

Making a vow such as this gives *us* power too because it aligns us with our deepest values. It's almost as if making this commitment carves out a clear channel for the energy of the compassionate heart to flow out into the world. With this deep congruence in place we will have the staying power to remain committed to compassion even in the face of fear.

Perhaps in our own ways we are all warriors of compassion like Chenrezig, because as soon as we undertake to open our heart to the suffering of ourselves and others, we must face our own fears. A warrior can be defined, in this context, as someone who is brave, who has courage (French 'coeur' — heart). This includes the bravery it takes to take a stand or move into unknown territory in service of those in need. A wonderful example of this is the American abolitionist, Harriet Tubman, who was born into slavery, escaped and then made 13 dangerous missions to rescue other enslaved people by using a network of anti-slavery activist safe houses called the 'underground railroad'.

Compassionate warriorship may show up in a more modest forms too, such as the bravery it takes to face the personal suffering of loss, trauma or illness, as in the following personal example of Fay Adams, a Mindfulness Association tutor.

Fay recalls clearly how at the age of 26 she went through a year of debilitating and constant headaches. The possibility of accepting the pain was unthinkable because she was stricken by fear that the pain would never go away. She remembers thinking that she *had* to find a way to make the headaches part of her ambitions in life — not just an obstacle — but she was in so much pain that doing anything was a struggle. She didn't yet know that in order to heal she would have to let go of her young person's life in London as a socialite and community worker. She didn't yet know that she would spend six years on a small island off the west coast of Scotland in a retreat centre. Here she would explore how to unwind the strictures that amplified her pain through the practice of meditation. She didn't yet know that this would be her baptism of fire, her initiation into being able to offer mindful compassion to others. To do this she needed to sit within the pain and face the fear of it with a compassionate heart.

When we are faced with difficult times, either personally or collectively, we can call on our compassionate warrior-self to find the courage we need. Then the ups and downs can begin to teach us how to open our heart. What would it be like if, when something difficult happens, we could open our heart to it, face the fear and stay present from the start? In essence this kind of bravery means *not to be afraid to feel*. This is the invitation of compassionate warriorship.

When Chenrezig broke into pieces at the bottom of Mount Meru, it was as if the suffering of the world was just too much — too shattering. And yet this shattering was part of the process; it was what had to happen for the full potential of Chenrezig's compassion to be realised. When he rose from this 'death' he was reborn with a thousand arms and on each of his thousand hands there was an eye. With these eyes he was able to clearly see the suffering of the world (remember the first psychology) and with his thousand arms he was able to take action with great fortitude (a super-charged version of the second psychology).

Warrior of Compassion Pledge

We are now at the point of completing our training in compassion. As we stand here, about to step out into the rest of our lives, it is a good time to make a pledge similar to Chenrezig's vow. This will symbolise the culmination of our journey of compassion and it will help us to feel a strong sense of purpose and commitment to act from our compassionate heart, as we go forward in our lives. You can find the practice of making the pledge in the practice section below.

The Exquisite Risk

'My soul tells me, we were all broken from the same nameless heart,
And every living thing wakes with a piece of that original
Heart aching its way into blossom.
This is why we know each other below our strangeness,
Why when we fall, we lift each other,

Or when in pain, we hold each other.
Why when sudden with joy, we dance together.
Life is the many pieces
Of that great heart loving itself
back together.'
by Mark Nepo (2005)

Practice Section

Formal Sitting Practice

Practice 32: Beholding the Basic Goodness (20 — 30 minutes)
Beginning by easing into your sitting posture. Find a balance between grounding, softening, and remaining dignified. Now spend a moment setting an intention for this practice such as connecting with universal basic goodness. Then connect with your compassionate motivation. See if you can experience it as a source of energy in your heart centre.

Now, imagine in front of you a person or animal that you know and feel a natural appreciation for. Either see an image of them before you or just feel that they are there. Resting in your heart see if you can behold this being in front of you with warmth and gentleness. What do you see? Perhaps imagine them doing something they love. Can you sense their spirit shining through? Can you see the liveliness in their eyes? Imagine them spending time with people they love. Can you see their care and dedication, perhaps in their actions, gestures or words? Imagine them expressing their affection for you. Is it possible to behold their basic goodness as a human being (or animal)? What positive qualities do you notice? Maybe their curiosity, creativity, loving affection, kind-heartedness, or loyalty.

Now just rest and notice how you're feeling. Do you sense any opening, tenderness or love in your heart. If you find that you can't make a natural connection with appreciation today, just let that be so. Sometimes it's like that in our practice. Perhaps be curious about what is there and respect that.

Would you like to make a wish for this being's wellbeing? You might gently repeat a few times: 'May you be happy, may you be at ease, may you be held in love and peace'. Find the phrases that resonate best with you. Then reconnect with the weight of your body resting on the earth and feel the gentle flow of the breath in your body.

Now turn your appreciative attention towards yourself. Is it possible to behold your own positive qualities. What do you appreciate about yourself? Imagine yourself doing something you care about or spending time with loved ones. What do you see? Be aware that your self-critic might show up and try put you down; if so, just recognise it and make space for it. Then shift your attention to beholding yourself just as a dear family member or friend might behold you. If it's helpful you can imagine looking at yourself through their eyes. Do you see your basic care and concern for others shining through in some way? What essential qualities do you see? Maybe bubbliness, confidence, gentleness, thoughtfulness, or sensitivity? Spend a moment or two resting in a sense of beholding your own basic goodness. What does this feel like? Can you trust it?

Don't worry if you find this hard to do. If any difficult feelings arise just give them space and breathe with them. You might place your hand on your heart and say 'soften, soothe, allow'.

Now make a wish for yourself: 'May I thrive, may I be happy, may I be at peace', or suchlike. Find phrases that resonate best with you. Then pause with how this feels in your body for a moment or two, drinking it in.

Now choose another person or animal that you'd like to spend a few minutes appreciating. Imagine them in front of you. See if you can really see them for who they are and acknowledge their positive qualities and gifts. What do you see? What do you love about them? It might help to imagine them doing what they love or spending time with people they love. Gently behold the sweetness of their unique humanity. What kind wish would you like to make for them? Then rest back into the body's presence held by the earth and be aware of the rhythm of the breath in your body.

Now spend a few minutes reflecting that every human being is in possession of this basic goodness. You can imagine this being like a core of love and caring in their heart. You might like to imagine a warm light or a candle flame inside the heart of every human being. Then you can imagine this warm light permeating all reality, especially nature and planet earth. Notice any 'buts' that may turn up — but there's so much ill-will ... but what about people who...? See if you can return to resting in an awareness of the basic care and goodness which can be seen and felt everywhere. This basic goodness within each of us is powerful and pervasive. It is the force behind compassionate activity. Imagine resting in a luminous sense of the warm light of basic goodness shining through all of reality, including your own heart.

Finally just rest with whatever feelings remain. Then dedicate your practice and close.

Practice 33: Releasing into the Earth and Reflection on Open Sentences (20 – 30 minutes)

From a lying down posture, supported by the steady presence of this ancient, life-giving earth, become aware of the in-breath while sensing into the body and noticing any tension or tightness or discomfort. On the out-breath there is a natural releasing, melting and dissolving of any tension down into the earth. Proceed in this way by beginning with the toes and moving incrementally up to the head and then finally opening to the whole body. Resting in this way, we may begin to experience the earth as receiving our body, holding it, and cradling it in nourishment and healing.

End this part of the practice with gratitude for this ever-present support of life beneath our feet and gratitude for our body itself, before coming to sit and reflecting either out loud (taking turns with a partner), or in writing by completing the following open sentences:

1. Things I love about our world, include...
2. Concerns I have about our world, include...
3. A perspective I find inspiring or empowering is...
4. a) Something I'd love to do to make a difference is...
   b) And a step towards this I can make in the next 7 days is...

Take some time to rest with whatever is present for you now, whether something clear has emerged or not. When you dedicate the benefits of the practice, you could include the earth we all call home and the future generations still to come.

Practice 34: Warrior of Compassion Pledge
Find a quiet space on a meditation cushion or chair, or in a park or coffee shop. Choose somewhere that feels supportive of reflection. Spend a while settling into your seat and coming into the body. Notice your environment too and feel life going on around you.

You may wish to write things down during the exercise, or you can choose to journey in your imagination in a more inward way and write at the end.

Now introduce the following contemplation: reflect on your life prior to this compassion journey. You can imagine you are a bird high in the sky able to look down on the winding pathway you have taken through life so far. You can go as far back as you wish. As you do this, think about what brought you to the point when you decided to embark on the path of compassion. Can you see the seeds of this endeavour starting a long time back, even in childhood? Allow your mind to meander through your storehouse of memories, impressions and feelings. Perhaps there's a story there, a bit like a fairytale with you as the hero or heroine.

Now look down on the point when you began this compassion journey. Perhaps you have a feeling or image of what made an impression on you at that time. Notice changes, difficulties and triumphs as you go on this journey. Do you have a sense of the place within yourself you have come to at this culmination point?

Now consider how all your experiences and learning are a rich resource for your future development and activity. What can grow out of this rich soil? How might you be able to crystallise this into the form of a pledge? Consider how this pledge might become a channel for the fruition of your compassionate motivation.

The pledge can be something quite practical (a psychiatrist chose to write a pledge to take a few minutes remembering his compassionate motivation between patients) or more practice-based ('I want to venture a little outside of my comfort zone each day', or 'I pledge to practise tonglen for 20 minutes every day').

Bear in mind that the pledge should not feel too easy. It's good to stretch yourself a bit, but it should not be so ambitious that it feels intimidating. You can have more than one pledge. Perhaps you can have practical pledges for daily life, and pledges from the 'think big' perspective! Perhaps you can write a kind of mission statement.

Finally write your pledge(s) on a piece of paper and keep it somewhere safe, perhaps in the place where you sit to practise.

Informal Daily Life Practice

Practice 35: Seeing Basic Goodness Everywhere
In daily life look out for basic goodness shining through the ordinary moments (and the extraordinary ones!). Focus

your attention on the small things: the cheerful manner of the postman, the way a loved one glances at you with mirth or appreciation, the care you might take in preparing food, witnessing someone's love for their dog in the park, noticing the devotion of a carer towards an elderly person, someone whistling while they work, or the simple presence of beauty in our environment — birdsong, the buzz of a city street, sun-dapples, sparkles on water, the fresh smell of rain, reflections in puddles, the moon rising.... Notice how you feel in your body and heart when you make this a practice.

What Next?

It can be really helpful to practise Compassion Meditation as part of a group. Many of our course participants comment how motivating it is to be part of a group of practitioners that come together and practise regularly.

You may be able to find a teacher locally, but make sure that they are properly qualified by ensuring that they are trained and that they practise according to the UK Good Practice Guidelines for Mindfulness Teachers. For more details see www.bamba. org.uk. This website lists the organisations, including the Mindfulness Association, that adhere to the UK Good Practice Guidelines and also includes a listing of Mindfulness teachers that meet these guidelines.

For information about the ongoing work of the Mindfulness Association and the range of courses that we offer, please visit our website www.mindfulnessassociation.net. We offer a free daily online meditation session, each weekday at 10.30am and 7.00pm, led by Mindfulness Association tutors, including Choden and Heather.

Mindfulness Association Membership

The Mindfulness Association has an online membership that you can join. This provides a variety of benefits including a weekly digest email curated to support your practice, monthly live online teachings, and two online membership weekends. These resources are designed to support a regular and effective Mindfulness and Compassion meditation practice.

Details can be found on our website: www.mindfulnessassociation.net.

References

Chapter Two: Why Practise Compassion?

Choden and Gilbert, P. (2013). *Mindful Compassion*. London: Constable Robinson.

Tsering, T. (2008). *The Awakening Mind: The Foundation of Buddhist Thought*. Vol. 4. Simon and Schuster.

Chapter Three: Building the Foundations

Choden and Regan-Addis, H. (2018). *Mindfulness Based Living Course: Eight Week Mindfulness Course*. O Books.

Rūmī, J. A. D. and Coleman, M. (2003). *Rumi: The Book Of Love: Poems Of Ecstasy And Longing*. CiNii Books.

Chapter Four: Compassionate Mess

Rob Nairn talk. Samye Ling, September 2009.

Akong Rinpoche (1994). *Taming The Tiger: Tibetan Teachings For Improving Daily Life*. Random House.

Chapter Five: It's Not Our Fault

Wright, R. (2017). *Why Buddhism Is True: The Science and Philosophy of Meditation and Enlightenment*. Simon and Schuster.

Chapter Seven: Self-Compassion

Germer, C. (2009). *The Mindful Path to Self-Compassion: Freeing Yourself From Destructive Thoughts and Emotions*. Guilford Press.

Germer, C. and Neff, K. (2019). *Mindful Self-Compassion (MSC). Handbook of Mindfulness-Based Programmes*. Routledge, pp.357-67.

Porges, S.W. (2011). *The Polyvagal Theory: Neurophysiological Foundations Of Emotions, Attachment, Communication, and Self-Regulation*. (Norton series on interpersonal neurobiology). WW Norton & Company.

Chapter Eight: Finding the Compassionate Friend Within

Williamson, M. (2015). *A Return to Love: Reflections on the Principles of 'A Course in Miracles'*. Harper Thorsons.

Chapter Eleven: Widening the Circle of Compassion

Chodron, P. (2009). *Perfect Just as You Are: Buddhist Practices on the Four Limitless Ones: Loving-Kindness, Compassion, Joy, and Equanimity*. Shambhala Publications.

Chapter Twelve: Taking and Sending

Chodron, P. (2003). *Start Where You Are: A Guide to Compassionate Living*. Element.

Trungpa, C. (2005). *Training The Mind & Cultivating Loving-Kindness*. Shambhala Publications.

Chapter Thirteen: Compassion in Action

Brach, T. (2020). *Radical Compassion: Learning to Love Yourself and Your World with the Practice of RAIN*. Penguin.

Bregman, R. (2021). *Humankind*. Bloomsbury Publishing.

Chodron, P. (2000). *When Things Fall Apart: Heart Advice For Difficult Times*. Shambhala Publications.

Claxton, G. (2015). *Intelligence In The Flesh: Why Your Mind Needs Your Body Much More Than It Thinks*. Yale University Press.

Evans, A. (2017). *The Myth Gap: What Happens When Evidence And Arguments Aren't Enough?* Random House.

Gabbatiss, J. (2017). 'Nasty, Brutish and Short – Are Humans DNA Wired to Kill?' in *Scientific American*, with permission from Sapiens Biology.

Hamilton, R. (2021). Book Review: *Humankind: A Hopeful History* by Rutger Bregman. US App–American Politics and Policy Blog: https://blogs.lse.ac.uk/usappblog/2021/02/14/book-review-humankind-a-hopeful-history-by-rutger-bregman/

Keltner, D. (2009). *Born To Be Good: The Science of a Meaningful Life.* W. W. Norton & Company.

Macy, J. and Johnstone, C. (2012). *Active Hope: How To Face The Mess We're In Without Going Crazy.* New World Library.

Macy, J. (Retrieved 2023). *The Work That Reconnects.* Network (https://workthatreconnects.org/).

Nepo, M. (2005). 'The exquisite risk' in *Constructivism in the Human Sciences,* 10 (1/2), p.177.

Further Reading

We can recommend the following books:

Diamond Mind by Rob Nairn (Founder of the Mindfulness Association).

Mindfulness Based Living Course by Choden and Heather Regan-Addis.

From Mindfulness to Insight by Rob Nairn, Choden and Heather Regan-Addis.

Mindful Compassion by Prof. Paul Gilbert and Choden.

MANTRA
BOOKS

EASTERN RELIGION & PHILOSOPHY

We publish books on Eastern religions and philosophies.
Books that aim to inform and explore the various traditions
that began in the East and have migrated West.
If you have enjoyed this book, why not tell other readers by
posting a review on your preferred book site.

Recent bestsellers from MANTRA BOOKS are:

The Way Things Are
A Living Approach to Buddhism
Lama Ole Nydahl
An introduction to the teachings of the Buddha, and how to make use of these teachings in everyday life.
Paperback: 978-1-84694-042-2 ebook: 978-1-78099-845-9

Back to the Truth
5000 Years of Advaita
Dennis Waite
A demystifying guide to Advaita for both those new to, and those familiar with this ancient, non-dualist philosophy from India.
Paperback: 978-1-90504-761-1 ebook: 978-184694-624-0

Shinto: A celebration of Life
Aidan Rankin
Introducing a gentle but powerful spiritual pathway reconnecting humanity with Great Nature and affirming all aspects of life.
Paperback: 978-1-84694-438-3 ebook: 978-1-84694-738-4

In the Light of Meditation
Mike George
A comprehensive introduction to the practice of meditation and the spiritual principles behind it. A 10 lesson meditation programme with CD and internet support.
Paperback: 978-1-90381-661-5

A Path of Joy
Popping into Freedom
Paramananda Ishaya
A simple and joyful path to spiritual enlightenment.
Paperback: 978-1-78279-323-6 ebook: 978-1-78279-322-9

The Less Dust the More Trust
Participating in The Shamatha Project, Meditation and
Science Adeline van Waning, MD PhD
The inside-story of a woman participating in frontline
meditation research, exploring the interfaces of mind-practice,
science and psychology.
Paperback: 978-1-78099-948-7 ebook: 978-1-78279-657-2

I Know How To Live, I Know How To Die
The Teachings of Dadi Janki: A warm, radical, and life-
affirming view of who we are, where we come from,
and what time is calling us to do
Neville Hodgkinson
Life and death are explored in the context of frontier science
and deep soul awareness.
Paperback: 978-1-78535-013-9 ebook: 978-1-78535-014-6

Living Jainism
An Ethical Science
Aidan Rankin, Kanti V. Mardia
A radical new perspective on science rooted in intuitive
awareness and deductive reasoning.
Paperback: 978-1-78099-912-8 ebook: 978-1-78099-911-1

Ordinary Women, Extraordinary Wisdom
The Feminine Face of Awakening
Rita Marie Robinson
A collection of intimate conversations with female spiritual
teachers who live like ordinary women, but are engaged
with their true natures.
Paperback: 978-1-84694-068-2 ebook: 978-1-78099-908-1

The Way of Nothing
Nothing in the Way
Paramananda Ishaya
A fresh and light-hearted exploration of the
amazing reality of nothingness.
Paperback: 978-1-78279-307-6 ebook: 978-1-78099-840-4

Readers of ebooks can buy or view any of these bestsellers by
clicking on the live link in the title. Most titles are published
in paperback and as an ebook. Paperbacks are available in
traditional bookshops. Both print and ebook formats are
available online.

Find more titles and sign up to our readers' newsletter at
www.collectiveinkbooks.com/mind-body-spirit. Follow
us on Facebook at facebook.com/OBooks and
Twitter at twitter.com/obooks